Chicken Soup for the Soul®

Teens Talk Tough Times

Our **101** BEST STORIES

Chicken Soup for the Soul® Our 101 Best Stories:
Teens Talk Tough Times; Stories about the Hardest Part of Being a Teenager
by Jack Canfield, Mark Victor Hansen & Amy Newmark

Published by Chicken Soup for the Soul Publishing, LLC   www.chickensoup.com

Cover photos courtesy of Corbis, iStockPhoto.com/helloyiying, Jupiter Images/photos.com

Cover and Interior Design & Layout by Pneuma Books, LLC
For more info on Pneuma Books, visit www.pneumabooks.com

Distributed to the booktrade by Simon & Schuster. SAN: 200-2442

Publisher's Cataloging-in-Publication Data
(Prepared by The Donohue Group)

Chicken soup for the soul. Selections.
    Chicken soup for the soul : teens talk tough times : stories about the
hardest parts of being a teenager / [compiled by] Jack Canfield [and] Mark
Victor Hansen ; [edited by] Amy Newmark.

    p. ; cm. -- (Our 101 best stories)

    ISBN-13: 978-1-935096-03-0
    ISBN-10: 1-935096-03-6

1. Teenagers--Literary collections. 2. Teenagers' writings. 3. Teenagers--Conduct
of life--Anecdotes. I. Canfield, Jack, 1944- II. Hansen, Mark Victor. III. Newmark,
Amy. IV. Title.

PS508.Y68 C293 2008
810.8/09283   2008929327

PRINTED IN THE UNITED STATES OF AMERICA
on acid∞free paper
16 15 14 13 12 10 09 08   01 02 03 04 05 06 07 08

Chicken Soup for the Soul

Teens Talk Tough Times

Our 101 BEST STORIES

Stories about the Hardest Parts of Being a Teenager

Jack Canfield
Mark Victor Hansen
Amy Newmark

Chicken Soup for the Soul Publishing, LLC
Cos Cob, CT

Chicken Soup for the Soul

Contents

❶
~Courage~

❷
~Tough Choices~

❸
~Being There~

❹
~The Little Things that Make a Big Difference~

❺
~Family~

❻

~Pushing Forward~

❼

~Lessons Learned~

❽
~Loss and Grieving~

❾
~Reaching Out~

⑩
~Second Chances~

⑪
~You Are Not Alone~

Chicken Soup for the Soul

A Special Foreword

by Jack and Mark

For us, 101 has always been a magical number. It was the number of stories in the first *Chicken Soup for the Soul* book, and it is the number of stories and poems we have always aimed for in our books. We love the number 101 because it signifies a beginning, not an end. After 100, we start anew with 101.

We hope that when you finish reading one of our books, it is only a beginning for you too—a new outlook on life, a renewed sense of purpose, a strengthened resolve to deal with an issue that has been bothering you. Perhaps you will pick up the phone and share one of the stories with a friend or a loved one. Perhaps you will turn to your keyboard and express yourself by writing a Chicken Soup story of your own, to share with other readers who are just like you.

This volume contains our 101 best stories and poems on tough challenges that face teenagers. We share this with you at a very special time for us, the fifteenth anniversary of our *Chicken Soup for the Soul* series. When we published our first book in 1993, we never dreamed that we had started what would become a publishing sensation, one of the best-selling lines of books in history.

We did not set out to sell more than one hundred million books, or to publish more than 150 titles. We set out to touch the heart of one person at a time, hoping that person would in turn touch another person, and so on down the line. We know that it has worked. Your letters and stories have poured in by the hundreds of thousands, affirming our life's work, and inspiring us to continue to make a difference in your lives.

On our fifteenth anniversary, we have new energy, new resolve, and new dreams. We have recommitted to our goal of 101 stories or poems per book, we have refreshed our cover designs and our interior layout, and we have grown the Chicken Soup for the Soul team, with new friends and partners across the country in New England.

In this new volume, we showcase our 101 best stories and poems on tough times for teenagers, drawn from our fifteen year history. We know that being a teenager is difficult even under idyllic circumstances. But when bad things happen, the challenges of being a teenager can be overwhelming, leading to self-destructive behavior, eating disorders, substance abuse, and other challenges. In addition, many of you are faced with illness, car accidents, the loss of loved ones, divorces, and other upheavals, and the obstacles to happiness can seem insurmountable.

We chose stories written by other teenagers just like you. We hope that you will find these stories inspiring and supportive, and that you will share them with your families and friends. We have identified the 20 *Chicken Soup for the Soul* books in which the stories originally appeared, in case you would like to continue your journey through your teenage years with some of our other books. We hope you will also enjoy the additional titles for teenagers in "Our 101 Best Stories" series.

With our love, our thanks, and our respect,
~*Jack Canfield and Mark Victor Hansen*

Chapter 1

Teens Talk Tough Times

Courage

*You, yourself, as much as anybody in the entire universe,
deserve your love and affection.*
~Buddha

Staying Strong

Walking through a quiet field on a dewy morning, you spy a wild horse. Slowly you walk up to him, and to your delight he doesn't run away. He lowers his head for you to pet and then motions with his snout for you to climb on his back. You ride away, hair and mane blowing in the wind behind you. You hear a voice, quite faint. You cannot tell what it is, but it is getting louder... louder... louder.

You awake abruptly from a relaxing sleep to the sound of your mother yelling, "Come on, we've got to go!" You wipe the gunk from your eyes and roll over to look at the clock. Seven A.M. It's time to leave for chemotherapy. You really don't want to go, so it is a struggle, but you make yourself get out of bed. Making all of the lovely "I'm not really awake yet" noises, you drag yourself to the bathroom. It is almost a ritual now, with no thought really involved. You step out of your clothes, turn on the shower, wash, step out of the shower and dry off, all the while wishing you were still asleep. You find your most comfortable clothes and put them on haphazardly. You're only going to the hospital, so who cares what you look like?

"We're going to be late if we don't leave right now!" you hear from down the hall. Walking down the hall you realize your stomach is growling and remember that you have yet to eat anything. Guess you'll just have to ask Mom to stop somewhere; what a pity.

You're in the car now, reclining and squinting to see through the sunlight in your eyes. You get your breakfast, and after eating, you perk up a little bit. Forty-five minutes later you arrive at the hospital clinic. Parking is an adventure in itself, so you get Mom to drop you off at the main entrance. You're not quite in the mood for battling blue-haired ladies for parking spaces.

As you enter the clinic, the first thing you notice is the smell: doctors, latex gloves, saline drips and disinfectant spray. After checking in, you scout out a nice seat to relax in. After settling on a brightly colored plastic couch, you realize that it is incredibly cold. Good thing you remembered to bring a sweater. You wrap it around your shoulders and wait for your mother to arrive. Once your mother returns from the parking lot battle, your nurse for the day comes into the waiting room.

"You ready?" she asks. "Oh yeah, you know it," you reply.

She leads you to the check-in room where you are instructed to stand on the scale. Oh boy, it looks like you've gained two pounds since last week, so you make a mental note to lay off the Twinkies from now on. The nurse takes your blood pressure and asks what medicines you are taking. You recount the oh-so-familiar list once again. You think they could at least remember twelve medicines from last week. She takes you into the "access room." You climb up on the lovely examining table, all covered in disposable paper. Lying back, you lift your shirt to reveal the semipermanent IV that is under your skin, located right below your bra line. This is more commonly known as a venaport, or to other patients as "the poison-control center."

You peel the Tegaderm off the area on and around your port, wincing all the while, as it pulls out the little hairs on your stomach. Taking a tissue, you wipe off the Emla Cream that had been applied earlier to numb the first two layers of skin. You watch as your nurse puts on her latex gloves and begins the procedure. She opens her "kit" and arranges everything the same way she does every week. Three syringes, the access needle and Betadine — all waiting to be used.

She walks over to where you are lying and begins. First she uses a giant cotton swab soaked in alcohol all around your port. Following this, she swabs you three times with Betadine, each time with a new swab so that she won't counter the disinfectant. Once again she swabs your port with alcohol and then waits fifteen seconds.

She prepares the needle and asks, "Are you ready?"

"Go for it," you reply.

You have done this so many times before. Still though, right before she presses the needle through the skin, your stomach clenches. You take a deep breath, close your eyes, and exhale as the needle goes in. A sense of relief comes to you; it didn't hurt this week! Your nurse places two cotton squares under the "butterfly" part of your port (the area up against your skin) and places a sheet of Tegaderm over the entire thing. She then screws a syringe into the tube attached to the needle, which is now in your port, and takes some blood. Now she takes a syringe of saline and slowly pushes it into your port; you ask her to do it faster because you want to get a head rush. After the head rush, she flushes your port with heparin. You begin to taste it inside your mouth as she pushes it in, and it doesn't taste good.

You are sent to a back room with chairs, TVs, VCRs and a wide variety of board games. You choose a seat, and your nurse hooks your port line up to a fluid drip. Some time passes, and the doctor arrives to examine you. He makes jokes while prodding you and feeling for lumps and bumps. Then he asks you the same questions he asks you every week: "Have you been nauseated? Have you had headaches? Back pain? Diarrhea? Constipation? Blood in your urine?"

All to which you answer a quick "No, no, no, no, no and no." He says you're looking good and to let him know if any problems arise, and then he leaves. A little while later your nurse returns with a copy of your blood counts. Your ANC (Absolute neutrophil count) is over five hundred, so you can receive your chemotherapy. Yippee for you!

Your nurse gives you a small push of Zofran, so that the chemo doesn't make you throw up, and then she hooks your port up to the bag of chemotherapy, or as it's more fondly called, "poison." You find it ironic that the nurse must wear special super-thick gloves to handle the bag of chemotherapy, yet they are pumping it into your body. You watch as the liquid runs through the IV line... slowly making its way closer and closer. Still tired from getting up so early, you doze off to the quiet sound of the IV machine pumping... pumping... pumping.

You awake suddenly to the sound of an alarm going off. The nurse comes into your room and messes with the IV machine, pushing buttons, and then the alarm stops.

"It looks like you're all done! Let's go de-access you."

You willingly obey, anxious to get home and lie back down. Already you are feeling the chemotherapy's effects on your body, and all you want to do is go back to bed. You lie on the table in the access room once again and peel the Tegaderm off from your port, again ripping out the little hairs on your stomach. The nurse puts on her latex gloves once again and flushes your port with some saline and heparin. Now it is time to take the needle out. She gets a good grip on the needle and asks you to take a breath and hold it. You do as she says, and as you hold your breath, she quickly pulls the needle out. You let your breath out, relieved that you finally get to go home. She places a Band-Aid over the port and says she will see you next week.

Your mother makes an appointment for next week while you stand there looking like you're about to fall asleep. Mom goes out to get the car, and you wait in the main waiting room. After about five minutes you walk out to the garage area and see your mother pulling up. She brings the black van of comfort, waiting to take you home to your bed. Climbing in, you sigh—your life is so different from everyone else's, yet so much the same. You remember with a smile that this will all be over soon, and then you drift off to sleep.

~Deiah Haddock
Chicken Soup for the Teenage Soul IV

Swimming with Dolphins

Animals are such agreeable friends —
they ask no questions, they pass no criticisms.
~George Eliot

"It's not easy to die when you are only fifteen."

Those were the words that began the story I heard from Robert White, a North Carolina factory worker. He and his wife were visiting their daughter Lee in the hospital as they did every evening, but Lee had already accepted her fate.

She knew she had an illness that would not spare her. She knew that, in spite of their finest efforts, the doctors couldn't save her. She suffered a lot, but never complained.

This particular evening, she seemed tranquil and composed, but suddenly she said, "Mama, daddy—I think I'm going to die soon, and I'm afraid. I know I'm going to a better world than this one, and I'm longing for some peace at last, but it's hard to accept the idea that I'm going to die at only fifteen."

They could have lied, telling her of course she wasn't going to die, but they didn't have the heart. Somehow, her courage was worth more than their pretense. They just cuddled her and cried together.

Then she said, "I always dreamed of falling in love, getting married, having kids... but above all I would have liked to work in a big marine park with dolphins. I've loved them and wanted to know more about them since I was little. I still dream of swimming with them, free and happy in the open sea."

She'd never asked for anything, but now she said with all the strength she could muster, "Daddy, I want to swim in the open sea among the dolphins just once. Maybe then I wouldn't be so scared of dying."

It seemed like an absurd, impossible dream, but she, who had given up just about everything else, hung on to it.

Robert and his family talked it over and decided to do everything they could. They had heard of a research center in the Florida Keys, and they phoned them.

"Come at once," they said. But that was easier said than done.

Lee's illness had used up all their savings, and they had no idea how they would be able to afford air tickets to Florida. Then their six-year-old, Emily, mentioned that she'd seen something on television about a foundation that grants the wishes of very sick children. She'd actually written down the telephone number in her diary because it seemed like magic to her.

Robert didn't want to listen. He thought it sounded like a fairy tale or a very sick joke, and he gave in only when Emily started crying and accusing him of not really wanting to help Lee. So he phoned the number and, sure enough, three days later they were all on an airplane and on their way. Emily felt a bit like a fairy godmother who had solved all their problems with a wave of her magic wand.

When they arrived at Grass Key, Lee was pale and terribly thin. The chemotherapy she'd been having had made all her hair fall out, and she looked ghastly, but she didn't want to rest for a minute and begged her parents to take her straightaway to the dolphins. It was an unforgettable scene. When she got into the water, Lee was already so weak she hardly had the strength to move. They had put her in a wet suit so she wouldn't get cold and a life preserver to keep her afloat.

Robert towed her out toward the dolphins, Nat and Tursi, who were frolicking about thirty feet away from them. At first they seemed distracted and uninterested, but when Lee called them softly by name, they responded without hesitation. Nat came over first, raised his head and gave her a kiss on the end of her nose. Then Tursi came over and greeted her with a flurry of little high-pitched squeaks of joy.

A second later they picked her up with their mighty fins and carried her out to sea with them.

"It feels like I'm flying!" cried Lee, laughing with delight.

Lee's family hadn't heard her laugh like that since before she became ill. They could hardly believe it was true, but there she was, gripping Nat's fin and challenging the wind and the immensity of the ocean. The dolphins stayed with Lee for more than an hour, always tender, always attentive, never using any unnecessary force, always responsive to her wishes.

Maybe it's true that they are more intelligent and sensitive creatures than man. What was certain was that those marvelous dolphins understood that Lee was dying and wanted to console her as she faced her great journey into the unknown. From the moment they took her in hand, they never left her alone for a second. They got her to play and obeyed her commands with a sweetness that was magical. In their company, Lee found for one last time the enthusiasm and the will to live. She was strong and happy like she used to be. At one point she shouted, "The dolphins have healed me, Daddy!"

There are no words to describe the effect that swim had on her. When she got out of the water, it was as if she had been reborn.

The next day she was too weak to get out of bed. She didn't even want to talk, but when Robert took her hand she squeezed it and whispered, "Daddy, don't be sad for me. I'll never be afraid again. The dolphins have made me understand that I have nothing to fear." Then she said, "I know I'm going to die tonight. Promise me that you'll cremate my body and scatter my ashes in the sea where all dolphins swim. They gave me the most beautiful moments of my life. They have left me with a great feeling of peace in my heart, and I know they will be with me on the long journey that lies ahead."

Just before dawn, Robert's little girl woke and whispered, "Hold me, Daddy, I'm so cold." And she died like that in his arms a few minutes later—passing from sleep to death without a ripple. They only realized her suffering was over because her body became colder and heavier.

They cremated her as she wanted and went out the next day to scatter her ashes in the ocean amongst the dolphins. They were all crying—not only Lee's family, but also the sailors on the boat who had taken them out into the bay. And then, suddenly, through their tears, they saw the great arching silver shapes of Nat and Tursi leaping out of the water ahead.

As Robert recounted, "They had come to take our daughter home."

~Allegra Taylor
Chicken Soup for the Nature Lover's Soul

Losing Myself

I was like any other average ninth grader. I was active in sports, had my circle of friends and got good grades. Until the day I was introduced to him. There was something in his eyes that attracted me. Somehow I thought that he needed me just as much as I needed to be loved. After flirting for months, we finally became a couple. We were together every single moment from that day on. Slowly, day by day, my family and friends saw me changing. I was in love.

After about two months, however, he started to try to control me and even raise his voice at me. I told myself it was okay because he really did love me. Or so I thought. The first time he ever hurt me, we were skiing with friends and had lost each other on the slopes. When he found me, he said it was my fault. He proceeded to push me and call me nasty names while people just stared at us. I ran into the bathroom with my best friend and cried my eyes out. The next thing I knew, he was in the bathroom hugging me, overflowing with kisses and saying how sorry he was. So I forgave him and put that day in the back of my mind.

Things did not go back to normal, though. He became possessive and jealous. He made rules stating I could no longer wear my hair down, wear shorts in the summertime or have any sign of another boy in my room. If another boy even glanced at me in school, he would yell at me. My grades dropped, I lost my ambition for sports, I started losing my friends, and my family became my worst enemy. I didn't want to listen to what they thought about my relationship or how much I had changed. I cried every single night because of the way I was beginning to feel about myself. He would yell at me or blame me for everything. A couple of times, I tried hurting myself because I felt I wasn't good enough for him and that there wasn't any other reason to be alive. I tried to justify his actions by believing they showed how much he cared about me. As a ninth grader, it made me feel important to be in love and have a steady boyfriend.

My parents tried taking me to counseling and talked to all my teachers about my relationship. I started skipping school. The violence escalated. He tried to choke me on several occasions, and once he tried to break my arm because his brother looked at me in my swimsuit. I felt hopeless and depressed. He had so much control over my mind that I could not accept anyone else's opinion of him. I told myself that they just didn't understand how much he loved me. He only did what he did because he cared.

The physical abuse continued to get worse. He forced me to do sexual things with him. He also hit, choked and pushed me around. He tried drowning me once. Fortunately, I fell on some rocks before he had the chance to get me under the water. He also cut my wrists because he was in the dumps. This went on for nine months.

Finally, my parents took me on a trip for a week. While I was on vacation, he cheated on me, and I built up enough courage to break up with him. One night, I lay in bed and thought of everything he had done to me. It was clear what I had to do.

I spent the last two weeks of summer break trying to get my old friends back before returning to school. When I went back to school, he was in my gym class. I was nice to him because I still feared him. When I got up the nerve to tell him that it was over for good, he went psycho, pushed me to the ground and kicked me several times. Nobody came to help me. The next day, I discovered an eight inch bruise on my leg.

It took me three days to show the bruise to my parents. To my surprise, after everything I had put them through, they helped me. They took me straight to the police station to file charges. I wanted to just let it go, but I was also determined that this should not and would not happen to anyone he "loved" in the future. At home, I continued to receive threatening phone calls from him saying that he was going to kill me. He told my parents that he would hurt me if he got the chance.

My court experience took over a year and was horribly painful. I found out that he had a violent past and that it wasn't the first time that he had abuse charges brought against him. I was never notified about the final court hearing, so it happened without me and, to my knowledge, nothing severe happened to him. The justice system let me down, but I chose to go on with my life.

I am very lucky to be where I am today. I am nineteen years old, and I have grown and healed a lot. It took me over three years to tell my parents everything that he did to me. My parents and I are very close now. The healing process may continue for years to come, but I deal with my pain by sharing my story with other young teens, hoping to help prevent this from happening to anybody else. I do not wake up every day hating him. I feel bad for him, and I know he needs help, wherever he is. I have learned instead to focus on living my life to the fullest and cherishing the people I truly love.

~Jenny Deyo
Chicken Soup for the Teenage Soul on Tough Stuff

Role Reversal

We must be willing to get rid of the life we've planned,
so as to have the life that is waiting for us.
~Joseph Campbell

It was a Friday night, and I had just returned from climbing one of the red rocks of Sedona. The night was chilly, the moon was high and I was looking forward to crawling into my warm bed. My faculty adviser, Bunny, approached me as I walked through the arches to my dorm room. She took me to her home, where she told me that my mother had been in a terrible car crash and had been taken to the intensive care unit of a nearby hospital in critical condition.

When I got to the hospital, my grandmother pulled me aside and said whatever I did, I mustn't cry in front of my mother.

A nurse unlocked the door that led down a wide hallway with machines all around. A strong smell of medicine brought a nauseous feeling to my already turning stomach. My mother's room was right next to the nurses' station. As I turned into the room, I saw her lying on her side, with her tiny back to me and a fluffed pillow between her bandaged legs. She struggled to turn around but couldn't. I slowly crept to the other side of the bed and said "hi" in a calm voice, stifling my urge to cry out.

The cadaverous condition of her body stunned me. Her swollen face looked like it had been inflated and kicked around like a soccer ball, her eyes had huge dark bruised rings around them, and she had tubes down her throat and in her arms.

Gently holding my mother's cold swollen hands, I tried to keep my composure. She kept looking at me and rolling her eyes into the back of her head as she pounded her hand against the bed. She was trying to tell me how much pain she was in. I turned my face away from her, trying to hide the tears that were rolling down my face. Eventually I had to leave her for a moment because I couldn't hold my anguish in any longer. That was when it struck me that I really might lose my mother.

I kept her company all day long; in time the doctors took the respirator out of her throat for a short while. She was able to whisper a few words, but I didn't know what to say in return. I felt like screaming but knew I mustn't. I went home and cried myself to sleep.

From that night on, my life completely changed. Up to that point, I'd had the luxury of just being a kid, having to deal with only the exaggerated melodramas of teenage life. My concept of crisis was now forever altered. As my mother struggled first to stay alive and then to relearn to walk, my sense of priorities changed drastically. My mother needed me. The trials and tribulations of my daily life at school, which had seemed so important before, now appeared insignificant. My mother and I had faced death together, and life took on new meaning for both of us.

After a week of clinging to life in intensive care, my mother's condition improved enough to be taken off the respirator and moved to a regular hospital room. She was finally out of danger but, because her legs had been crushed, there was doubt that she would be able to walk again. I was just grateful that she was alive. I visited my mother in the hospital as often as I could for the next two months. Finally, a sort of hospital suite was set up in our family room, and to my relief and joy, she was allowed to come home.

My mother's return home was a blessing for us all, but it meant some unaccustomed responsibilities for me. She had a visiting nurse, but much of the time I took care of her. I would feed her, bathe her, and when she was eventually able to use a toilet, would help her to the bathroom. It struck me that I was pretty much playing the role of mother to my own mother. It wasn't always much fun, but it felt good to be there when my mother really needed me. The difficult part for me was trying to always be upbeat, and to keep my mother's spirits up when she became frustrated with the pain and her inability to do simple things for herself. I always had a smile on my face when, really, I was suppressing tears in my heart.

My mother's reliance on me changed our relationship. In the past, we had more than our share of the strains of mother-daughter relationships. The accident threw us into a relationship of interdependence. To get my mother back, I had to help her regain her strength and ability to resume an independent life. She had to learn to accept my help as well as the fact that I was no longer a child. We have become the closest of friends. We genuinely listen to one another, and truly enjoy each other's company.

It has been over two years since my mother's crash. Although it was devastating to see my mother go through the physical pain and emotions that she still continues to experience, I have grown more in that time than in all the years before. Being a mother figure to my own mother taught me a lot about parenthood: the worries, the protectiveness and, most of all, the sweetness of unconditional devotion and love.

~Adi Amar
Chicken Soup for the Teenage Soul II

Stuck with No Way Out

A t five feet, three inches tall, and well under a hundred pounds, I looked at myself in the mirror and thought, How did I get to be such a pig? At that moment it struck me, I don't know where the clarity came from, but, looking back on it, I am grateful it did come. I thought, I need help. This need for perfection and this compulsive behavior was literally going to kill me.

• • •

When I started college the stress began to take its toll and I started overeating. I was living away from home, I was separated from most of my good friends, and I was in a big school taking premed classes. I was facing many adult responsibilities that came from living away from home for the first time, and my class load was heavy. Food became my comfort, fast food became my excuse—I had to eat! Chips and cookies were my reward for good grades. And, where I had shied away from eating anything closely resembling candy in the past, I now found myself frequenting snack machines and stocking up on candy bars. It was energy food, I told myself. My newfound diet, along with my sedentary life of study, conspired to put the weight on. By the beginning of my sophomore year, I weighed in at 150 pounds. I couldn't believe my eyes when I stepped on the scale at the doctor's office for my yearly checkup. I had gained forty-five pounds in one year.

I was so depressed. I was back home for the holidays. Between the horror in my mother's eyes upon seeing me, the horror in my own eyes when I saw the numbers on the scale, and becoming the butt (obvious pun intended) of all my brothers' jokes, I did what any normal, red blooded, American girl would do: I pigged out for the holidays.

I went back to school armed with every diet book known to man from my well-meaning mother and a handful of recipes (as if I was going to cook). I could handle this. Taking off weight was never a problem for me in the past. What I didn't realize was that in the past I only needed to lose five or ten pounds at the most. I was now looking at trying to take off forty! When it didn't come off as quickly as I thought it would, I became even more desperate. I was hungry all the time, frustrated at my lack of success and facing summer — shorts and bathing suit season?! I don't think so!

My dorm mate convinced me that if I just purged for one meal a day I would see a huge difference. The thought of bulimia terrified me. But she became very convincing in her argument. "Just once a day. You'll get nutrition from your other meals. You just won't be so hungry all the time." She was right in one regard, the dizziness I was experiencing from the lack of food was beginning to take its toll. I needed to pull down really good grades if I was going to get into a good medical school.

Purging one meal became purging two, sometimes more. The weight was dropping off. I was so excited and encouraged by seeing my waist again, I joined a gym and began to work out three days a week. Between studying until all hours of the morning, running my body ragged on a treadmill and bingeing and purging, I had become a full-blown bulimic. But I couldn't even admit it to myself. I was in denial.

When I went home for a few weeks in the summer, the accolades from my brothers and the sudden, unexpected visits from their friends, while flattering, only made it worse. I wanted to be even thinner. My mother, however, didn't like what she saw. She was worried about the dark circles under my eyes and the pallor of my skin. Plus, my naturally calm, easygoing personality had given way to a cranky, argumentative nightmare of a person. I exploded when she questioned me about it. "What more do you want from me? I got straight As this term, lost all the weight that you were bugging me about, and I had to do it all living away from home!" My screaming fit gave way to tears and I broke down. The stress had taken its toll. My mother held me like I was three years old again. I felt comforted but trapped. How could I stop this behavior without giving up everything I had worked so hard for? Besides, I didn't want to be fat again—ever.

I assured my mother everything would be all right and I went back to school. I convinced myself that I could handle this problem, but in truth, I couldn't. I would abstain from my purging behavior for only a few days. Because I hadn't changed my eating habits—in fact they were worse—my weight would begin to go up again. I couldn't stand it so I would begin purging again. Even my dorm mate, the friend who gave me the idea in the first place, suggested that I was out of control. Out of control? How could I be out of control when I've never felt so in control of my life and circumstances? I liked everything about this behavior—almost.

Suddenly, I stopped having periods. My body was screaming at me and I wasn't getting the message. I was taking anatomy and biology classes learning everything about the body, except how to take care of my own. One day I passed out in my dorm room while just sitting down studying. That was it. I looked at myself in the mirror and the warped part of me, the part that was responsible for this behavior, saw a girl who needed to lose more weight. But some wisdom forced its way through and I knew I needed help.

I ran over to the counseling office and grabbed the phone number for the eating disorder hotline. Even though I felt like a grown-up with all these new responsibilities and being away at college, this was my first real adult act.

• • •

After being in a group for three months, I was changing my behavior. I found my way out of the darkness with people who cared and professionals who were trained. I continued with the group throughout college and received enormous support for all kinds of life-changing situations I faced. I learned so many things from this experience—it's okay to be scared and you don't have to be alone or do it alone. I took all this wonderful information into my practice and it has served my patients and me well.

When I went home for the holidays that year I was glowing. My mother hugged me and I could tell that she was enormously relieved. We stayed up until all hours of the night and talked about everything. By being honest about my circumstances, I had everything to gain. I was back, and, magically—much to my delight—so were all my brothers' friends.

~Rosanne Martorella
Chicken Soup for the College Soul

Panic

*The only courage that matters is the kind that
gets you from one moment to the next.*
~Mignon McLaughlin

One October day, in eighth grade English class, I sat taking notes while my teacher explained prepositional phrases for what felt like the eightieth time. Suddenly, my forehead and fingertips became numb, as if a crazed dentist had injected them with Novocain. I tried to concentrate on the teacher's lecture, but his words sounded garbled, like he was speaking through a long cardboard tube. My heart raced, and I couldn't breathe. I was either going to throw up or pass out.

It seemed like I was having a dream. Was I really sitting in English class? I turned my head to look at my classmates. They were moving slowly, like a film being viewed frame by frame. I touched the smooth Formica desk and squeezed my pen. I wasn't dreaming. What was wrong with me?

My friend touched my arm. "Are you okay?" she asked. "You're completely pale."

I raised my hand; it felt detached from my body. "Can I go to the nurse?" I asked. The voice came from my throat, but I didn't recognize its sound. Our teacher had told the last guy who asked for a pass to the nurse to wait until the bell. Before that could happen, he had hurled into his desk.

"Sure, go ahead," the teacher told me.

I rushed out of the room. The hallway's spotted floor seemed to slant under my feet. I rested my forehead against the cool turquoise tiles of the wall. What was happening?

The nurse had me lay down on her fake leather couch, and she popped a thermometer in my mouth. I prayed that I had a fever and could go home. After a few minutes, the nurse read my temperature. "No fever. Better go back to class," she told me.

"No, I can't," I nearly shouted. "Please, send me home," I begged.

The nurse frowned at my urgent tone. She paused a moment, then telephoned my mother.

Once I was home, I felt fine. I cuddled under my down comforter, read one of my favorite horror novels and then watched a soap opera on TV. My mother served me strawberry Jell-O and sliced bananas for dinner. I was an only child, and my mom spoiled me. She gave me a hug. "You'll be up and around tomorrow," she assured me. At home, I was safe.

The next day, I convinced my parents that I was too weak to return to school, but I was really just afraid. "Okay, just one more day of rest," my mother told me, "but make sure you do the homework. You don't want to ruin your A average."

The following morning, my mother said, "Get up and get dressed, have a bit of breakfast and see how you feel." I knew this trick. She'd been using it on me since I was a kid. Once I had pulled on some clothes and had eaten, she'd say, "If you're healthy enough to be out of bed and keep cereal down, you're well enough to go to school." And that's exactly what happened.

One afternoon a few days later, one of my classmates asked me to her house for dinner. Supper at her house was a foreign experience for me. She had a big family, and they all talked at the same time, fighting to be heard.

Suddenly, the hum of the kitchen lights became loud and drowned out their voices. Their faces looked too clear in the unnatural light. My cheeks began to go numb, and I felt like the floor was caving in under my feet. It was happening again. Maybe one of the blood vessels in my brain is slowly leaking blood, I thought. I had to get out. I had to find help. I mumbled, "Excuse me. I feel sick," and I bolted from the house.

I ran all the way home. I slammed the front door behind me and collapsed on the family room sofa. "What in the world are you doing home so early?" my mother asked.

"I don't feel well, again," I told her. I felt tears well in my eyes. "What is wrong with me?"

My parents were concerned about me, but not as worried as I was about myself. They scheduled an appointment with my doctor. I explained the scary episodes to him. He ordered a test for diabetes. I had to swallow this super sweet, cola-flavored glucose drink, and I had blood taken from my arm. I went for stomach X-rays, where I had to drink a chalky barium milkshake. Finally, he sent me for a full neurological exam.

When the test results were in, the doctor telephoned.

"I'm glad to say that you are perfectly healthy," the doctor told me. My parents thought that was great news, but I wasn't sure.

The next morning, I couldn't face going back to school and the frightening possibility of another episode. I lied and told my mother that my stomach hurt. "The doctor said you are healthy," she reminded me. "He didn't test me for the stomach flu," I insisted. That nonexistent stomach virus bought me two more days at home.

When the third morning arrived, I just couldn't drag myself to class. For two weeks, I refused to go. Each day, I cried, screamed and begged. At first, my parents tried to reason with me; then they threatened to punish me. My father yelled, and my mother dissolved into tears. Again, they turned to my doctor for help, and he suggested that I see a psychologist. Oh, great, I am totally insane after all.

I was queasy with nerves at my first appointment with the psychologist. He was an old guy, but he was funny. He told me about a time that he was giving a speech at the local high school. "My microphone wouldn't work, so the janitor hopped up on the stage to check out the equipment. After a bit of fiddling, the janitor shouted, 'There's a screw loose in the speaker!'" I giggled and the knot in my stomach disappeared.

He listened quietly as I told him about my problem. "Your racing heart, tingling hands and your need to escape sound like classic symptoms of a panic attack," he told me. "In a panic attack, your body reacts like someone just jumped out of the closet and scared you, but, really, no one is there. Many people suffer with panic disorder. With some work on your part, and courage, it is a condition that can be overcome."

I leaned back into the chair's overstuffed cushion. I felt so relieved to have a name for what was happening to me.

I was having panic attacks, and I wasn't the only one in the world, either.

The next few times I met with my therapist, he taught me relaxation exercises. He told me to close my eyes and picture a calm place. "I'm lying on the beach on a sunny July Fourth day," I told him. "Just leave before the fireworks," he joked. Then I had to imagine that my muscles were so relaxed and heavy that they were sinking into the warm sand. I was supposed to breathe deeply and slowly. We talked about how to use these techniques until a panic attack ended.

When I mastered these exercises, the psychologist took me to a 4 P.M. field trip to my school. I sat at my desk in the empty classroom and practiced my relaxation. We walked around the school until I felt comfortable.

"Tomorrow, you'll have to try a full classroom," he said.

My stomach tightened. "What if the teacher won't let me leave the class if I have to? What if the nurse won't let me go home?" I asked.

"We can take care of those fears," he assured me. My therapist made special arrangements with my teachers. They agreed that I could leave the room without asking for a pass, and the nurse would let me call home, no questions asked.

I was shaking the first morning when I entered homeroom, but my friends gathered around me and told me how great it was to have me there. "I've missed you guys," I told them. I was glad to be back.

It wasn't easy, though. The panic attacks were still the scariest things I'd ever experienced. Sometimes, I could stay in the classroom and relax through them. Other times, I slipped out the door and sat in the hall until they passed.

The popular kids made a warped game of trying to gross me out so I would leave the class. They would make disgusting vomiting noises or stare at me with their eyelids turned inside out. I was so mad that I forced myself to stay in my seat. In a twisted way, their being mean actually helped me.

My real friends stood by me, though, and every day got a bit easier. Before my eighth grade graduation, there was a school talent show. I played the piano in front of a full auditorium. When the judges handed me the first place trophy, my parents and friends gave me a standing ovation. I felt so proud of myself, not because I'd won, but because I'd beaten the panic attacks. I couldn't wait for high school.

~Marie-Therese Miller
Chicken Soup for the Preteen Soul 2

I Said No

I may not have gone where I intended to go,
but I think I have ended up where I intended to be.
~Douglas Adams

I was eighteen years old when I left home for the first significant period of time. As a college freshman, I spent the five hour drive upstate arguing with my mother about the speed limit and the radio. When we arrived, I was eager for her to depart.

Growing up, I had been shy, reclusive and insecure. I viewed going to college as a chance to wipe that slate clean. Despite my parents' reminder that "we take our hang-ups everywhere we go," I wanted to become an entirely new person, outgoing and confident. I began to introduce myself with my middle name instead of my first, about which I had been teased for years.

I met Brian my first day on campus. A tall, charming senior, this Texan lived right down the hall and helped me move my things in. Although I was suspicious of the endless string of compliments he drawled, I was also quite flattered. I had never believed I was beautiful, though my family told me so all the time. I didn't date much in high school—just the occasional movie date with this boy or a walk around the mall with that one. I felt special when Brian called out, "Hey, gorgeous" even when I was wearing my glasses instead of my contact lenses.

My roommate, Tara, had turned out to be a disaster. Tara was a homesick Bostonian who cried all day about how she should have joined the Peace Corps. Frankly, I also rather enjoyed the idea of her departing for some far-off country. The tension between us made Brian's room a haven of sorts for me. He would fix me screwdrivers, which I sipped while he downed beer after beer and talked about scamming people for money. I knew he was bad news, but at the time that just made him more appealing.

One night he came into my room and lifted me over his shoulder. He carried me, kicking, screaming and laughing, into his room and began tickling me. The next thing I knew, we were kissing.

We began fooling around every day. He was much more experienced than I, who had never done more than kiss. I was upfront about my virginal status, and he said he was fine with it. Then one night things got out of hand.

I remember certain things, like we were watching *The Cutting Edge*, and I was wearing my white ribbed tank top. I had been hinting all week about wanting to discuss "where we stood," but he kept dodging the subject in that sly way of his. It was like pulling teeth, but I finally got an answer—only it wasn't the one I was hoping for. He didn't want a girlfriend because he was graduating in the spring.

I felt stupid and used. All I wanted was someone to love me. We started discussing sex again, but I knew I wasn't ready, especially with someone who wouldn't commit to me. He said there were other things we could do, to which I finally consented, even though I knew it was against my better judgment.

It happened so fast. One minute we were making out, doing "other things," then before I knew it, it was all over. I wasn't a virgin anymore. I was so shocked, I couldn't move or speak. I was so angry, so scared, so confused—and I couldn't quite believe it had happened.

After it was over, Brian made me swear not to tell anyone. At that time, I was so humiliated, I couldn't imagine telling another soul. I was sure my friends and family would lose all respect for me because I had sex with a guy I had only known for a short while. It took me a while to accept that what happened to me wasn't sex.

Most of us have a stereotyped image of sexual assault. In the TV movie of the week, rape is about being grabbed in a dark alley by a stranger. It is always violent and always leaves physical scars. That isn't what happened to me. As with most women who are sexually assaulted, I knew my attacker. The scars left by "acquaintance rape" are emotional, yet the scars last just as long as, or longer than, physical scars.

After it happened, I had tests done for STDs and pregnancy, all of which were fortunately negative. I moved to another dorm, all the way across campus, where I would no longer be greeted with Brian's sheepish, "Hey, kiddo, how's it going?" I talked to my friends. I went to a counselor. It's a process, and it makes me angry that I have to live with it for the rest of my life. But it's fading. I am moving past it.

One thing that really helped me was the "Take Back the Night" march on campus, where victims, their friends and anyone opposed to rape joins in a rally. Afterward there was a speak-out, and girl after girl got up to tell her story. It shocked me to see how many young women have experienced some version of what I went through.

All of our stories are different, yet the same. While I wish this had never happened to any of us, it makes me feel better that I can be available to help someone else who may experience something similar.

~Natasha Carrie Cohen
Chicken Soup for the College Soul

Lumps

If you don't like something, change it;
if you can't change it, change the way you think about it.
~Mary Engelbreit

It's strange how it takes realizing your life will never be the same again to see how great each day really is. I was fourteen years old, and I had been diagnosed with Hodgkin's lymphoma, a cancer of the lymph nodes.

Last winter, I made frequent visits to different doctors for several problems. I had a severe case of asthma and allergies and rashes on my legs. I had hip pains that kept me up at night. I was anemic, too. One afternoon, I went in to see my doctor about my hip pains and some swelling in my throat. We thought I had tonsillitis. My doctor took a few X-rays and said everything looked fine. He looked inside my mouth and found a mild case of thrush, an infection, which he said would probably go away in a couple of weeks. When he felt my throat, he became concerned. I had several, hard-as-rocks lumps in my neck, chest and shoulders, where the lymph glands are. They weren't tender (if they were, that would have been because of a cold) and when I tilted my head, you could see lumps sticking out of my neck. He told my mother on the phone that night that he wanted me to be seen at Children's Hospital.

That night I went out to see a movie with my boyfriend at the time, Matt. I had a great time. I didn't even know that I was going to the hospital the next day. When I woke up the next morning, my mom told me to get ready. The whole way to the hospital, I had this weird feeling in my stomach, as if I were going up one of those tall roller coaster hills.

It took us forever to find a parking space. When we made it inside, it didn't look like those hospitals in movies, all spic-and-span clean and wall-to-wall white. It was kind of warm and cozy, just like a hospital for small people should be.

When we went into the waiting room, a little bald girl with bright blue eyes and a smile walked out. I thought to myself, "Oh, how cute. I wonder what she is here for." Then, I saw a boy from my school walk in who I didn't know very well. I knew he had cancer the year before. I knew his name was Matt, just like my boyfriend, and I knew that all the schools in the city we live in had heard about him and the disease he had. After he sat down, a little boy walked in wearing a black beanie hat. I eavesdropped on his conversation with his mother.

"Eric, wasn't it funny what Daddy told you to do this morning?" his mother asked.

"What did he tell me to do?" he responded.

"He said, 'Go upstairs, get dressed, brush your teeth and brush your hair!' Remember what you told him?" she asked.

"I don't have any hair!" Eric said with a smile.

Just then I realized where I was and why I was there. I was in the cancer clinic because of the lumps on my neck. I knew from listening to my doctor's "Mmm-hmm"s and "Uh-huh"s that things weren't normal. After my mom filled out some papers, they finally called me in. This really pretty, blond doctor named Jennifer felt around my neck, underarms, shoulders, stomach and pelvic area. She measured the lumps on my neck and wrote stuff down on a piece of paper.

She had this worried look on her face. "You have such pretty hair, nice skin and your weight is healthy. I'm worried about those lumps on your neck, though, sweetie. We're going to have to do a biopsy on some of those lumps. It's a procedure where we make a small incision in your neck and take some out to do tests. I'd also like to do a bone marrow test while we're at it."

I started crying and looked at her. "Am I going to die?" I asked.

"I doubt it," she said. "This cancer is 90 percent curable."

She gave me a hug and helped us schedule the biopsy. All the way home, my mom and I cried. When I got home, I called all of my friends and told them.

I went back to the hospital for my biopsy, and they put a bracelet on me and put me in bed to watch some movies while I waited. I watched *Ever After*, *Clueless* and the beginning of *A Bug's Life* before they came in to tell me what was going to happen. They gave me a Valium to relax me, which made me pretty sleepy. I tried to go to the bathroom and, when I got out of bed, I tripped because I was so dopey. My speech was slurred, too.

They hooked me up to an IV and rolled my bed down a large hallway and into a small, white room. There were several doctors in there, all wearing funny hats. They put a mask on me and told me to breathe deeply. It seemed like I blinked and then realized I was in the recovery room. It wasn't like in those movies where the people just automatically flutter their eyes and wake up to see lots of people around their bedside, looking at them with presents, teddy bears and balloons. Waking up felt like trying to bench-press five hundred pounds with my eyelids. And I wasn't so glamorous, either. I remember saying, "Ow... Oww... OWW!" Then I heard people talking about morphine to take away the pain. It did make me feel a little better. My mom helped me put on my clothes and they wheeled me out to my mom's car. I crashed on the couch as soon as I got home.

The next day I went to our school's Winter Ball and my boyfriend, Matt, dedicated the song "Let's Get It On" by Marvin Gaye to me, just to make me laugh. I didn't really dance that night because I was still tired and I was in a lot of pain, but I had fun.

A couple of days later, I went back to the hospital to see how the biopsy turned out. I had this feeling in my stomach. I knew I had cancer. I was right. I did have cancer. I burst into tears again because I knew my life would never be the same. I knew my hair was going to fall out; I knew I was going to have to endure chemotherapy; I knew all of it. And I just wanted to pretend I was dreaming.

I'm halfway done with my cycles of chemotherapy now and I'm not bald yet, but my hair is incredibly thin and still falling out. Matt and I broke up a couple of months ago. I was going out with this guy, Lucas, for a while but then he broke up with me. I'm okay with it, though, because there will be new romances. I will have new relationships. There's lots of life to live. I've told all of the people who I love that I love them. I wrote letters to those people I had stopped writing to. I've tried things I was once scared to do. I pretty much have a normal, fourteen-year-old teenage girl's life. I've been able to go to school pretty regularly except I'm not there a few Mondays a month. I just keep on saying to myself, "I'm a fighter, not a victim of cancer." People have complimented me on how strong I am. Now that I think of it, maybe they're right.

~Christina Angeles
Chicken Soup for the Teenage Soul on Tough Stuff

Not Alone

*What life means to us is determined not so much by what life brings to us
as by the attitude we bring to life;
not so much by what happens to us as by our reaction to what happens.*
~Lewis L Dunnington

Dear Chicken Soup,

I'm entering my senior year in high school. I'm approaching college and getting ready to leave behind many rough memories of my high school days.

My struggles started in seventh grade when I began passing out. I had various tests done to see why. I was told I had low blood pressure, which causes a rapid heartbeat. I tested many medications and finally found one that helped. My average blood pressure was about 80/60 on a good day. To this day, I continue to battle this problem.

Then, two years ago, I was diagnosed with fibromyalgia, a muscle disease that is not really helped by medication. It's like having a pulled muscle and when your muscles flare up, it can last as long as three months. There are eighteen points in the body where it can occur. I have it in twelve of the eighteen points. I was bedridden for a month two years ago. Cold weather, rain, or physical or emotional stress can trigger the flare-ups.

It's hard enough to be a healthy teenager and go through the typical changes with friends, family, relationships, school, etc. Add to that missing two to three months of school a year, and it can make things very difficult. The hardest part was, on the outside I looked normal like everyone else; however, on the inside I was in horrible pain. Some teachers have passed judgment on me thinking that since my physical appearance is fine I must be okay. One teacher even told my class when I was absent one day that I was faking my heart problem. Those judgments hurt me more than anyone will ever know. I felt like I was always having to prove myself to everyone. I have lost friends, but I have also realized who my true friends really are.

I battled with depression as well, because I felt like an outsider, a freak, isolated from the rest of the world. I longed to be normal and healthy. I even developed an eating disorder. In the beginning, I had lost a lot of weight because of my heart condition. I went from a size eleven to a size six in one year. For the first time, I felt like I was attractive because I was skinny. I was receiving more attention than ever. I felt like people liked me more because I was skinny and that mindset was a large part of my eating problem. I would still feel depressed, though, because of all that was going on in my life, and I would eat a lot hoping the stress would go away. But then I would throw up the food so I would still look good. Eventually I overcame both these problems with the help of family, friends and a wonderful job.

My mother, who is an amazing woman, stuck by me and encouraged me in all my times of need. She has truly inspired me. She took the time to try and understand all that I was feeling and was there for me when I felt like I had no one. Having her believe in me helped me to believe in myself. She helped me get a job at the retirement home where she worked. I had grown up around this place but working there changed my life. To help these elderly people and see the sparkle of appreciation they got in their eyes was wonderful and motivating. I found a purpose knowing I had something to give to these people. I gained a confidence that was disassociated from my looks. I was loved by them unconditionally. This gave me the strength to overcome my depression and my eating disorder. This also helped open my eyes and see that my real friends didn't care if I was skinny or not; they loved me for who I was on the inside.

Life can be so overwhelming, but I feel much stronger now having overcome these obstacles. I have had plenty of time to dig deep into myself to find the person I am. I have been able to figure out what I value in my life — that I don't need to prove myself if someone doesn't understand me. A goal in my life is to help other young people find positives in their lives even when faced with certain obstacles.

Your books have helped me to realize that I'm not alone in my struggles; that there are other people out there going through similar adversities. So many teenagers have found the strength they need in the stories in these books. I am hoping my story might do the same — that would make me feel good.

Sincerely,
~Andrea Blake
Chicken Soup for the Teenage Soul Letters

Teens Talk

Tough Times

Tough Choices

Sometimes if you want to be a winner,
you have to be willing to bear the scars from the fight.
~Petra Salvaje

A Sobering Place

The journey of a thousand miles must begin with a single step.
~Lao Tzu

"What will you have?" the waiter asks.

"A Shirley Temple," I shoot back. When I go out I always order the same drink. The sparkling Sprite with grenadine and a maraschino cherry allows me to pretend, to fit in with my friends somehow, to cast aside the hurt of my childhood.

I don't drink and I've never been drunk, but now and then I do wonder what it would feel like. I'm afraid, though, that one sip might lead to many more, and that one day I might become an alcoholic.

That's what my mother is.

The sweet Shirley Temple hides a bitter past and a picture etched in my memory: Mom is sitting on the couch, legs crossed, drinking malt liquor. I tend to forget that I was the one who grabbed it from the refrigerator for her. I tapped the top, even tilted it to the glass and poured it for her. At five years old, I was my mother's bartender.

When I was a little girl, I had long hair, and I thought that made me pretty.

"More hair," Mom would say, as she braided the last of four ponytails.

"Grow longer," I'd answer, while she wrapped yellow ribbons around my braids.

But we didn't have our little ritual on weekends. On weekends Mom got drunk. She was a mean drunk and didn't clean the house or comb my hair. She broke lamps, cursed Dad and even threw things at him. The arguments always ended the same way: She'd leave, dressed to the nines in high heels and a sleek dress that showed off her long legs. I cried when she left. She would be gone for one, sometimes two days at a time, partying. I would wonder if she was ever coming back.

She always did. Groggy, tired. I didn't care. I was just glad Mom was back. I hated her drinking, but I didn't hate her. I loved her then and I love her now. I separated my mom from the alcohol, decided the liquor was the monster.

When I grow up, I vowed to myself, I won't curse out my husband or act mean with my children. I won't drink.

The message never rang so loud in my head as it did when I was sixteen. When most kids were circling the local McDonald's on Friday and Saturday nights, I was out cruising the city streets with my dad, looking for Mom's car. Dad, a career military man, searched for hours, fearful she would drive home drunk, get a DUI or have an accident. But when he found her in a club, she would refuse to leave. So I'd slide over into his seat and put the car in gear. He'd slip into the parking lot and drive out in her car. I would follow him home, pull into the driveway behind him and slam the door, thinking about Mom out there stranded in some nightclub. It didn't make sense.

Mom would get drunk; Dad and I would leave her. I didn't think that either of them was right.

My mother had been raised poor in the Deep South. She had been shuttled from house to house until she was a teenager, and she had no idea who her father was — these were her demons, and she was unable to drink them away. So she tried again and again to rehabilitate herself. Once I even spent a week with her in rehab, telling my side of the story, trying to help. The scene always played out the same way: She would enter an angry woman and leave as my mother, the woman who had tied yellow ribbons in my hair. But soon the demons would find a home in her again, pushing her down those twelve steps she had so painstakingly climbed.

They say alcoholics have to hit rock bottom before they can change. Mom didn't land there until after she divorced my father. My father left, taking my little brother and me with him to South Carolina. Alcohol had won, and she had lost everything—her marriage, her children, her home. My brother and I had never truly bonded with our father, whose work took him to Korea and later to Operation Desert Storm in the Middle East, but we decided to live with him anyway.

After losing her marriage and her children, my mother continued to drink for another seven years. Mom doesn't drink anymore. "I just got tired, Boo," she said recently. "Getting up drunk, going to bed drunk, I got tired of living that life."

Nearly three decades after she sipped her first rum and Coke at a military dance, she stopped. No more malt liquor, no more brandy, no more whiskey sours. She's a devoted participant in a Twelve-Step program and hasn't had a drink in nearly five years.

Meanwhile, I kept my promise. I didn't drink, either. I stepped outside my mother's footsteps and walked in another direction. It took me, literally and figuratively, to a sobering place. Occasionally, I get an urge to leave there. When I do, I grab something sweet—a Shirley Temple.

~Monique Fields
Chicken Soup for the Teenage Soul on Tough Stuff

My Toughest Decision

Good decisions come from experience,
and experience comes from bad decisions.
~Author Unknown

Mistakes, mistakes, mistakes. Everyone makes them. No one saw mine coming.

Overall, I was a really good kid. At fifteen, I was a sophomore at a Catholic high school and a member of the National Honor Society. I played softball and ran cross country. I had, and still have, aspirations of becoming a doctor. If someone had told me that at the age of fifteen I would become pregnant, I would have said they were crazy. Why would anyone do something so foolish? It's still hard for me to believe, but it happened.

October 11th was the day my daughter was born. I took one look at her, and it was love at first sight. It was so overwhelming—a flood of emotions that I have never experienced. I loved her in a way that could only be described as unconditional. I looked at her, and in my heart I knew that I could not give her all the things that she needed and deserved to have, no matter how badly I wanted to. Physically, emotionally and in every other way, I was not capable of being a mother. I knew what had to be done. Putting all my emotions aside and doing what I felt was best for my daughter, I decided to give her up for adoption.

Placing my baby in the arms of her mother was the hardest thing I've ever had to do. My very soul ached. Even though I still get to see my daughter because I am blessed with having an open adoption, the pain is still there. I can feel it burning inside me every day when I think about Katelyn. I only hope that when she gets older, she realizes how much I love her. I love her more than anything in the world.

Today is my daughter's first Christmas. I won't be there to share with her the joy of this season, or to play Santa and open her presents for her (she's only two months old). In fact, I won't be there to see her first step, or hear her first word. I won't be there to take pictures on her first day of kindergarten. When she cries for her mommy, it won't be me that she wants. I know in my heart that I made the right choice. I just wish with all my heart that it was a choice I never had to make.

~Kristina Dulcey
Chicken Soup for the Teenage Soul II

A Step Toward Healing

We must try not to sink beneath our anguish... but battle on.
~J.K. Rowling

I look at my reflection in the bathroom mirror and think, Will I be missed if I die? Do I really have a purpose in this superficial world?

"Hurry up, Yaa, you're going to be late for school again!" my mom screams from downstairs.

I take my bag and head for school. I sit in class and listen uninterested as my first period teacher rambles on about the speed of light. Lately I have lost interest in everything including after-school activities. My mind is consumed with the hopelessness of ending my life. I look at the teacher and curiously wonder if she can detect the grief in my eyes.

At school, I don't belong to any specific clique. Even though I am a cheerleader, I don't really hang around with them anymore. I don't belong with the drama students despite the fact that I am in the drama club, or the computer kids even though I like learning about computers, not even the Goths, although I listen to heavy metal. I simply can't bring myself to be with a particular circle of individuals. I just walk around the hallways, occasionally stopping to chat with some "friends." I don't even have a best friend. At lunch, I sit and listen to people talk and sometimes even try to participate in the conversation so no one will be suspicious of my sudden change in behavior.

After cheerleading practice, I go home up to my room and cry and cry because I don't understand where this feeling of depression is coming from, and it's overwhelming. I listen to sad songs because I feel better when the pain is directed somewhere else. Every night, before my mom comes home, I wash my face to hide any evidence of tears because I know how hard she works and the last thing she needs is to worry about me. We always eat dinner together, and during that time I assure her that my health, classes, school and everything in general is fine.

She always says, "Yaa, I know high school can be tough, and if anyone or anything is bothering you, you can talk to me and let me know."

It's every time she says these words that I open my mouth and try to tell her about what I am going through, but I am so convinced that she will never understand it and that no one will ever understand me because I don't even understand myself.

Late one night as I lie in bed, I look up at the ceiling and think of the many ways to end this misery. I finally come to the conclusion to end my life. As is customary with those who've decided to kill themselves, I decide to leave my mom a suicide note.

I start with the words "I am sorry," and I continue writing, listing my reasons, my everyday sadness and my lack of interest in everything. I tell her I love her and it's best for me to do this and that we will meet up in heaven someday. As I begin to fold the letter, I realize what I am about to do, and I'm not scared; in fact, it's comforting to me. Then I think of my mom. I realize I am her only source of hope and happiness in this world. I realize how much pain she will go through. She tries so hard to make me—her only child—happy. My father left us six months ago to get married to another lady. I cry when I see my selfishness, cry some more when I reread the letter out loud. I collapse on the floor. Maybe death isn't the road to regaining my happiness, because I remember there was a time in my life when I was happy. I sway my weary body as I cry. I wipe away my tears and head to my mom's room. I knock on the door.

"Yaa, is that you?" her tired voice asks.

"Yes, Mom," I respond. I start crying as I walk toward her.

"What's wrong?"

I tell her everything. She cries and hugs me, and I feel relieved.

After that night, we sought help together, and I met a lot of kids in my same situation, and I understood how much better life could be. Ending my life was not the solution to my freedom and happiness. Talking about it, no matter how hard, was a giant step toward healing.

~Yaa Yamoah
Chicken Soup for the Teenage Soul IV

Dangerous Depression

Adversity introduces a man to himself.
~Author Unknown

"Blah, blah, blah, blah, blah..." was all I heard while my Spanish teacher lectured the class about verb conjugation or something like that. Someone raised his hand to ask a question. I struggled to keep my eyes open. "You need to listen to this," I thought to myself. Our teacher went off topic, again, and started telling us a really interesting story that had nothing to do with learning Spanish. I looked at the clock. There were still thirty minutes of class left. But a minute later, the bell rang. It couldn't possibly be the dismissal bell.

"Is there an earthquake or fire drill today?" I thought to myself. Usually the teachers forewarned students about drills, but this bell rang longer than it should have. There could only be one reason that a bell like that would ring: a lockdown drill.

After locking the classroom door, our teacher immediately called the office to ask them what was going on. They didn't know, but they did say that the bell was not for a lockdown drill but for an actual lockdown! Everyone in the class got scared. The students began to talk among themselves, including me. One girl, Joyce, had to go to bathroom really bad, but no one was allowed to leave class. An armed gunman could be walking the halls for all we knew. Before I knew it the dismissal bell rang, but we couldn't go to break because no one could leave class. Joyce just couldn't hold it anymore. So our teacher asked for an administrator to escort one of her students to the restroom—it was an emergency. It wasn't too long after Joyce came back that a girl in my class got a cell phone call from her friend, and we found out what was going on.

In Room 309, another classroom just two halls away, a boy stood up with a loaded gun, pointed it at the teacher, and started talking about how horrible his life was and how stupid his family was. While he was speaking one of the teacher aides snuck out of the classroom with about five students and ran to the office. It was then that the lockdown bell rang. The boy with the gun waved it around while the teacher and his friend tried to calm him down. The boy pointed the gun at a student named Greg. His friend saw this and, although terrified, jumped on the boy. Greg, seeing that the boy was distracted, immediately grabbed the gun. An administrator came in, and soon after the police arrested the boy.

I called my parents and left school early that day, along with half of the school. The students from Room 309 went to counseling for the next few weeks, which brought them behind in their classes.

The boy with the gun is now in jail; he will never participate in a graduation ceremony. However bad his life was, it cannot be worse than it is now. I wish he knew there are other ways to cope with trauma than by using a weapon on yourself or others. Help is always there.

~Rosie Ojeda
Chicken Soup for the Teenage Soul: The Real Deal School

14

That Warm Night

I was invited to a party,
a few roads across town.
I thought I'd meet my friends there,
but they were not around.
So I hopped into my beat up car,
ready for adventure.
My mom came racing to my door,
I was ready for my lecture.
Instead she told me softly,
to be careful that warm night.
I promised her that I'd drive safely,
that everything would be all right.
I arrived at the location,
and accepted a small drink.
I didn't really want it,
but I didn't stop to think.
Soon I was gulping cocktails,
feeling lighter with each sip.
And I felt so free, invincible,
as I swallowed the last drip.
The room was spinning freely,
as I danced across the floor.
And I wondered why I hadn't ever
drank this much before.

Then, despite my happiness and fun,
my head began to ache.
I found my car keys in my purse,
'cause my brain was going to break.
I stumbled across the gardens,
unlocked my beat up car.
Started up the engine,
headed across town once more.
But something tragic happened,
I didn't see the light.
I didn't see the people, either,
crossing that warm night.
As I slid across the pavement,
I knew my time had come.
My head just kept on spinning—
all this for just some fun.
The next moments were quite hazy,
as I lay mangled in the car.
Pain shooting through my body,
never thought it'd go this far.
Heard sirens in the background,
rushing to my aid.
But as I closed my tired eyes,
I knew it was too late.

As I saw the world below me,
my heart just filled with dread.
I saw the people that I hit,
and knew that they were dead.
I cried so hard on that warm night,
as I floated through the sky.
Knowing that it was my fault,
and I never said goodbye.
Now I'm floating up to heaven,
where I really don't belong.

Brought so much pain to others,
did something really wrong.
I killed six happy people,
four kids, a man and wife.
And I'm lying in a coffin,
because I lost my precious life.
I see my mother's upset face,
her eyes so filled with tears.
"This wasn't supposed to happen,
this is exactly what I feared."
I was just a normal teen,
who had too much to drink.
I had a boyfriend, did well in school,
but that night I didn't think.
So the next time you're invited
to a party with your friends,
Please remember this could be
the night when it could end.
I learned all this the hard way,
and made a terrible mistake.
So please don't do what I did,
and drink as much as you can take.
I had so much before me,
a great future straight ahead.
I wanted to be an actress,
but I can't because I'm dead.
It happened all so quickly,
didn't even get to fight.
Didn't know how fast my life could end,
I'll always remember that warm night.

~Sarah Woo
Chicken Soup for the Teenage Soul on Tough Stuff

15

Independence Day

I can still hear our prepubescent voices calling out to one another in the camp's swimming pool. Back in the days when getting our ears pierced and owning Cavarichis determined whether we were cool, the closest we came to cigarettes was fake smoking with pretzels.

We were children who thought we knew everything but really knew very little. Stubborn, we believed the New Kids on the Block and Vanilla Ice were the coolest groups around and couldn't fathom our tastes ever changing, ourselves ever changing.

The years passed. We graduated from high school and went off to different colleges, where we did change. Some of us became vegans, others atheists. We changed our majors, from Spanish to communications to international relations... and some of us began toweling our doors so the RAs wouldn't detect we were doing hands-on experiments for our drugs and human behavior class.

I suppose I shouldn't be surprised that my childhood friends have grown up to smoke everything that doesn't smoke them first. I remember my elementary school had a representative from D.A.R.E. (Drug Abuse Resistance Education) come and warn us against the dangers of drug use. He explained about everything from shooting heroin to huffing common household products. Apparently his warnings backfired, for I recollect one of my classmates inhaling a bottle of Wite-Out during recess.

It's not that I expected everything to stay the same. In fact, I welcomed change and was eager to go off to college and begin a new life. I knew some of my friends and I would grow apart, but I never could have predicted how I would feel when I saw one of them snorting coke.

I was visiting a friend at her college and had become aware of changes in her since high school. She now smoked like a chimney, which was actually mild in comparison to the other toxins she routinely put in her body. As she lit up her zillionth cigarette of the day, I made a cancer comment to which she rolled her eyes and flippantly responded, "Well, I guess if I ever get suicidal, I'll be well on my way."

We were in one of her friends' off-campus houses, and, just like the movies, white powder was carefully laid along a mirror and cut with a razor. I was offered a line but shook my head no and watched in shock as my chain-smoking friend expertly snorted one.

Minutes later, bustling with energy, she rambled, "People think cocaine is a really big deal, but now you see it's not. I'm just really happy and alive right now, that's all."

I felt sick to my stomach seeing her like this and high-tailed it out of there, spending the night with a friend who had also declined the drug. Personally, I have found cocaine to be especially terrifying ever since childhood, when I read a Sweet Valley High book in which one of Elizabeth Wakefield's friends tries coke at a party and dies of a heart attack. If the writers intended to scare children away from coke while they were still impressionable, they sure accomplished that with me.

I think how we've changed and why we've changed since going off to college, and I've realized some things. Peer pressure is not like an after school special where a group of bad kids with a joint surround a younger, smaller kid, saying, "Come on, don't be a chicken. Try it! You know you want to." It's more the internal pressure of feeling like a loser for being scared and wondering whether it can really be that bad if your friends are all doing it.

When you're living on your own for the first time, it's easy to get caught up in the moment. (Just look at the number of college girls flocking to the health center Monday morning for the morning after pill.) A part of me wants to believe drugs really aren't that big a deal, that you're only young once and yada, yada, yada. But then I see the death tolls of kids my age and sometimes younger. And it scares me—it really does. I see the flashing lights of ambulances, and it seems kind of ironic that drinking oneself into alcohol toxicity is how we try to show our independence.

When it comes down to it, living on your own is about making decisions—not always the right ones, but, hopefully not so many wrong ones that you lose your chance.

~Natasha Carrie Cohen
Chicken Soup for the College Soul

16

No Longer a Child

Hold a true friend with both your hands.
~Nigerian Proverb

Jordana was a twelve-year-old girl like every other; she worried about her clothes, hair and boys. She always had a smile on her face and a warm hug to share. What most people did not know about her was that this little girl had some very grown-up problems. Her father caused these problems. He had sexually abused her when she was five and physically abused her for years after. The emotional scars left her in hidden shambles. Her mother and father divorced when Jordana was eight, leaving her mother with sole custody.

When we met in seventh grade, years after the abuse had stopped, she seemed like every other twelve-year-old girl. We became instant best friends, gossiping about movie stars, rock bands and boys. Jordana seemed happy living with her mother and stepfather, and when I asked about her father she only told me that she did not see him anymore.

One June day, I found out one of her biggest secrets. It was hot that day after school, and we went in Jordana's backyard to tan in tank tops and shorts. It was then that I noticed cuts on her arms, mirrored by scars of cuts that had already healed. When I asked her where she received the cuts, she turned to me and began to cry stories of the past, horrors flowing from her lips as fast as the tears fell from her eyes. Jordana told me that she had cut herself because she felt so much anger towards her father. She told me about the nights of terror, about beatings and the bruises. I didn't know what to do so I just listened, consoled and counseled to the best of my ability.

Not until I had gone home did I realize what had just happened. Jordana had trusted me with information that she had hidden deep inside for a dozen years. She had chosen my hand to reach out to and pleaded silently for me to reach back.

As the weeks went on the cuts became more frequent, as if she was using her body as a personal canvas. I became increasingly scared. I was too young to handle this myself. I realized soon that I did not have the means to help her, and my decision lay before me like a shallow grave. That day after school when Jordana was at basketball practice I went to her house and knocked on the door and reached out the only way I knew how, "Mrs. Brown, I have something I have to tell you." It was then that I realized I was no longer a child.

~Hilary E. Kisch
Chicken Soup for the Teenage Soul III

Sixty Second Flashback

Remember, if you're headed in the wrong direction, God allows U-turns!
~Allison Gappa Bottke

I sit in my Honda Civic stopped at a red light, staring straight ahead, when I catch a glimpse of a white Subaru. Out of habit, I turn my head to see if it is someone I know, someone I love deeply but haven't seen in three months — to see if it is Zach, my older brother, my other half. The man driving the Subaru reminds me an awful lot of Zach, but it's not Zach.

Suddenly, I drift off into my memories and remember all the things about my brother I love and miss so much. I think of how his dishwater blond hair would curl, and how he would try so hard to straighten it by wearing a baseball hat until his hair was dry, or by plastering it with gel, only to make it curl even more. I think of how he would get angry with me for trying to wear his baggy pants and shirts so I could look like him. He wanted to be his own person. I remember how, whenever I was down, he would hug me and tell me how beautiful I was and then cheer me up even more by cracking some off-the-wall joke. He had a sense of humor that, no matter how upset somebody was, could always make that person laugh.

I recalled a conversation he and I had when I was fourteen and he was eighteen. We were both going through a tough time with our parents, though our situations were different. We were driving in his Subaru, practically brand-new then, and for the first time he opened up to me. I felt like he looked at me as his equal instead of his little sister. He began talking to me about how much he loved music and how music was his outlet for stress when things got too rough for him to handle. He looked me in the eyes, which he rarely did because he usually avoided direct eye contact, and he told me that I also possessed something deep down that would allow me to create when I felt I had nowhere to turn. He told me I just needed to search my soul, and I would find it. At that moment, I looked at him and wished so much that I could play the guitar or draw like him. He seemed to possess so many talents that I envied, and to hear him say that he saw creativity inside of me made me want to hug him. I didn't, though.

I remember him always being holed up in his room whenever he was home, which wasn't very often. He preferred going out partying with his friends. He was messing around with different kinds of drugs, which made him moody and difficult to tolerate. When he was around the house, there was a constant tension because he didn't want any of us telling him what to do; he didn't want to hear a thing we had to say. I guess that's why I was so surprised when he took me with him that day in the car and spoke to me with such sincerity.

My eyes begin to well up with tears as I remember the time, not too long ago, when his dog of ten years got cancer and had to be put to sleep. He slept in the garage with her for the last week of her life, and we were all together when she died. The look of loss in his eyes and the river of tears that flooded his cheeks told more about his love for his dog than any words he could have spoken. As he bent over and held her limp, lifeless body in his arms, his own body began to shake, and I realized how attached to her he was. As he stood up, I put my arms around him, hoping he would realize I was there for him, but he was distant and in his own world.

Later that day, he came walking through the garage door with sunglasses on, even though it was a rainy day, so that we couldn't see his red, puffy eyes. He always wore choker necklaces, but he had another necklace on that hadn't been there earlier. He pulled the necklace out from under his shirt and showed us that he was wearing his dog, Annie's, name tag.

I cry even more as I begin thinking about why we haven't spoken for three months. I had to set boundaries. I vividly recall the night when I awoke to hear him calling someone a bitch and a whore. I stood in the hallway and heard my brother calling his girlfriend names, thrashing all around the kitchen like a mad rabbit. He was incredibly drunk. The hurtful words that spewed from his mouth were ones I would only expect a deranged lunatic to say. They were not words that should be spoken to a loved one.

The next day I decided we needed to discuss the previous night. He stood in the family room with a vacant, yet defiant, look in his eyes as I began pouring open my soul about how much I worried about his alcohol consumption. It seemed the more I said, the further away he went. Finally, he looked at me, told me I was overreacting and that he was perfectly fine. I stood and listened to him deny my concerns, knowing that his denial was just a way to convince himself there was no problem. I gathered all the courage I had and proceeded to tell him that until he quit drinking and got help, there could be no brother-sister relationship between us. The look he gave me said more than words could ever express. I knew he thought I was over-reacting and that I wouldn't follow through—after all, I never had before.

He moved out two weeks later when my parents and I gave him the ultimatum of living at home sober or moving out. He chose the latter of the two. He was furious with us for making him choose. He has stayed away for three months now.

The light turns green, and I begin to cross the intersection while looking into the windows of the white Subaru. The man driving the car is built just like Zach. I realize how much I want to see him and wonder if I made the right decision. Then I think to myself what my dad told me the day Zach left: "Tiani, he may not realize it now, but he will thank you one day for loving him so much, that you put your foot down and let him know how things were going to be. Your mom and I love you and respect you for being so strong and caring that you would risk not talking to him to make him face the facts and get better." At that moment I knew I made the correct decision, and I said a little prayer that I would see my brother again soon.

~Tiani Crocker
Chicken Soup for the Teenage Soul on Tough Stuff

[*Editors' note*: We received the following update from Tiani: "Zach's drinking is no longer a problem; it has stopped controlling his life as well as our relationship. He has since moved back to Washington, is attending massage school, and is focusing on his health and fitness. He has grown in amazing ways—he has a stronger, healthier connection with the entire family, and we are all proud of him. I feel blessed to have our relationship back stronger than before, but even more blessed to have him as a male role model for my son."]

18

April 15th, the Worst and Best Day of My Life

Dear *Chicken Soup for the Teenage Soul*,

April 15th was the worst day of my life. I was nineteen years old. My body felt achy, my mind was cloudy and I felt as if I couldn't go on any longer. My face was pale, and my nerves were frazzled. It was on that day that I faced the biggest decision I have ever made.

Although I had dealt with depression before, it wasn't until the last few years when it really hit hard. It had become so bad that most days it was all I could do to keep breathing. On the outside I looked like a smart, happy and talented teenager. On the inside I was wilted and dying.

Things just kept on getting worse. I got to the point where I truly hated myself. I started to become self-destructive and ended up in therapy. My therapist tried to help me, and although I attended my weekly session and took my medication, it didn't help. I started to binge and purge and lost thirty pounds. I started to cut myself, using knives and sharp items to make me bleed. Because I couldn't understand or handle the emotional pain, I preferred the physical pain because I knew where it came from. My days were filled with thoughts of how I'd end my life and what I'd write in my suicide note. I also began to hurt my family and friends, pushing them away and saying hurtful things to them. I wanted them to hate me as much as I hated myself. They were only trying to help, but I couldn't, wouldn't accept help from anyone, not from my therapist, my friends or my family. I was too afraid to open up. I let all my emotions and feelings stay bottled up inside me. I had hit bottom — I was broken down and couldn't go any further into my hole. I didn't know what else to do.

So on April 15th, after a sleepless night, I had to make a decision that would affect the rest of my life. As I saw it, I had two choices — to give up and give in, or to fight.

After showering and trying to make my body look human, I got into my car and drove. I cried, and my mind was spinning. I felt like I was going to pass out, but I had made my choice and I promised myself I'd follow through no matter what. I finally arrived at my therapist's office, and spilled out the whole story: the cutting, the suicidal thoughts, everything. I felt as if my self-constructed dam of emotions had burst. Old pent-up emotions and feelings came rushing out and wouldn't stop. It came as a surprise to both of us — I hadn't talked much in therapy. It had been so hard to allow myself to be vulnerable with someone, and now I was letting her in on my darkest pain. And it was such a relief.

I drove home exhausted. I knew I had to tell my parents everything that was going on and I knew how hard it was going to be. It would hurt them to hear, just as much as it would hurt me to tell the truth. They were wonderful. That day and for days after, my large, extended family and friends surrounded me with love and support. They let me know how much I mattered to them — and for the first time in my life, I felt true love and happiness. Being honest about my feelings wasn't nearly as painful as I thought it would be; it actually felt incredible to finally express myself openly.

It's been a long road. Even now, I still get down and have hard days, but it's different. The darkness doesn't last as long and the depression isn't as bad. I'm twenty now and in my second year of college. I work part-time, sing in a choir and teach drama to junior high kids. I can finally let people love me and allow myself to love them back. I'm looking forward to becoming all that I can be. April 15th was the best day of my life, and I'll always remember it.

Thank you so much for your books. I hope my story will be one that helps others as much as certain stories have helped me.

Sincerely,

~Laurel Walker
Chicken Soup for the Teenage Soul Letters

Teens Talk Tough Times

Being There

*Friendship is the inexpressible comfort of feeling safe with a person,
having neither to weigh thoughts nor measure words.*
~George Eliot

19

Donna and Claudia

While we try to teach our children all about life,
our children teach us what life is all about.
~Angela Schwindt

Donna is my sister, and I always thought of her as beautiful. Our father called her his princess. When Donna entered high school, with her long blond hair and incredible blue eyes, she caught the attention of the boys. There were the usual crushes and school dances, phone calls and giggles, and hours of combing and brushing her hair to make it glow. She had eye shadow to match the perfect blue of her eyes. Our parents were protective of us, and my father in particular kept close watch over the boys she dated.

One Saturday in April, three weeks before Donna's sixteenth birthday, a boy called and asked her to go to an amusement park. It was in the next state, about twenty miles away. They would be going with four other friends. Our parents' first answer was a firm no, but Donna eventually wore them down. On her way out the door, they told her to be home by eleven, no later.

It was a great night! The roller coasters were fast, the games were fun and the food was good. Time flew by. Finally one of them realized it was already 10:45 P.M. Being young and slightly afraid of our father, the boy who was driving decided he could make it home in fifteen minutes. It never occurred to any of them to call and ask if they could be late.

Speeding down the highway, the driver noticed the exit too late. He tried to make it anyway. The car ripped out nine metal guardrails and flipped over three times before it came to a stop on its roof. Someone pulled Donna from the car, and she crawled over to check on her friends. There was blood everywhere. As she pulled her hair back from her eyes so she could see better, her hand slipped underneath her scalp.

The blood was coming from her. Practically the entire top of Donna's head had been cut off, held on by just a few inches of scalp.

When the police cruiser arrived to rush Donna to a nearby hospital, an officer sat with her, holding her scalp in place. Donna asked him if she was going to die. He told her he didn't know.

At home, I was watching television when a creepy feeling went through me, and I thought about Donna. A few minutes went by, and the telephone rang. Mom answered it. She made a groaning noise and fell to the floor, calling for my father. They rushed out the door, telling my sister Teri and me that Donna had been in a car accident, and that they had to go to the hospital to get her. Teri and I stayed up for hours waiting for them. We changed the sheets on Donna's bed and waited. Somewhere around four o'clock in the morning, we pulled the sofa bed out and fell asleep together.

Mom and Dad were not prepared for what they saw at the hospital. The doctors had to wait until our parents arrived to stitch up Donna's head. They didn't expect her to survive the night.

At 7:00 A.M., my parents returned home. Teri was still sleeping. Mom went straight to her bedroom and Dad went into the kitchen and sat at the table. He had a white plastic garbage bag between his legs and was opening it up when I sat down at the table with him. I asked him how Donna was and he told me that the doctors didn't think she was going to make it. As I struggled to think about that, he started pulling her clothes out of the bag. They were soaked with blood and blond hair.

Some of the hair had Donna's scalp attached to it. Every piece of clothing she had worn that night was soaked with blood. I can't remember thinking anything. All I did was stare at the clothes. When

Teri woke up, I showed them to her. I'm sure it was an awful thing to do, but I was in such shock that it was all I could think of.

At the hospital later that morning, Teri and I had to wait outside for a long time before we could see Donna. It was an old hospital and it smelled old, and Teri and I were afraid of it. Finally we were allowed in to see our sister. Her head was wrapped in white gauze that was stained with blood. Her face was swollen, which I couldn't understand because she had lost so much blood. I thought she would look smaller. She reached up and touched my long brown hair and started to cry.

The next day, I called a neighbor who was a hairdresser and asked her to cut my hair. It's a funny thing—I loved my long brown hair and it curled just right, but I never, ever missed it or wanted it back. All I wanted was for Donna to come home and sleep in the clean sheets that Teri and I had put on her bed.

Donna was in the hospital for two weeks. Many of her friends went to see her, especially Claudia, who was there a lot. Mom and Dad never liked Claudia—maybe because she seemed "fast," maybe because she spoke her mind; I don't really know. They just didn't like her being around.

Donna came home with the entire top half of her head shaved. She had hundreds of stitches, some of which came across her forehead and between her left eye and eyebrow. For a while she wore a gauze cap. Eventually she had our hairdresser neighbor cut the rest of her hair. It had been so soaked and matted with blood that she couldn't get it out. The hairdresser was such a kind person. She found Donna a human hair wig that perfectly matched her hair.

Donna celebrated her sixteenth birthday and went back to school. I don't know where rotten people come from, and I don't know why they exist, but they do. There was a very loud-mouthed, self-centered girl in some of Donna's classes who took great pleasure in tormenting my sister. She would sit behind her and pull slightly on Donna's wig. She'd say very quietly, "Hey, Wiggy, let's see your scars." Then she'd laugh.

Donna never said anything to anybody about her tormentor

until the day she finally told Claudia. Claudia was in most of Donna's classes, and started keeping a close eye on my sister. Whenever that girl got close to Donna, Claudia would try and be there. There was something about Claudia that was intimidating, even to the worst kids in school. No one messed with her. Unfortunately, though, Claudia wasn't always around, and the teasing and name calling continued.

One Friday night, Claudia called and asked Donna to come spend the night at her house. My parents didn't want Donna to go — not just because they didn't like Claudia, but because they had become so protective of Donna. In the end, they knew they had to let her go, even though they probably spent the whole night worrying.

Claudia had something special waiting for my sister. She knew how awful Donna felt about her hair, so Claudia had shaved off her own beautiful long brown hair.

The next day, she took Donna wig shopping for identical blond and brown wigs. When they went to school that Monday, Claudia was ready for the teasers. In a vocabulary not allowed inside school walls, she set them straight so that anyone ready to tease my sister knew they would have to mess with Claudia. It didn't take long for the message to get through.

Donna and Claudia wore their wigs for over a year, until they felt their hair had grown out enough to take them off. Only when Donna was ready did they go to school without them. By then, she had developed a stronger self-confidence and acceptance.

My sister graduated from high school. She is married and has two great kids. Twenty-eight years later, she is still friends with Claudia.

~Carol Gallivan
Chicken Soup for the Teenage Soul II

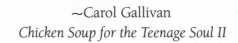

20

Jerry

B ack in early fall 2000, I met a person who would change my life forever—my friend, my brother, Jerry. Jerry was different from other kids. He had been born with such severe health and mental problems that his mother and family couldn't take care of him, and he was placed in foster care.

When I met Jerry at a residential treatment facility in Pittsburgh, he was thirteen years old and only four feet seven inches tall. He had very short black hair and big brown eyes. I loved him immediately. For the next month or two, we visited him in Pittsburgh, and he came to our home to visit us. During his short visits with us, Jerry and I talked, went to the store and watched TV. Jerry became one of my foster brothers four days before Christmas 2000.

Over the next two years, the bond between Jerry and I grew. He became more than a friend to me—I thought of him as a brother. Despite Jerry's physical limitations, we would play wiffle ball and go swimming. We would go camping with the family. At night, Jerry needed to be hooked up to oxygen to help him breathe, and a machine monitored his pulse. If he stopped breathing, an alarm would go off and wake us so we could help him.

Mom showed me how to hook up Jerry to the machines, and every night at bedtime, Jerry would hop on my back and I'd carry him downstairs to his room. The machines were noisy, and my room was right next to his, but I didn't mind. Jerry would yell "goodnight" to me, and I would yell "goodnight" back. I lay in bed and listened to his machines until I fell asleep.

Jerry had a reputation for being a troublemaker, but I loved him anyway. Eventually, he was placed back in and out of institutions and group homes because of his behavior. I continued to visit him in these institutions all over Pennsylvania. At some point, Jerry ran out of institutions in Pennsylvania due to the extreme level of care he required, so he went to a home in Oklahoma. Before he left, he was allowed a short home visit with us. I saw him for only two hours. That was the last time I would see Jerry, even though I talked to him on the phone every now and then and told him that I loved him.

On June 1, 2003, we received a call from the group home in Oklahoma saying that Jerry had died. I completely broke down. I didn't know what to say. I couldn't breathe. It felt like the walls were closing in on me. We went to Jerry's hometown for the viewing and funeral. We finally got to meet Jerry's real family—his mom, brother, sister, cousins, grandparents and nieces. At the viewing, his family had made a collage that included pictures of all of us, and we all had a chance to say one last goodbye to my friend, my brother, Jerry. Even though he's gone, I'll always love him... just like a brother.

~Andrew Woods
Chicken Soup for the Teenage Soul: The Real Deal Friends

21

For Such a Time as This

A true friend never gets in your way unless you happen to be going down.
~Arnold Glasow

My friend is so beautiful but she is blind to it. She has exotic dark features with full lips and flashing eyes. Her figure is one that many girls would kill to have, and her sense of style is undeniable. Although her beauty is so evident on the outside, it's what she has inside, her heart, that draws so many people to her: her kindness and compassion, her spirituality, and especially her sense of humor. She can make me crack up with a certain face or a noise. And this girl's voice is that of an angel. Talented in innumerable ways, she plays sports, dances and is an honor student. From group to group she flits, a social butterfly, unaware of the cliques, thinking each group is a different type of exquisite flower, each having different, but equally delicious nectar. Her many friends are constantly vying for her attention and approval, advice and comfort. She is popular not through fear, but by friendliness and authenticity. Which is why I can't understand how this wonder of a woman can possibly feel the way she does: worthless.

Not many know the self-loathing she feels. I am one of the few who have been granted a tiny peek into her mixed up world. I say mixed up because my friend just can't see her loveliness and realize her value. Stress runs her life, and anxiety is her constant companion. Pressure, she feels, is unavoidable. She wants it all to end, her pain to be banished forever, but she covers these unfathomable contemplations with extra smiles and laughter. There is no laughter when she is all alone and her mind is telling her she's nothing; the smiles are replaced with blank stares, and the sense of nothingness returns.

What do I do when I see my friend like this, a shell of what she once was? How do I convince this miracle of the beauty she possesses and that she is loved by others, when she can't love herself and look herself in the eye? This girl doesn't know how much she means to me: lifting me up countless times, cheering me on, listening to my sobs and crying with me. If this girl is taken away from me, I will be dead inside, for we are joined by something greater. Nothing can replace what we have, and I will stand by her side always, lifting her up, cheering her on, listening to her sobs and crying with her. I will repay her for what she has done for me, and I will strive to keep her alive. I have been placed in her life for such a time as this.

~Sarah Klapak
Chicken Soup for the Teenage Soul on Love & Friendship

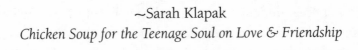

22

A Call for Help

The most important thing in communication is to hear what isn't being said.
~Peter F. Drucker

My dear friend Lindsay: she had been part of my life since kindergarten. We met over her ninety-six pack of Crayolas, a big thing to a five-year-old. She was a constant fixture in my life. She was a born comedian, with more talent, creativity, laughter, love and curly red hair than she knew what to do with. The greatest thing about our friendship was that we completely understood each other. We always had a smile, a joke, a shoulder or an ear to lend one another. In fact, our favorite thing to do was to have our parents drop us off at a restaurant, where we would have these outrageously long talks over Mountain Dews, Diet Cokes and the most expensive dessert our babysitting money would allow.

It was over one such talk in seventh grade where the subject of suicide came up. Little did I know that this would be a conversation that would forever change our relationship. We talked about how weird it would be if one of our friends ever committed suicide. We wondered how families could ever get over such a tragedy. We talked about what we thought our funerals would be like. This conversation was definitely the most morbid one we had ever had, but I did not think about it too much. I assumed that, at one time or another, everyone wonders who will cry and what will be said at their funeral. It never entered my mind that this talk was a cry for help from my beloved friend. Whenever this topic came up, I had the same frame of mind as my mother—we could never understand how one's life could get so desperate that the only alternative is death. However, we ended our talk with a laugh about how we were too "together" to ever do something so drastic, and we parted with a hug and a "Call me if you need anything."

I didn't think about our conversation until three weeks later, when I received a phone call from Lindsay. I immediately knew something was wrong when she did not begin the conversation with a bouncy hello and a good story. She came right out and asked me if she was important to my life and if she meant anything to this world. I answered with an energetic "Of course! I don't know what I'd do without you!" Lindsay then told me something that sent chills up my spine and neck. She told me that she felt lost, confused, worthless, and that she had a bottle of pills in her hand. She said that she was fully prepared to take them all to end her life. Was this the girl who sat next to me in English class and with whom I loved to get in trouble? Was this the girl who loved bright colors, laughing, and striking up conversations with anyone in the world? Was this my wonderful, funny friend who was so bubbly and light that she practically floated through life?

My reality then came into focus and I realized that this was my friend, and for that reason, I had to keep her on the phone. I then started the longest phone conversation in my life. Over the next three-and-a-half hours, Lindsay told me her troubles. And for three-and-a-half hours, I listened. She spoke of how she got lost in her large family (fifteen children, and she was the baby), how her self-confidence was low from her appearance (which I thought was beautiful and unique), how she was anorexic the summer before (I was too busy playing softball to notice), how she was confused about her future—whether or not she would follow her dreams or her parents' wishes, and how she felt completely alone. I kept telling her over and over how original, beautiful and important her dreams and personality were to our lives. By this time, we were both crying: she was frustrated, I was pleading for her life.

My mind then reached out at what I assumed was my final

chance at helping Lindsay; I told her three simple things. I first told her that everyone has problems. It's a part of life. That overcoming these problems and moving onto greater heights is what life is all about. The second thing I told her was that if life was as bad as she said, then things couldn't possibly get worse. There wasn't room for any more failure—things had to improve. The final simple thing I told her was that I, or someone else close to her, would always be there, no matter what trials may come. I told her that the fact that we were having this conversation, that she wanted me to know what was going on, proved my theory that she really wanted to live. If she wanted to end her life, she would have just done it. But, since she took time to call, her mind was saying "Help! I want to keep my life!" After I finished that last statement, I heard the best sound in the world—Lindsay flushing the pills down the toilet.

I went to her house, and we talked about how she could start putting her life back together. We got her some help, and eventually, Lindsay overcame her issues. I am proud to say that Lindsay and I will be starting the eleventh grade together in the fall, she is getting excellent grades, and is a happy teenager. The road there wasn't easy, and we both slipped a few times. But the important thing is that we raised ourselves up and arrived.

~Jill Maxbauer
Chicken Soup for the Teenage Soul II

23

SPF 1,000

Cameron and I met in the ninth grade, at a time when we were both covered in acne and our mouths were full of metal. Until I met Cam, I had a few good friends with whom I shared many of the same interests, but never in my life had I experienced a friendship quite like the one I shared with her.

"I'm Cameron. Friends call me Cam," she said, introducing herself to me.

"Cool, I'm Lauren. Friends call me Lauren or Lauren."

Cam and I shared everything. At times it even seemed like we shared a brain. Cam and I both had a thing for snapping photos of our shadows in the moonlight. Some nights we would ditch everyone else, and walk around school, the park, even train tracks with our cameras—searching for the perfect shot of our shadows, imprinted on the sidewalk beside us.

A few months before I met Cameron, I was diagnosed with a rare nervous system disease that progresses if left untreated. I was misdiagnosed for months. Consequently, a lot of time was wasted on the wrong treatments and I was getting worse and worse. Cam was the first friend I ever told about my situation.

"Eventually I might not be able to walk, be in the sun, digest food, eat like a normal person. Or worse," I said as we sat on a bench one day after school. She was quiet for a moment.

"Well, if you can't walk, I'll push you and if you can't eat, I'll have a food fight with you anyway, and if you become allergic to light we'll still be able to go shadow-hunting. I'll be your emotional sunscreen—SPF 1,000."

"My SPF 1,000, huh?"

"Yup," she laughed.

I hugged her. "Thank you."

Days turned into weeks, weeks turned into months and my health deteriorated. It was getting increasingly difficult for me to get around. Soon I lost the ability to walk entirely. Cam was there with me, every "step" of the way. Finally, things got bad enough that I was forced to leave school. Over the next four years, I was in and out of the hospital. It became my home away from home and I was often there for months at a time. I was very sick and unable to stay in contact with friends, even Cam.

I remained bedridden for those four years but eventually gained a lot of my strength back. I had a nurse who gave me my medicine and made sure I was okay. I was never "alone" but that didn't change the fact that I felt lonely. I needed someone to talk to, a friend.

"Cam, it's me."

"Lauren, oh my gosh. How are you? I have missed you so much. How are you feeling?"

Hearing Cam's voice filled me with an inner peace I hadn't felt in a long time.

"I'm fine, now," I said, relieved. Everything was going to be okay.

Things slowly began to improve. I received a power wheelchair for my eighteenth birthday, which for me meant FREEDOM! Finally, I could get around again! I could go outside at night, smell the grass, feel the wind against my face. I could take photographs with a flash. I could live. I called Cam and told her the news.

"I'm on my way!" she said.

That night, I took my first walk in four years. Cam brought her camera and I brought mine. We walked and talked and laughed like we were kids again. We made shadow puppets in the dark with our hands, against the pavement.

Having her back was a relief. There were so many things I wanted to tell her, so many questions I had about myself.

"Sometimes I wonder about my purpose, Cam. Why am I here? What's going to happen to me? I mean, I'm lucky to be alive. I'm appreciative of every moment and every day. The thing is, though, I don't just want to 'exist.' I want more than that. I want to break free. I'm tired of being the patient patient. I want to change the world. I want to be great, I want to help people and I don't want to be alone. It's just that, I'm terrified of being alone again..." I trailed off.

"You will never be alone, Lauren," she said shaking her head, smiling. "You will be great. You will do whatever you want to do and you will never, ever be alone." She paused to snap a picture of a tree and then continued. "Think of me as your shadow. No matter how far you walk, no matter how dark the night becomes, I'll always be behind you."

We stopped and took pictures of our shadows. She looked at the screen on her digital camera. "Hot!" she exclaimed. "I think we finally got the perfect shot!"—two forms, dancing across the sidewalk, side by side, best friends back together again.

I looked over at Cameron and laughed. "What would I do without my SPF 1,000?"

She kissed me on my cheek and we kept on down the road.

~Lauren Henderson
Chicken Soup for the Teenage Soul IV

24

Kim

A friend accepts us as we are yet helps us to be what we should.
~Author Unknown

We both lie sideways on her bed, the screen door slapping open and shut with the California breeze. We thumb through fashion magazines, laughing at the hairstyles and smelling the perfume samples. It seems like any other Sunday between girlfriends; laughter filling the room, a half-eaten carton of cookies between the two of us. This was my Sunday afternoon ritual, the two of us and our magazines, and from the time I was twelve, I lived for these afternoons. She was my friend, but more than that, she was a safe place, an unconditional love, and she was an adult.

I had known Kim most of my life. For the first ten years of my life, Kim wasn't one of the closest adults in my life, but her husband John doted on me and was one of the only "grown-ups" to understand my fearless and abundant energy.

When I was twelve, I moved to Los Angeles to live with my father. Kim and John also lived nearby, and soon after my move, I began spending time at their home. Kim was fun; she liked to laugh and talk about boys. She listened to me while I talked about my crushes and fights with my family. She spoke to me as an equal, as a friend, not a child.

As I grew older, these visits became more important. I would cry over heartbreaks and whine about the latest rejection. The gap in age between us stayed the same, but the space between us grew closer.

I called her with secrets, which she kept, and went to her when I couldn't handle my world for a while.

I think my parents went through periods of jealousy and hurt regarding Kim and our friendship, because they wished they could be the ones to whom I came with my stories. I had reached an age where it was harder to relate to my parents, but I still needed guidance. Kim offered that guidance; she didn't force feed it.

Soon I was sixteen, and things began to change. I sunk into sadness, and I was slipping away from everyone, including Kim. I was taken to the hospital after swallowing a bottle of pain medication, and there, without question, was Kim. She was two hours away when the call came, and she showed up at the hospital with hair things and, of course, magazines. We didn't talk about the incident, but when she pulled my hair up for me, I saw in her eyes true fear and heartache. She used to say to me, "You wouldn't want to spend so much time with me if I really was your mom." I didn't understand those words until that day when she offered me the feeling of love without obligation. She wasn't my mom; she wasn't obligated to love me, she just did.

After my suicide attempt, things between us, though unspoken, began to change. I stopped spending Sunday afternoons at her house. I called, but not as often. I didn't feel good about myself, so I couldn't feel good about our friendship. I figured I had grown up and that we had just grown apart. Like any normal friendship, it had transformed, and I believed that I no longer needed Kim or the friendship.

The summer before I left for college, I went to say goodbye to Kim. Though we hadn't been as close for the last two years, we both cried when I left. I walked down the walkway from her house, and she called out from the kitchen window, "Call me if you need anything." I knew she meant that.

My first semester was hard. I was far from home, a little lonely, and things began to swing back down for me. With pure instinct, I picked up the phone. It was late. Kim picked up the phone, and I asked, "Were you sleeping?" She replied, "Yes, but it's okay. What's wrong? What do you need?" What I needed was Kim. I needed to hear her voice, and feel that California breeze in her back bedroom. I needed to tell her that our friendship had finally surpassed the age gap.

We talked about once a week after that, every Sunday afternoon. I called with the stress of my finals and with my newest boy problem. When I returned home for the summer, I went to Kim's, and we read magazines and ate cookies. I had become an adult, what she had always been. When I was younger, she had related to me on a level that I needed at that time, and now she relates to me as an equal. She was right; things would have been different if she were my mom. I didn't need another mom. I had one. I needed exactly what she gave: love, unconditional. And because she wanted me in her life, not because she had to have me.

~Lia Gay
Chicken Soup for the Teenage Soul III

25

Take Back the Night

W e met under unfortunate circumstances—in a girls' group for survivors of sexual abuse. Her name was Kimmy, and she was twelve years old. I was thirteen. While there were six other girls in the group, Kimmy and I immediately connected and began sharing with each other. I had a connection with her that was unlike any with my other friends—we both were survivors of sexual abuse.

For the next five months, Kimmy and I met weekly at our group. We shared many laughs and long talks, and participated in activities with all the other girls. Outside our group, Kimmy and I had sleepovers together. Kimmy opened up to me and shared the details of what she went through. She invited me to her birthday party, while I invited her to spend time with me at my summer house. Our group eventually had to come to an end, but it was just the beginning of our friendship.

Kimmy was always a phone call away. There were many nights I needed someone to listen to me, and she was always there. Together we experienced sixteenth birthday parties, getting our driver's licenses, boyfriends... even getting together with other girls from our girls' group. Although we went to different high schools, it never affected our friendship.

Before long, it was time to graduate high school. My graduation party was held at my summer house in Wisconsin. Dozens of friends showed up for the big day, including Kimmy. When we talked about college, we were shocked to find out that we'd both decided on the same university.

Today Kimmy and I attend college together, building more memories and often looking back on how our friendship began in such unusual circumstances. We find ourselves laughing at some of the childish things we did when we were younger.

Kim and I took part in Take Back the Night at our university. The night is for survivors of sexual assault and others to go out and take to the streets, chanting powerful words about being survivors and bringing awareness to sexual violence. To my amazement, Kimmy and I were asked to lead the march. With hundreds of people behind us, Kimmy and I held two lit torches and marched into the night. Every now and then we looked over at each other, smiling, knowing just how far we had both come in life.

I believe that everything happens for a reason. If Kimmy and I had never gone through the difficult things that we had, our paths would never have crossed. In some ways, I see my past as a blessing. Kimmy is one of those blessings... a friend I will hold close to my heart forever.

~Erin Merryn
Chicken Soup for the Teenage Soul: The Real Deal Friends

26

The Tragic Reunion

An apology is the superglue of life. It can repair just about anything.
~Lynn Johnston

I almost dropped the phone when I heard the words. "Julia's father died today." After I hung up, I walked to my room in a daze and fumbled with my CD player, hoping that the sound of my favorite songs would provide some comfort.

Although I had known this day was coming, I still felt as if the wind had been knocked out of me. As I sat on my bed, the tears came. My mother came quietly into the room and held me in a gentle embrace.

As I sat cradled in my mother's arms, I thought about last summer. I had gone with Julia and her parents on a trip to an island off the coast of South Carolina. We'd had a great time together, sharing breathtaking sunsets on the beach, eating at posh restaurants and biking along the rugged coastline. Julia's dad had taken it upon himself to fulfill our every desire.

Now I knew that beneath all the laughter and fun, Mr. Yolanda must have been suffering. One night, as Julia and I were getting ready to go out, Mrs. Yolanda came into our room looking upset. She told us that Mr. Yolanda was sick and was not up to coming with us. Julia didn't seem alarmed, and we went out as we had planned without her father.

The next day Mr. Yolanda appeared to be his usual self: soft-spoken, generous and on the go. Since his illness was not mentioned again, I didn't think about it any more for the rest of that wonderful trip.

When school started, my friendship with Julia began to change.

I watched as she became caught up in making new friends. She didn't include me in her new plans, and I felt left in the dust. Pretty soon, we were no longer best friends. In fact, we were barely friends at all.

One day, my mother sat me down and told me that Mr. Yolanda had terminal pancreatic cancer. Shocked, my thoughts turned to Julia. At school she seemed a happy-go-lucky teen. Her sunny exterior displayed no sign of any turmoil, but now I knew it had to be present somewhere within her. Not wanting to upset Julia in school, and still feeling separate from her, I didn't say anything to her about her father. But inside, I wanted to run up to her in the hallway, give her a hug, and let her know that I was there and that I cared.

Now I wondered, as I walked nervously into the funeral home, if it was too late. Wakes make me uncomfortable, probably because they make death so real. And the thought of seeing Julia in this setting, knowing what a very private person she was, also made me uneasy. As my friends and I got in line to pay our respects to Mr. Yolanda, I noticed pictures of the Yolandas surrounding the casket. One photograph in particular jumped out at me. It was of Mr. Yolanda and Julia on our vacation in South Carolina.

The photograph triggered an overwhelming sadness in me, and I began to weep. I simply could not understand why God would take a parent away from his child. Julia found me then and seeing me in tears, she too began to cry.

Even though I told her how sorry I was about her father, I realized I could never fully understand what she was going through. What was it like to come home every day to a house where someone you loved was dying, or to head off to school each morning not knowing if your father would be alive when you got home? I couldn't imagine. But I did know how to express support and compassion. It wasn't too late.

Julia apologized for her neglect of our friendship, and we vowed to be friends again. A funeral is a strange place to make up with a friend, but I guess a tragic reunion is better than none at all.

~Amy Muscato
Chicken Soup for the Teenage Soul II

Why Rion Should Live

High school didn't frighten me. Oh sure, the endless halls and hundreds of classrooms were overwhelming, but I took it in with all the pleasure of starting a new adventure. My freshman year was full of possibilities and new people. With a class of nearly two thousand newcomers, you just couldn't go wrong. So I, still possessing the innocence of a child concealed in a touch of mascara and lipstick, set out to meet them all.

Spanish One introduced me to Rion. By the student definition, he was a "freak": the black jeans, the well-worn Metallica shirts, the wallet chains, the works. But his unique personality and family troubles drew me to him. Not a crush, more of a curiosity. He was fun to talk to, and where interrupted whispering sessions left off, hours of phone conversations picked up.

During one of these evening conversations, "it," as we like to address the incident, unfolded. We were discussing the spectacular height of Ms. Canaple's over-styled bangs when I heard Rion's dad yelling in the background. "Hold on," Rion muttered before a question could be asked. I could tell that he was trying to muffle the receiver, but you could still hear the horror as if his room were a dungeon, maximizing the bellows. Then the line went dead.

Shaking, I listened to the flatline of the phone for a minute before gently placing it in its cradle, too scared to call back for fear of what I might hear. I had grown up in an ideal family setting: a mom and a dad and an older sister as a role model. This kind of situation took me by surprise, and I felt confused and helpless at the same time. A couple of tense hours later, after his father had gone to bed, Rion called me to apologize. He told me his dad had received a letter from his ex-wife, Rion's mom, saying she refused to pay child support. Having no other scapegoat, he stumbled into Rion's room in rage.

"I can't take this anymore. All the fighting... it's always there...." His voice had trailed off, lost in painful thought. "All I have to do is pull the trigger, and it will be over."

"No!" I screamed. "Don't talk like that! You know you have so much to live for." It was becoming clearer every second how threatening the situation was. A cold, forced chuckle came from the other end of the line. "Yeah, right," was his response. We got off the phone, but only after promising to go right to sleep.

Sleep, however, was light years away from me. I was so worried and had a feeling I was Rion's only hope. He had told me repeatedly that it was hard to open up to anyone but me. How could someone not want to live? I could literally list the reasons why I loved waking up every morning. Frantically, I racked my brain for ways to convince Rion of this. Then the lightbulb clicked on. I took a piece of notebook paper and entitled it, "Why Rion Should Live." Below, I began listing every reason I could think of that a person had to exist. What started as a few sentences turned into twenty, then thirty-two, then forty-seven. By midnight, I had penned fifty-seven reasons for Rion to live. The last ten were as follows:

48. *Six feet of earth is pretty heavy.*
49. *They don't play Metallica in cemeteries.*
50. *Braces aren't biodegradable.*
51. *God loves you.*
52. *Believe it or not, your father loves you, too.*
53. *Spanish One would be so boring.*
54. *Two words: driver's license.*
55. *Satan isn't exactly the type of guy you want to hang out with for eternity.*
56. *How could you live without Twinkies?*

57. *You should never regret who you are, only what you have become.*

Believing that I had done my best, I crawled into bed to await tomorrow's chore: saving Rion.

I waited for him at the door to Spanish the next day and handed him the paper as he walked in. I watched him from the opposite side of the room while he read the creased sheet in his lap. I waited, but he didn't look up for the entire period. After class, I approached him, concerned, but before I could say a word, his arms were around me in a tight embrace. I hugged him for a while, tears almost blinding me. He let go, and with a soft look into my eyes, he walked out of the room. No thank you was needed, his face said it all.

A week later, Rion was transferred to another school district so that he could live with his grandmother. For weeks I heard nothing, until one night the phone rang. "Sarah, is it you?" I heard the familiar voice say. Well, it was like we had never missed a day. I updated him on Ms. Canaple's new haircut, and he told me his grades were much better and he was on the soccer team. He is even going to counseling with his dad to help them build a stronger relationship. "But do you know what the best part is?" I sensed true happiness in his voice. "I don't regret who I am, nor what I've become."

~Sarah Barnett
Chicken Soup for the Teenage Soul III

The Right Thing

The counselor was late for our appointment. I sat in one of the hard plastic chairs in her office that, despite a few squirming attempts to rearrange myself, continued to be uncomfortable. I glanced at the boy who sat beside me, my partner in crime. He looked upset and unsure, wounded by the decision that we had finally made out of desperation. Friends for many years, we now offered each other little comfort as we sat lost in our own thoughts and doubt.

My tingling nerves heightened my senses, and I took in everything around me. From the smell of freshly sharpened pencils to the sight of the overly organized desk, the room oozed with the aura of a disciplined junior high school counselor and I found myself again questioning our judgment in choosing this complete stranger to help save our friend.

She entered in a cloud of smiles and apologies for being late. Sitting down across from us, she looked at us expectantly. I felt as if she were waiting for us to announce that she had just won the lottery rather than tell the story of pain and frustration we had both been holding in for so long.

I was overcome for a moment by the fear that had nested in my stomach. It was hard to imagine how my best friend Suzie would react when she found out that the two people she had trusted most in the world had betrayed her. But selfishly, I was also concerned about how this betrayal would affect me. Would she hate me? Would she even speak to me? As much as the pain that she would feel, I contemplated whether or not I would have a best friend the next day.

"Why don't you begin, Kelly, by telling me why you're here?" the counselor suggested. I cast one more glance at my friend; his sad eyes confirmed that we were doing the right thing.

As I began to tell Suzie's story, my uncertainty gave way to a feeling of relief. Carrying the emotional burden of a friend who was slowly killing herself was a lot for a fourteen-year-old to handle, and more than I could stand any longer. Like an exhausted runner, I was passing on the baton for someone else to carry.

By way of my emotional and broken telling, Suzie's story came out. How we laughed at her strange habit of breaking all her food into tiny little pieces, not realizing that by splitting her food up, she could take more time to eat less. How we went along with her self-deprecating jokes about how overweight she was, without realizing that deep inside, she wasn't joking.

The guilt rose in my throat as I related fact after fact, knowing now that all these things should have made us aware months earlier that Suzie actually had a very serious problem. We had pushed it away as she had deteriorated a little at a time. It wasn't until it was almost too late that we had finally understood the big picture.

I explained that the depression that typically walked hand in hand with anorexia had closed in on Suzie a few weeks earlier. I had sat by her side, avoiding the sight of her dark-circled eyes and gaunt cheekbones as she told me that she now ate practically nothing at all, and that for no explainable reason, she would often cry for hours.

It was then that I too began to cry. I couldn't stop my tears as I explained how I hadn't known how to stop my friend's tears, either. She had reached a point that terrified me, and the terror in my voice was plain as I revealed the last thing I knew, the thing that had cemented my determination to tell someone: She was looking for an escape from the pain, sadness and feelings of inadequacy that were now constant for her. She thought that killing herself might be that way out.

My part completed, I sat back in disbelief. I had just poured out secret after secret that I had been told with the understanding that I would never speak them again. I had shattered the most sacred aspect of our friendship: trust. A trust that had taken time, love, and good and bad experiences to build had just been destroyed in ten minutes, broken out of helplessness, desperation and the burden that I could no longer bear. I felt weak. I hated myself at that moment.

So did Suzie.

She needed no explanation when she was called to the office. She looked at me, at her boyfriend sitting at my side, at the concerned look of the counselor. The tears of fury that welled up in her eyes said that she understood. As she began to cry out of anger and relief, the counselor gently sent Aaron and me back to class, shutting the door behind us.

I didn't go back to class right away, but instead walked the hallways of the school trying to make sense of the emotional ramblings going through my head. Though I had just possibly saved my friend's life, I felt less than heroic.

I still can recall the overwhelming sadness and fear that surrounded me, as I was sure that my actions had just cost me one of the best friends I'd ever had. But an hour later, Suzie returned from the counseling office, and with tears in her eyes, headed straight into my arms for a hug that I, perhaps even more than she, needed.

It was then that I realized that no matter how angry she was at me, she would still need her best friend to help her get through what was going to be a very difficult journey. I had just learned one of my first lessons of growing up and being a true friend—that it can be hard, and even terrifying, to do what you know is the right thing.

A year later, Suzie handed me my copy of her school picture. In it, she had color in her cheeks again, and the smile that I had missed for so long spread across her face. And on the back, this message:

Kel,

You were always there for me, whether I wanted you to be or not. Thank you. There's no getting rid of me now — you're stuck with me!

I love you,

~Suzie

~Kelly Garnett
Chicken Soup for the Teen Soul II

Forever Beyond a Goodbye

You learn to like someone when you find out what makes them laugh, but you can never truly love someone until you find out what makes them cry.

~Author Unknown

I waited patiently until the mailman placed the mail into each of the mailboxes and drove away before I cheeked to see if my much anticipated college acceptance letter had arrived. I truly believed that since my abusive father had finally moved out of the house a month before and I was developing an unbreakable bond with my mother and brother, that things were finally on the right track and nothing could go wrong. I wasn't ready to handle any additional downers in my life.

I opened the mailbox with drops of water from an afternoon rain shower tracing through my hands. I searched anxiously through every envelope. My eyes finally landed on a small envelope with the name of my hopefully future college printed on its face. I vaguely remembered someone saying that the small envelopes only contained letters of rejection. I quickly muted that thought. As I opened the tiny envelope, all my fears were born into reality, and drops of water now traced my face all leading up to my eyes.

I jumped into my truck, afraid to go home and see the disappointment written across my mom's face. I drove to my only place of comfort and support—my best friend Dave's house. My stomach was doing so many flips that I had to stop the truck several times to catch my breath and regroup. I finally arrived at Dave's house, trying my hardest to keep my composure. I spent the next few hours sobbing to Dave about my lost future. He said all the right things that a best friend could say.

I was so full of anger and shame that I decided tonight was going to be my last night on Earth. I knew that if I were to wake up the next day, I would see a smile on my dad's face celebrating my lack of success—the only kid in the family who couldn't get into college—a bum with no future. I could not stand that my past, consisting of anger and sadness, was catching up with me.

I decided that it was time to leave Dave's house. I got up to say my goodbyes forever but before I could open my mouth he grabbed me and gave me a huge hug and told me that he loved me, in a brotherly kind of way. As I sat in my truck to leave, he cradled my head in his hands and gave me a kiss on the side of my head. I closed my door and left—my eyes so filled with tears that I could barely see. As I left his driveway I whispered, "Goodbye forever," hoping that maybe he heard me.

I walked into my room and saw my butterfly knife staring at me, screaming that it was the answer. I then got in my truck and drove to a place where I knew I would be alone. I opened the butterfly knife and rested it on my wrist, contemplating the amount of pain that I could encounter before my life would end. I tightened my arm with a "no turning back" expression painted on my face. Just as I placed the edge of the knife on my wrist, my cell phone rang and interrupted my focus. I couldn't understand why anyone would be calling me this late. I answered it.

Dave's voice cracked through my cell phone. "I'm just calling to tell you that I love you. I don't know what I would ever do without you."

With tears once again welling in my eyes, I said, "I love you, too."

I put the knife away, drove home and went to sleep. A few weeks later, the first time either of us spoke of that night, Dave told me that he had an urgent feeling that he should call me and tell me he loved me. He called it a gut feeling or an intuition. I broke down and told him what his gut feeling had done for me, and for the first time I saw my best friend with a tear in his eye and a smile on his face as he told me life would just be "life" unless we experienced it together.

I now have a steady job with a future in the culinary arts. I live on Maui with my other best friend, my brother. I can never fully thank Dave enough or understand what kind of miracles actually took place that night, or what's going to happen now since we live so far apart. But I do know he will be my best friend forever.

~Adam Cohen
Chicken Soup for the Teenage Soul on Love & Friendship

Chapter 4

Teens Talk
Tough Times

The Little Things that
Make a Big Difference

Be faithful in small things because it is in them that your strength lies.
~Mother Theresa

Losing Hope

All kids need is a little help, a little hope and somebody who believes in them.
~Earvin Johnson

"Hope is the hat rack upon which I hang my dreams...." Oh, please! I crumple up the paper and fling it across my bedroom. I can't believe I kept my hopeless seventh grade attempts at poetry. I thought I was a poet that year. Obviously I wasn't, and never will be.

"Here they are," I mutter, pulling a stack of yearbooks from the depths of the drawer. They go all the way back to elementary school. Lauren will like these. Best friends since first grade, she's not talking to me now, but I'm sure she'll want these... after....

"You're hopeless, Carrie," she yelled at me over the phone Friday night. Because I don't see everything exactly her way, because I tell her things she doesn't want to hear. The way I think best friends should. Now I don't even have a best friend. And I can't stand losing her friendship.

I peer into the drawer, empty of yearbooks but still containing the debris of my life. Now what would Josh want from me? According to him, nothing. "There's no hope, Carrie," he told me that night two weekends ago. The night he broke up with me, practically pushing me away as I begged him for another chance. "No," he shook his head at me. "No, it's over. No hope for us." He hasn't spoken to me since. I can't stand losing him, either.

I slip my hand into the pocket of my robe and finger the little container of pills. My stepfather takes these for his back, and I've heard his repeated warnings to my little brothers never to touch them, how dangerous pills like these can be. He never warned me, knowing that I'm old enough, knowing that I understand about things like dangerous pills.

A knock on my door makes my hand fly from the pocket. Of course, my mother barges right in before I can respond.

"Carrie," she says in her exasperated tone, "we're all waiting for you out by the tree. You know we can't open the presents until we're all together." The faint melody of a Christmas carol and the scent of hot cocoa waft into my room through the open door.

"Honestly, Carrie, can't you dress up a little for Christmas Eve? Or at least get that hair out of your eyes," she continues. "Sometimes I think you're hopeless." She sighs—loudly, dramatically, as if otherwise I wouldn't understand the depths of my hopelessness. "Well, hurry up."

With that, she closes the door and leaves me screaming silently after her: Yes, Mom, I know I'm hopeless, like you always tell me. Every time I forget to empty the dishwasher, fold the laundry, get the hair out of my eyes, whatever.

So they're all waiting for me. Mom, my stepfather, Dave, and Aaron and Mark. Waiting for me to join in the singing of carols and unwrapping of gifts. Sure, I'll go. I'll unwrap a few presents. Not that they'll mean a thing to me. But it's Christmas. I'm supposed to be happy. I can pretend. After all, I took drama class last semester.

Ah, school. Another one of the victorious arenas of my life.

"I'm sorry, Carrie, but it's hopeless," Ms. Boggio told me the last day before winter break. "You'd have to get an A on every test for the rest of the year to raise that D to a C." Then she left me alone in the biology lab, staring at my latest test, the latest record of my failures.

I tossed the test away. "I won't even have to show Mom," I thought. "I won't have to hear that lecture again. The one about how I'm ruining my chances for college. That there will be no hope for my future if I keep going on this way. In fact, I'll never have to hear another lecture again. The problem will be solved before school starts in January."

How about a note? Would they want one? I used to think I was some great writer. I'd spend hours filling notebook after notebook with my stories and poems, sometimes just my thoughts and ideas. That's when I felt most alive—writing and dreaming of being good at it, of having other people read my words. And having my words mean something to them. But that was before the hopelessness of being Carrie Brock swallowed me up.

"Just a lousy note," I remind myself. That's all I have to write now. Or ever. I've lost everything: my best friend and my boyfriend. Or I've messed it up: my grades, even my hair. I can't do anything right, and I can't stand facing the reminders of my failures anymore.

"Come on, Carrie," Aaron's voice cries through the door. "I want to open my presents."

Oh, all right. I'll do the note later. I drag myself up and tighten the belt on my robe. As I walk down the hall, the pills make a satisfying clicking noise in my pocket.

I sink into the couch and watch as Mark, my younger brother, tears open his gifts, flinging wrapping paper everywhere. Then it's Aaron's turn. That's the tradition in our family. Youngest to oldest. Everyone oohs and aahs over Aaron's gifts.

"Your turn, Carrie," Mark informs me.

"Can you bring them?" I ask. "I'm tired."

Mark carries over a rectangular box. Clothes, of course. From Mom. I mumble the appropriate thanks. My gifts are few this year. Nothing from Lauren or Josh, of course. Trinkets from Aaron and Mark.

"Okay, I'm done," I say.

"No, wait, here's another one," Mark says, handing me a small package.

"Who's it from?"

"Me." My stepfather speaks up. Dave, the man who resides in the background of my life. A good guy, he treats me well. I've never regretted my mom marrying him.

I tear off the paper, revealing a book. But opening it, I find there are no words inside.

"It's blank," I say, looking up at Dave.

"Well, not quite. There's an inscription up front. But it's a journal, Carrie. For your words."

I flip to the front and find Dave's handwriting in one corner. I read the inscription silently.

To Carrie:

Go for your dreams. I believe in you.

~Dave

I look up at Dave again. He shrugs slightly, as if embarrassed. "Well, I know you want to be a writer, Carrie," he explains. "And I know you can do it."

His last words are almost lost in the noise my brothers are making, digging under the tree and coming up with my mother's presents. But Dave's words are not lost on me.

Somebody believes in me and in my dreams, even when I've stopped believing in them myself. When I thought I was beyond all hope. I clutch the journal to my chest and a feeling I haven't felt for a long time returns. I do want to be a writer. But most of all, I want to just be.

I watch the rest of the presents being opened, thinking there's something I need to do, but I can't quite figure out what. I can slip the pills back into the cabinet later, so that's not it. Then I know.

I grab a pen from the coffee table and open my journal. On that first blank page I write my words: "Hope is the hat rack I hang my dreams upon."

H'mm, I think. Kind of sounds like a country song. Maybe it's not that bad after all. I look up and smile at Dave, even though he's not looking my way. He's just given me the best Christmas present ever. I've gotten my dreams back. Maybe there's hope for me, after all.

~Heather Klassen
Chicken Soup for the Teenage Soul II

Change

Wherever you go, no matter what the weather,
always bring your own sunshine.
~Anthony J. D'Angelo, The College Blue Book

]f change is a scary thing, then I can honestly say that I was nearly scared to death at the age of sixteen. We had to leave the only home and friends I had ever known and move. "We'll all make a new start, Carrie," my parents kept saying. Just because my parents had decided to work on their marriage and "start over," I didn't see why I had to give up everything.

I pouted and protested until they sold the house, boxed up our lives and moved. Then I just shut up; I had no choice. But I didn't give up. Purposely, I let my grades slip, didn't join in any social activities, and, above all, I never admitted that anything was as nice here as it had been in our old hometown.

That strategy didn't last long, not because I had tons of new friends or was won over by this new town they called home. It was because my parents began fighting, and they were fighting about me. "Discussing" is what they called it, but fighting is what it was. Loud disagreements followed by tension filled silences were becoming the norm.

Believe me, my parents needed to work on their marriage. They had separated and come back together so many times that I classified my birthday pictures as "they were separated that year," or "that's the year they were trying to work it out again."

I guess I was just tired of trying to guess if a slammed door meant my father was out of our lives again or just going for a walk to let off steam. Or if my mother's smile was a happy one or the forced one she used to reassure me that "we'll be just fine without your father."

It was bad enough that they kept splitting up. But I couldn't handle being the reason for this dreaded occurrence. So I cleaned myself up, worked hard in my classes and began to meet friends. Things at home mellowed out, but I was afraid to think or feel anything that might cause so much as a ripple. It was my turn to be the keeper of the peace.

Things seemed to be getting back to "fine," until one night the front door slammed and my mother's morning smile was the "we'll-be-just-fine-without-him" one. I had been the best I could be, and it hadn't been enough.

At night, I crawled into bed exhausted with nothing to fill me, nothing to renew me for the next day. The hollow me crumbled in on itself.

Then I met the little girl next door.

I was alone on the front porch steps, trying to work up the energy just to go inside. The rhythm of her jump rope clacking on the sidewalk as she counted out her skips had a calming effect on me. Her hair was fanned out behind her and shining in the setting sun.

"Forty-eight, forty-nine, fifty," she counted, half out of breath. How simple she made it all seem.

"Sixty-three, sixty-four... oh no!" She looked over at me, distressed. "Look, the handle came off! Can I call a do-over? I was skipping my best ever. The miss shouldn't count. It wasn't my fault it broke."

I knew exactly how she felt. I was doing my best when my parents' marriage broke.

She plopped herself on the step next to me. "So, what do you think? Do I get a do-over?"

She was so serious. I wanted her to know that I understood the weight of her question, but I just couldn't hold back the smile that had welled up within me. She looked up, waiting for my answer.

"Well, I know you didn't step on the rope and make the handle pull out because I was watching you." She gave a serious nod. "And it isn't as if your shoe came off because you didn't tie it tightly enough." She studied her shoes and nodded again.

"So, given all the circumstances, I do believe that you're entitled to a do-over."

"Me too," she said, dropping the handle and rope into my lap. "You fix the handle, and I'll let you keep count for me. I stopped at sixty-four, and I bet I can skip over a hundred and that's my highest good counting number."

So I fixed her rope and counted her do-over up to one hundred and twelve.

"One hundred and twelve!" She gave me a high-five. "That's higher than Amy at school, and she's a grade ahead of me!"

That is when the miracle happened. It was a little thing, heartfelt and easily given. She hugged me! The warmth of her hug made my heart smile and, just like the sun coming out from behind the clouds, I understood.

"Meet me tomorrow," she said, completely unaware of all she had just given me.

My parents did get a divorce, and it was very painful. But it wasn't me who caused it, and there was nothing I could have done to prevent it. With my new understanding that came from the innocence of a little girl, I too had earned a do-over.

~Carrie Hill as told to Cynthia Hamond
Chicken Soup for the Teenage Soul on Tough Stuff

Beautiful, She Said

People will forget what you said, people will forget what you did, but people will never forget how you made them feel.
~Bonnie Jean Wasmund

I never thought that I understood her. She always seemed so far away from me. I loved her, of course. We shared mutual love from the day I was born.

I came into this world with a bashed head and deformed features because of the hard labor my mother had gone through. Family members and friends wrinkled their noses at the disfigured baby I was. They all commented on how much I looked like a beat up football player. But no, not her. Nana thought I was beautiful. Her eyes twinkled with splendor and happiness at the ugly baby in her arms. Her first granddaughter. "Beautiful," she said.

Before final exams in my junior year of high school, she died.

Seven years earlier, her doctors had diagnosed Nana with Alzheimer's disease. Our family became experts on this disease as, slowly, we lost her.

She always spoke in fragmented sentences. As the years passed, the words she spoke became fewer and fewer, until finally she said nothing at all. We were lucky to get one occasional word out of her. It was then that our family knew she was near the end.

About a week or so before she died, her body lost the ability to function at all, and the doctors decided to move her to a hospice. A hospice: where those who enter never come out.

I told my parents I wanted to see her. I had to see her. My uncontrollable curiosity had taken a step above my gut-wrenching fear.

My mother brought me to the hospice two days later. My grandfather and two of my aunts were there as well, but they hung back in the hallway as I entered Nana's room. She was sitting in a big, fluffy chair next to her bed, slouched over, eyes shut, mouth numbly hanging open. The morphine was keeping her asleep. My eyes darted around the room at the windows, the flowers and the way Nana looked. I was struggling very hard to take it all in, knowing that this would be the last time I ever saw her alive.

I slowly sat down across from her. I took her left hand and held it in mine, brushing a stray lock of golden hair away from her face. I just sat and stared, motionless, in front of her, unable to feel anything. I opened my mouth to speak but nothing came out. I could not get over how awful she looked, sitting there helpless.

Then it happened. Her little hand wrapped around mine tighter and tighter. Her voice began what sounded like a soft howl. She seemed to be crying in pain. And then she spoke.

"Jessica." Plain as day. My name. Mine. Out of four children, two sons-in-law, one daughter-in-law and six grandchildren, she knew it was me.

At that moment, it was as though someone were showing a family filmstrip in my head. I saw Nana at my baptism. I saw her at my fourteen dance recitals. I saw her bringing me roses and beaming with pride. I saw her tap dancing on our kitchen floor. I saw her pointing at her own wrinkled cheeks and telling me that it was from her that I inherited my big dimples. I saw her playing games with us grandkids while the other adults ate Thanksgiving dinner. I saw her sitting with me in my living room at Christmas time, admiring our brightly decorated tree.

I then looked at her as she was... and I cried.

I knew she would never see my final senior dance recital or watch me cheer for another football game. She would never sit with me and admire our Christmas tree again. I knew she would never see me go off to my senior prom, graduate from high school and college, or get married. And I knew she would never be there the day my first child was born. Tear after tear rolled down my face.

But above all, I cried because I finally knew how she had felt the day I had been born. She had looked through what she saw on the outside and looked instead to the inside, and she had seen a life.

I slowly released her hand from mine and brushed away the tears staining her cheeks and mine. I stood, leaned over, and kissed her and said, "You look beautiful."

And with one long last look, I turned and left the hospice.

~Jessica Gardner
Chicken Soup for the Teenage Soul II

My Own Thing

Wooden sticks slapping against each other, sharp metal blades cutting through snowy ice and heavy metal music blaring from the PA system.... It's like my very first hockey game remains with me wherever I go.

My father had just been diagnosed with cancer; his life and that of my family was thrown into complete flux. I was thirteen years old, and I couldn't grasp that my dad's time on this earth was growing short. There was no fathoming it.

For more than thirty years he was a teacher—he taught science to his classes and life to my sister and me, two jobs he would pour his heart and soul into. Two jobs he was holding onto ever so tightly because he could feel them beginning to slip away.

At the center of my relationship with Dad were sports... baseball, basketball, a little football... but never hockey. That was, until his school offered a class trip to see the New Jersey Devils.

When Dad first mentioned the idea of going, I was apprehensive. "Hockey? Really? Hockey?" By the time the ticket reservation deadline arrived, Dad had convinced me.

When that cold night in December fell upon us, and the hour of departure neared, my father was alas too ill. His mind said "try," but it could not deny his weakening body's ultimate wish to remain in bed. The sense of normalcy he was hoping to provide with this outing was escaping him just like everything else. With a look of mortality in his eyes he said, "I'm sorry, Son. I just can't make it tonight." And perhaps even worse, he continued, "Your mother will take you...."

And so I stepped onto a bus filled with a group of impassioned, anxious high school boys... and what felt like a thousand suspicious eyes turned toward my tiny frame. "What is this awkward kid doing on our bus with his mom?" they whispered among each other. A good question, really... it was the very same question that was running through my own mind as I slouched in the bus seat next to my equally shy mother. All of a sudden I couldn't wait for this night to end.

Somewhere between the suburbs of New York and the swamps of New Jersey a much older, intimidating high school freshman turned toward me and asked the most obvious question on the face of the earth. "You don't go to Ramapo, do you?" I was too nervous to reply... my mother intervened, "This is Neil, Mr. Katcher's son. It's his first hockey game."

"Oh," responded the boy. "Where's Mr. Katcher?"

"He's not feeling well tonight," my mother replied. The boy nodded and got really quiet for a moment... as if he knew about Dad's condition.

Within moments he started a new conversation, this one about hockey. For one night he would act as a substitute.

As we entered the arena, a shiver passed through me. A sense of excitement was filled with the smell of hot dogs and beer. I was in the Meadowlands. The Brendan Byrne Arena.

As the game began to unfold a few tiers below our discounted seats, my bearings and my instincts began to kick in. I was in the world of sport. Questions started flowing from me. "What's icing? What's off-sides? Who's that guy, he's good." I needed to understand this game, and my new mentor was always ready with the knowledge I craved. The game was the fastest, most enthralling sport I had ever witnessed.

I learned that I was watching the underdog New Jersey Devils getting dominated by the big burly Philadelphia Flyers... the game flooded through my blood and into my very DNA. Midway through the game there was this one play... a defining moment, hour, day in my life. One of the Flyers, maybe it was Peter Zezel, Rick Tocchet or even Tim Kerr, made a spin-o-rama move. With the puck sitting on the blade of his stick, this Flyer made a 360-degree maneuver past a Devil and then fired a shot past a flailing goaltender into the rippling twine!

As the red siren light behind the goals spun, I jumped to my feet.... My mentor tugged at me, "Kid, don't cheer for them. They're the enemy." Lost in the game, I replied, "Did you see that?!!"

Upon returning home, I ran as fast I could up the thirteen creaky, carpeted steps to my parents' bedroom. I called out, "Dad! Dad!" At first there was no answer until I realized he was in the adjoining bathroom. I went right up to the door and knocked, "Dad? Can I come in?"

"No... how was the game?" he managed to reply. I must have talked his ear off through that bathroom door. I talked as much as he's probably heard me talk in my entire thirteen years. The last thing I said was, "What team do you root for?"

"The Rangers," replied Dad... after all, fandom was not something one chose in our family, it was passed down from one generation to the next, like an heirloom. And so, from that moment on, the Rangers became my team... and the game of hockey seemed so magical that it could stop time itself.

Over the next five years my father would fight for his life, my family would fight to remain a family... and my heart would find its shelter in a 200-foot by 85-foot arena. Inside that space, every season and every game became a reason to dream—if for just a few hours at a time.

Recently, my father lost his battle with cancer, but even as I grow toward adulthood, hockey remains my beacon of hope. And it was that one chilly December night in the swamps of New Jersey that showed me that my father's spirit would continue to teach and comfort me... even in his absence.

~Neil Katcher
Chicken Soup for the Teenage Soul IV

34

Nintendo Master

The only disability in life is a bad attitude.
~Scott Hamilton

When I first saw you, I thought—Nintendo Master. There was this intensity about you. Your piercing blue eyes and the way your hands moved rapidly along the control buttons were subtle hints of your expert skill.

You didn't appear too different from all of the other video crazed teens out there, but you were. I guess the fact that it was summer, and we were both stuck in the oncology ward of the hospital cruelly betrayed the normality with which you tried to present yourself. Or maybe it was the fact that we were prematurely robbed of the innocence of childhood, and it comforted me to know that there was someone else out there just like me. I can only speculate, but all I know for sure is that I was drawn to your energy and zest for life.

That was the summer of my first post-cancer surgeries. The doctors were trying to fix my left hip joint, which had shattered under the intense bombardments of chemotherapy treatments. It wasn't the only thing that had shattered. I had misplaced my usual optimistic attitude about life and was surprised at how nasty I could be. This did not help to endear me to anyone in my presence.

My surgery had gone "well," the doctors said, but I was in excruciating pain.

I saw you again in physical therapy, realizing only then the extent of what cancer had done to you. I wanted to scream, "Let him go back upstairs and play his video games, you idiots!" But I just sat there in stunned silence. I watched you get up and start walking with the aid of the parallel bars. Prior to your entrance into the room, I had been sitting in my wheelchair, wallowing in self-pity—"Wasn't the cancer enough? Now my hip is screwed up, and I really don't care anymore. If I get up, it is going to kill."

You will never know me, but you are my hero, Nintendo Master. With such courage and poise, you got up on your one remaining leg. Some might have the audacity to call you disabled or even crippled, but you are more complete than many can ever wish to be. After you had your walk for the day, a walk that was perfectly executed on your part, and you were safely tucked into your bed and were enjoying your video games once again, I decided that it was about time that I get up and take a walk myself. You see, Nintendo Master, it dawned on me then that you had innately known what it takes most of us a lifetime to grasp—life is like a game, you can't win them all and yet the game goes on, forcing all to play it. Nintendo Master, you play it better than most!

~Katie Gill
Chicken Soup for the Teenage Soul II

35

The Turning Point

Sometimes being a brother is even better than being a superhero.
~Marc Brown

I stomped out of the house and the screen door slammed shut behind me. My face was wet with tears. As I started out down the street, I heard my mother call after me, "Dani, take your brother with you." I was in the middle of complete emotional distress and now my brother was trotting down the driveway behind me. This is exactly why my parents had no idea what was going on. They only talked to me to tell me to take my brother with me or to clean up my room. They had no idea of the pain I was enduring.

I walked down the block to my best friend Mike's house. I was going to say goodbye. I didn't want to be here anymore; I couldn't stand that no one understood what I was going through.

Mike opened the door and immediately embraced me in the biggest, tightest hug of my life. My younger brother, whom I had been ignoring, wandered off to play with Mike's brothers.

Mike and I went into his living room to sit down. He didn't ask for an explanation or try to console me; he just held me and let me cry on my shoulder. I sobbed until my sides hurt. I cried about how lonely I was. I cried about how my family didn't seem to understand me at all. And when I was all cried out, I realized that part of the hurt was gone.

It dawned on me that I had been crying and talking with Mike for hours. I called home, and my mother screamed at me for being out past curfew. But instead of picking a fight, I grabbed my brother and started the walk home.

There was something strangely calming about that walk home. Because of this new sense of calm and warmth I was feeling, I decided to tell my brother everything. My brother and I rarely talked, and when we did, it had only to do with him tagging along or arguments over the remote. But on that walk home, I spilled my heart to my sixth grade brother, someone I had never before looked to for advice or comfort.

He didn't yell at me or lecture me. He didn't tell me my feelings were wrong or that I was wrong for feeling them. He just said, "Please don't die. That would make me sad." It was then, walking hand in hand with my kid brother that I decided I wanted to live.

The next day I turned fifteen.

~Dani Allred
Chicken Soup for the Teenage Soul III

36

Kind Words

Dear Ms. Kirberger,

It is very difficult for me to talk about this. I have never really shared my feelings about this with anyone, but I really feel I need to. Like any teenager my life revolved around my friends. I was busy going to parties, seeing movies, having sleepovers with my girlfriends and worrying about the pettiest things. I was a normal teen despite a rough beginning.

I was born with a number of heart complications. These complications required different operations throughout my life, especially within my first few years. My situation was life-threatening but, with the help of excellent medical care, I was able to survive. I have lived my whole life with this heart condition, so I'm comfortable with it. I'm not able to do everything my peers can, but I know my limits and live with them. My friends have always been aware of my medical history, and it has never come between our friendships. I have always lived a fairly normal life like everyone else my age... until recently.

Last year my mother noticed I was constantly tired and took me to the doctor as a precaution. My doctor noticed I had poor color. I had never taken the time to stop and notice these changes in myself. I was going to bed earlier and waking up tired. Blood tests showed I was low in iron, which seemed to be a reasonable explanation for my loss of energy and poor color.

As the weeks passed, I started experiencing cramps in my stomach. They progressively got worse and worse. I was reassured that iron, which I was now taking to bring up my red blood cell count, was hard on the stomach and it was a normal side effect. I continued the iron and dealt with the pains in my stomach. I returned to the doctor after a period of time, hoping to hear that the iron had improved my body. Instead of my hemoglobin rising, it had fallen for reasons unknown to all of us at the time. I was sent to different specialists around the city to help find answers for my situation. I received blood test after blood test.

The doctors still had no definite answers for me. Soon they were talking about a bone marrow test. I was scared and, for the first time in a long time, worried. In the past, I always knew I would get better, but now it was different. I wasn't sure I'd ever be better. It got to the point where I was walking around hunched over because of the horrible pain. I could not go out with my friends. I would get up in the morning and go lie down on the couch with a hot water bottle. That seemed to be how I spent my days.

My pain worsened. The school year was over, and I was looking forward to sleepover camp. I was so excited to be able to see all of my camp friends that I don't normally see during the year and have a change of environment. I was determined to leave home for camp despite my pain. However, my parents told me I would not be able to attend summer camp that year. I was extremely upset and I didn't want to hear of it, even though deep down I knew it was not possible for me to go in my condition. I remember saying to my mother the first night of the camp session, "If I were well, I'd be sleeping in a bunk bed tonight." She turned and said to me with tears in her eyes, "Karen, I wish you were in a bunk bed tonight, too." I knew it hurt my parents to see me in pain and missing out on all the fun I should have been having that summer.

After more and more tests, seeing more doctors and being challenged by more pain, I was seen by a gastroenterologist at Sick Children's Hospital. I was finally given a diagnosis: Crohn's disease. It wasn't life-threatening like my heart, but it would affect my everyday quality of life. Believe it or not, the news came as a relief to my family and me. Sure, I was upset about what was happening to me. I had to make difficult changes in my life in order to get better, but at least now they knew what was wrong with me and I could follow the right path to feeling better again. I was given a steroid medication along with some antibiotics that were supposed to give me some quick relief. I went home from the hospital hoping and thinking I would feel better soon. Unfortunately, that wasn't the case. The medication wasn't helping, and I was having even more extreme pain. It got so bad that I was taken to the hospital by ambulance and admitted to the ward. I was taken off all food and given an IV. The IV failed to work. At this point, I was really depressed. I felt awful. Nothing was working. I was so discouraged. I couldn't see myself ever getting better.

A tube-feeding treatment was now introduced. Of course, the idea of inserting a tube down my nose, into my throat and to my stomach was not ideal and was very hard for my family and me, but I tried it anyway. The treatment actually worked, and I eventually learned to insert the tube myself. I continued my nightly feedings through the tube for the next six months.

I wasn't having pains anymore, just the discomfort. I only did the tube feedings at night and overall I was so much better, but it was still difficult going back to school and seeing my friends. I had lost over twenty pounds. I still wasn't able to eat anything, and it was hard for me to concentrate.

I was doing better, but my medication gave me many side effects. My face retained water, which made me look extremely fat. I knew the kids at school noticed, but most were polite and didn't say anything. My friends were so supportive of me. I couldn't have asked for a better group of friends, but I could sense that things were uncomfortable for them. My face had become so fat that I didn't even recognize myself. I didn't want to go out with them because of this and many other reasons.

I started to eat a few solid foods again, but seeing my friends binge on candy and french fries pushed me away from them. I had been through so much that summer. I felt twenty years older because of what I had struggled through. I had to be mature about things. My friends were worrying about movies, boys and themselves, much of what I worried about before I got sick. Now my whole life revolved around Crohn's disease, feeling good and keeping a positive mental attitude. I felt that I couldn't really relate to them anymore even though they had been so good to me. I was pushing myself away from them and as I pushed away, they thought I didn't want to be with them and they pushed away from me. I missed my friends and old life so much.

As the months passed, I lowered my medication and started to look like myself again. Things were getting better. I was feeling good and tried to make more of an effort to be a kid again and just hang out with my friends. I was starting to feel more in the loop of things, and one friend of mine contributed to that in the largest way. As we were walking out to recess one day, she turned to me and said, "You know what, Karen? After all that you have been through this year, I think it's so great that you can still laugh and joke with us." Just those few lines meant the world to me. That changed everything. For the first time, I felt a friend understood how hard things had been for me and recognized how difficult it was for me to return to being a friend who could laugh and joke. I realized then that I didn't want to push away from my friends any longer. I wanted to be the person I used to be — the one who could kick back and have a good time.

Now, a year later, I'm feeling great and have returned to my normal self and my old life. I have triumphed over the barrier that held me back from being happy. A positive attitude, determination and a few special words from a special friend can really make a difference. This past year I was lost and this friend helped to find me and return me to my life. I doubt she knew what an impact her words had on me, but I will never forget them. To that special friend of mine, I thank her and I love her.

Thank you for letting me share this with you, and hopefully other teens will be able to read this and know how important a few kind words can be.

Sincerely,

~Karen
Chicken Soup for the Teenage Soul Letters

Teens Talk Tough Times

Family

*You don't choose your family.
They are God's gift to you, as you are to them.*
~Desmond Tutu

What Siblings Know

When I was twelve and my brother David was seventeen, we were home one Halloween night watching a horror movie we'd rented. It was an entertaining but silly movie about a woman who becomes a witch. The woman who played the witch was young and looked like a model. Every time she cast a spell, her long red hair whipped around her face and her eyes got bright green. Once when this happened, my brother said, "Wow, she looks really hot."

I stared at him. I was astonished at what he'd said. I hadn't noticed it before, but until that night I'd never, ever heard my brother voice an attraction to women, even though he was a teenager and supposedly in the prime of his life.

This is what I remember when people ask me when I first knew my brother was gay. I didn't realize he was different until I heard him saying something that most guys his age would say without a second thought.

My brother tried to like girls. The thought of him trying—even by saying something as trivial as "She looks hot" about an actress on a television screen—breaks my heart. All that time he was trying, through middle school and high school and into college, he couldn't tell me or my parents how hard it was for him. He was all alone.

When I was twelve, David went out of state for college. He came home for holidays and a few weeks in the summer, and he called every week, but every year he seemed to pull farther away from me and my parents. When he was home, he was quiet and distant, and on the phone he was polite but tense, the way people get when they are hiding really big secrets.

My parents were slow, but they weren't stupid. A couple of years after David left for college, when they still hadn't heard mention of any girlfriends or even dates, they became suspicious. My mother started asking me questions, thinking that I must know something she didn't know, because siblings tell each other things they don't tell their parents. But David hadn't told me anything. He never had, not even before he left for college. I always knew he loved me, but he was more independent than the rest of us, and I never felt he needed me.

The next time David came home, I did a terrible thing. I wanted to borrow his leather backpack and I knew he wouldn't let me if I asked him, so I just took it. But before I filled it with my things, I had to take out his things to make room. There were some schoolbooks and a fancy notebook bound with a rubber band. I was curious. I pulled off the rubber band and started reading.

Immediately, I found myself immersed in a world of sup-pressed anger, self-loathing and tentative romances. I learned more about my brother in those pages than I ever could from him, at least back then. I learned that he'd known he was gay his entire life, but that not until he escaped to college did he admit it to another human being. That human being was his roommate, Rob. I remem-bered him mentioning how Rob had transferred dorm rooms in the middle of the semester, and when I read my brother's journal I learned that Rob changed rooms because he didn't want to live with someone who was gay.

It was a little while—a few pages into the journal—before my brother told anyone else. He joined a campus group and made some gay friends, and slowly his life forked into two lives. There was the life my parents and I saw—a life with lies and friends who didn't know him, and no one to love—and there was a second life, a life with friends and crushes and dates. A life where he was happy.

I put the backpack—and the little notebook—back in my brother's room, and I never told him what I'd learned. But my parents continued to badger me about David and his lack of love life—they knew he was gay, I'm sure, but denied it even to themselves—and eventually I called him up. "David," I said, "you have to tell them."

He didn't ask me how I knew, and I didn't tell him. But looking back, I understand that reading my brother's journal—a horrible crime I would never commit again—only filled in some of the details. Somehow, I already knew the story. Maybe it is true that siblings know each other better than their parents know them. I like to think so.

The next Thanksgiving, after a pretty typical family meal, my brother suggested we all take a walk. We walked past the end of our street and onto the grounds of the high school, then onto the track. Then my brother stopped. "I have something to tell you," he said. I felt my parents' hearts skip a beat—they wanted so badly, back then, for it not to be true. "I wanted to tell you that I'm gay."

My parents were pretty rational, considering. They told David that he was just experimenting, that eventually he'd find a woman he wanted to marry. He listened to them, then politely but firmly said that this was something that wasn't going to change. They argued but never raised their voices, and eventually we went home and took naps in separate rooms. The following days were very quiet. Then David went back to school, to his happy life.

It was five years before my parents came to truly accept my brother. My brother was fortunate to be out of the house during that time, but I was not so lucky. My parents fought more than ever, my father drank a lot, and I spent time out of the house. But slowly—very slowly—my parents got used to the idea. After a year, my mother told one of her friends about David, then my father told one of his. They received love and support—David was a great kid, said my parents' friends. That hadn't changed. Secretly, I'm sure they were relieved that it wasn't their kid who was gay. After my parents learned not to hide it, there was still the matter of being proud of David, of not only tolerating hearing about his romantic life, but wanting to hear about it.

About a week before Christmas one year, my brother called home to ask my parents if he could bring a friend home for the holiday. A boyfriend. My parents told David they'd think about it, then called him back and said absolutely not. My brother felt hurt and rejected, and when he came home, relations between him and my parents were strained. Then he and my father got into a fight on Christmas Eve, and David took an early flight back to school. Christmas Day was sadder and lonelier than it had ever been.

I called David a few days later. "You can't rush them," I said, feeling guilty for defending them.

"It's been three years," said David. He was frustrated, which I understood. So was I. I didn't understand why my parents couldn't just get over it. It seemed simple. Every time my mother asked me how a date had gone or said she liked a boy I'd introduced to her, I thought, What's so different between me and David? Don't you want him to be happy, too?

But David's patience paid off. My mother joined a support group for parents of gays and lesbians, and soon she was succeeding in dragging my father with her to the meetings. She was even asked to speak at a conference for high school teachers about being unbiased toward homosexuality in the classroom. Time passed. My parents eased into not only accepting the fact that David wasn't ever going to be straight, but also that it wasn't a bad thing at all. That for David, it was a very good thing.

Then they did the craziest and most wonderful thing. I still laugh when I think about it. They made a list of all the people they hadn't told about David, including old friends, siblings and their own parents, and they planned a three-week road trip across the country. They had news to deliver, and they wanted to deliver it in person and do some sightseeing in the meantime. They'd gotten this idea in their heads that it wasn't enough for David to come out of the closet. He would never feel they'd truly accepted him until they came out of the closet, too, as the loving parents of a gay son.

David's apartment was the last stop on their journey, and I took an airplane up to meet them when they arrived. We took another family walk, and David told us about his new boyfriend and I told them about mine. Finally, after so much pain and hard work, my brother's two lives started to merge.

~Danielle Collier
Chicken Soup for the Teenage Soul on Tough Stuff

Good Night, Dad

If you were going to die soon and had only one phone call you could make,
who would you call and what would you say? And why are you waiting?
~Stephen Levine

"Y ou afraid of heights?" my dad asked, as I climbed up the seemingly unstable ladder to the second-story rooftop. I was up there to help him fix our TV antenna.

"Not yet," I replied, as he climbed up after me with tools in hand.

I didn't have much to do up there on the roof — mostly I just held the antenna still and handed my dad tools — so I began to talk to him as he worked. I could always talk to my dad. He was more like a big kid than an actual adult. In fact, he looked much younger than his forty-one years. He had straight black hair and a mustache, with no signs of graying or balding. He stood at a strong six feet and had dark green eyes that seemed to always be laughing at some secret joke. Even my friends, whom he'd make fun of without mercy, loved him. Most of my peers would be embarrassed to have their dad hang around with them, but not me; in fact, I took great pride in him. No one else had a dad as cool as mine.

After he finished working on the antenna, we went inside, and I began to get ready for bed. As I entered my room, I looked over and saw my dad working intently at his computer in his office, which was adjacent to my bedroom. As I watched him, I had the most incredible urge to just poke my head in and tell him that I loved him. I quickly brushed that urge away and continued into my room. I couldn't possibly say to him "I love you"; I hadn't said that to him or anyone else since I was seven, when my mom and dad would come and tuck me in and kiss me goodnight. It just wasn't something a man said to another man. Still, as I walked in and closed my bedroom door behind me, the feeling continued to grow inside of me. I turned around, opened my door and poked my head into my dad's office.

"Dad," I said softly.

"Yes?"

"Um..." I could feel my heartbeat rising. "Uh... I just wanted to say... goodnight."

"Goodnight," he said, and I went back to my room and shut the door.

Why didn't I say it? What was I afraid of? I consoled myself by saying that maybe I'd have the courage to say it later; but even as I told myself that, I knew it might never happen. For some reason I felt that was going to be the closest I'd ever come to telling my dad I loved him, and it made me frustrated and angry with myself. Deep within me, I began to hope he'd know that when I said "Goodnight," I really meant to say "I love you."

The next day seemed like any other. After school, I began to walk with my best friend to his house, as I frequently do. However, his mom surprised us by picking us up in the parking lot. She asked me whose house I was going to, and when I said "Yours," she paused and said, "No, I have this feeling that your mom probably wants you home right now." I didn't suspect anything; I figured she had something she wanted to do with her own family so I shouldn't butt in.

As we pulled up to my house, I noticed a lot of cars in front and quite a few people I knew walking up our front steps.

My mom greeted me at the front door. Her face was streaming with tears. She then told me, in the calmest voice she could manage, the worst news of my life. "Dad's dead."

At first, I just stood there as she hugged me, unable to move or react. In my mind, I kept repeating "Oh God, no; this can't be true! Please...." But I knew I wasn't being lied to. I felt the tears begin to run down my face as I quickly hugged some of the people who had come over, and then I went upstairs to my bedroom.

As I got to my bedroom, I looked over into my dad's office. Why didn't I say it?! That was when I heard my little three-year-old brother ask, "Mommy, why is my brother crying?"

"He's just feeling a bit tired, honey," I heard my mom tell him as I closed my bedroom door behind me. She hadn't told him yet that Daddy wouldn't be coming home from work again.

Once in my room, I hurt so badly that my body went numb and I collapsed on the floor, sobbing. A few moments later, I heard a scream from downstairs and then my baby brother's voice crying out, "Why, Mommy?!" My mom had just told him what had happened. A few seconds later, she came into my room and handed my crying baby brother to me. She told me to answer his questions while she stayed downstairs to greet people who came over. For the next half hour I tried to explain to him why Heavenly Father wanted our dad back with him, while I simultaneously tried to pull myself together.

I was told that my father had died in an accident at work. He worked in construction and somehow, he had been knocked off the crane he was inspecting. Some workers nearby said they didn't hear him shout or anything, but had run over to him when they heard him land. He was pronounced dead on arrival around eleven o'clock that morning.

I never really told my dad I loved him. I wish I had. I miss him very much. When I see him again after this life, I know that the first thing I'm going to say to him is "I love you." Until then, "Goodnight, Dad."

~Luken Grace
Chicken Soup for the Teenage Soul II

39

A Birthday Gift

She lived a life of solitude.
She lived a life in vain.
She lived a life in which there was
A strong, ongoing pain.
She had no friends on which to lean
And cry her problems to.
She had no friends to give her love
And hope and kindness, too.
She thought about it day and night;
She lay upon her bed.
Her mind made up, she grabbed a gun
And put it to her head.
Just then a ring came from the phone.
She pulled the gun away.
Her mom was on the other end
And wanted just to say,
"Happy Birthday, my dear girl.
Today is just for you.
I care for you with all my heart,
I hope you know that's true."
These words ran through her mind so much.
The gun was down for good.
She changed her mind about her life
And then she changed her mood.

She thought about this special day
And what her mom had said.
The gift her mom gave her that day
Was the gift of life, again.

~Thad Langenberg
Chicken Soup for the Teenage Soul III

40

The Unexpected

Could we change our attitude, we should not only see life differently, but life itself would come to be different.
~Katherine Mansfield

In September of the year I turned nineteen, my parents drove up unexpectedly one Sunday afternoon to my college dorm. My mother sat down, quietly sniffling, while my dad, truly uncomfortable, cleared his throat, paused for a moment, and told me that they had received a letter from the Social Security Administration.

The letter said that Daniel Frazier—and for a moment, a heartbeat moment, I couldn't remember who he was—had died, and I was entitled to Social Security benefits. Oh yes, he used to be my father. Well, my birth father. I don't even remember him.

A part of me stood in the corner of the room quietly watching as this surreal scene unfolded. The person who I regarded as my true father, who had raised me from a child—my stepfather—was telling me about Daniel Frazier's death. Another part of me was summing up what I felt at this moment, which was nothing—no sorrow, no sadness. Only a sense of melancholy that sometimes comes when reading a stranger's obituary. Despite the chaotic thoughts scuffling around in my head, all I could think was that this isn't how I thought it would end. I always thought I would see him again, at least once.

This was the second and final time I had lost him. He left my mother, my six-year-old sister and two-year-old me, promising to be back in two weeks—walked out the door and never looked back.

When I turned six, my mother married a man who happily took on an instant family, and when our family grew through the addition of a baby brother, my sister and I happily spoiled our little prince.

But always, my thoughts would return to this missing man. I had wildly conflicting views on exactly how I should feel about Daniel Frazier. For a long time, I hated him. Despised him for walking out our front door and never looking back, never calling. I sometimes thought that perhaps he would silently be watching us at school or home, ashamed to show his face, lurking around the edges of my life, interested in how I was growing and my emerging chrysalis personality.

But the saddest thing is that I really have no memories of him. My sister recalls holding his hand and walking with him on a rainy October evening, the streetlights reflecting off the water-slicked streets. They stopped at a large building, where he pointed to one of the windows and said, "That's where your mommy and baby sister are." And that is as much as she can recall. But at least she has something, a bonafide picture captured in her heart. I find myself envious of her for that small glimpse.

My family had such an authentic core of sheer love that it was outside my understanding that someone of such looming importance to me could simply not care. Well, he didn't. Care, that is. But what was not apparent to me when I found out about his death was how unspeakably troubled his life was. Only years later did the details of his life emerge.

My mother's most hidden fear was that he would reemerge to haunt the lives of my sister and me, and only because he had died did she reveal some of his past. It turns out he had, for years, been manic depressive, undiagnosed and untreated during their marriage. My mother found out that he died alone in a hotel room after taking an overdose of sleeping pills.

I know truth is often blurred in interpretation and no one knows what anyone's final, most intimate thoughts are before exiting this world. But I want to believe he achieved some sort of redemptive grace before he died. Only lately, as I've gotten older, can I understand how utterly terrifying his world must have seemed. The chasm between him and a normal life must have seemed incalculable. How defeating it must all have been. With the added, overwhelming responsibilities of parenthood, he simply unraveled. All semblance of reality sloughed off of him, and during his last few years, he evidently lurched between medicated and nonmedicated crises. He had no friends, no family, no one to hold his hand at the end of his life.

It's taken me a long time to be able to write these words. And only after I went through some troubled times in my own life did I begin to comprehend his pain. I found myself understanding how he could walk out that door and not look back. And not call, not write, not be part of our lives. He had nothing left to give, except his own grief and madness. I'd like to think he knew this. So, as my sister and I talked about him last weekend, we realized that we forgave him for leaving us. We had finally stopped looking for the reasons why he went away.

He will always be the first man who broke my heart, but today as I write this, I can finally accept him with all his flaws.

~Julie Lucas
Chicken Soup for the Teenage Soul IV

Healing with Love

O n a bitterly cold and cloudy winter's day in upstate New York, I saw my brother again for the first time in a year. As my father and I pulled up to the reform school after four hours of driving, his attempts at cheerful commentary did nothing to ameliorate the dismal apprehension that I felt. I had little hope that my brother would be changed and, furthermore, I had convinced myself that any appearance of change would not necessarily be genuine.

Being with my brother after so long was like getting to know him all over again. Over the next couple of days, I felt a kind of peace developing between us, and, for the first time, I wasn't tense around him, nor was I scared of what he would do or say next. It seemed as though I would finally find a friend in my brother, and, more than that, I would find a true brother in my brother. While part of me rejoiced in his transformation, another part of me thought it was too good to be true, and so I remained skeptical of his seeming progress. Two days was surely not enough time to erase the hostility that had built up between us over the years. I showed this cynical front to my father and brother, while the hopeful voice remained hidden deep inside of my heart, afraid to appear, lest it should be trampled upon. My brother himself commented several times on my depressed disposition, but I knew he would never understand the complexity of my feelings, so I remained elusive.

I wrapped myself in this same protective silence during what was for me the most emotionally trying part of the visit. Meals at the school were more than just meals. They were chaperoned with two teachers at each table, and provided a forum for judging the students' progress and/or continued delinquency. My father had told me that these meals often lasted for an hour or two, as each student was treated separately and with the full attention of the table. As we sat down for lunch, I knew I wouldn't be able to make it through the meal without crying.

Several boys and girls were "brought up" in front of the table for transgressions they had committed, but a boy named Brian touched me the most. A fairly new arrival at the school, he hadn't yet lost the initial anger and bitterness at having been brought there against his will. He was an attractive boy, about sixteen years old and was, my father whispered to me, an exceptional soccer player with a promising future in the sport. As the head teacher at our table conducted a heavy interrogation of him, Brian shifted his weight nervously every two seconds, and I saw in his eyes what I had become so good at reading in my brother's. They darted anxiously about the room, resting upon everything except the man addressing him, and I knew that he was searching for someone or something to blame. He wasn't yet aware that only when he stopped looking for excuses could he truly hear and learn from those trying to help him.

Suddenly, out of the corner of my eye, I became aware of a bearded man standing at the closed door and peering in apprehensively at our solemn gathering, which must have looked more like an AA meeting than a meal. The realization that it was Brian's father trying to catch a glimpse of his son precipitated the first tear I had shed all weekend.

"Why is Brian here?" I whispered softly to my father.

"Oh, you know, the usual; drugs, violence... I think the last straw was when he hit his father in the head with one of his soccer trophies.... He was chosen for the National All-Star team, you know.... Must be quite a player."

As the tears flowed more freely down my face, Brian looked straight ahead at the wall and told us that he had refused to see his father who had driven for many hours to see him.

Then the teacher spoke, "Brian, I talked to your dad, and he says he brought you your puppy because he knows how much you must miss him. He's willing to accept the fact that you don't want to see him, but he wants you to know that you can see your puppy."

I was screaming inside. I wanted to stand up and tell Brian how lucky he was to have a father who obviously loved him so much, and who loved him enough to do the hardest thing a parent ever has to do: send his child away. I was bursting to enlighten him, but I knew it was something he would have to learn on his own, so I remained still and just let the overwhelming sadness spread over me like a dark cloud.

That afternoon, I saw my brother waving goodbye as we pulled up the dirt drive and out of the gates of the school. I couldn't look back, as I was too busy trying to suppress the emotion that I felt creeping up on me with the force of a tidal wave. I was filled with hopelessness and empathy for these kids who had somehow gotten lost along the way. I knew there was a fine line between them and me, a line I had walked like a tightrope at several times in my life. Indeed, part of my sadness lay in the guilt I felt for not having such a heavy load to bear and for never being able to fully comprehend the nature and sheer weight of this load my brother carried.

Several months later I returned to the school, this time in early spring and accompanied by my whole family, including my mother and two sisters. Everything looked brighter and more colorful in the sun. Wildflowers bloomed on the hillside looking out over the valley, and the water in the pond sparkled like jewels. I closed my eyes, held my face up to the sun and smiled. It was my family's first reunion in over a year. As it was family weekend, everywhere I looked I saw proud, attentive parents and beaming kids. This is when the full force of what I was experiencing hit me. For the first time in a while, I didn't feel the despair and hopelessness of these kids' lives, but the tremendous amount of love and support that surrounded each one of them. After a whole year spent doubting that my brother would ever be able to function normally in society, I allowed the seeds of hope to germinate in my mind, as well as in my heart.

Moments later, my new outlook was strengthened and forever cemented by the most beautiful sight I think I have ever seen. At first I couldn't believe my eyes. Brian and his father were walking arm in arm across the grass towards the pond and seemed to be in quiet discussion about one of those everyday, mundane things that is the business of fathers and their sons. A golden retriever, now fully grown, wagged its tail in delight as he trotted after them.

~Cecile Wood
Chicken Soup for the Teenage Soul III

Losing Mom

When I was twelve, my parents separated, and I thought that was hard. Then I realized that something else is even harder: losing someone you love very much.

In my opinion "cancer" is the worst six-letter word in the whole dictionary. My mom was first diagnosed with mouth cancer. She spent Mother's Day in the hospital that year recovering from major surgery. Then, four months later, she was diagnosed with lung cancer. I remember the day so vividly.

When I came home from school that day, my mom's side of the family was there. They were all crying. My mom said, "Come and sit by me," and she started crying, too. My heart began to pound really hard and my eyes filled with tears. I definitely knew something major was wrong. My mom was too upset to explain so my grandpa told me. My mom had cancer in both lungs, and she only had a short time to live. My mom and I just sat there and cried together.

My family had to watch my mom go through so much: chemo-therapy, radiation, oxygen treatments and the loss of her beautiful hair. She suffered so much, and we couldn't do anything about it. She couldn't talk without coughing or losing her breath. She was weak, and she was just slowly dying.

We knew it would happen someday, but not as soon as it did. Everything was over in eight months. I came home from school one day, and my mom wasn't there. She was always my first concern when I walked through the door. She had been taken to the hospital in an ambulance. We went up to see her that night. I didn't get my homework done, but I didn't care.

The next day, my brother Robert and I were called out of school because my mom wasn't doing well. I went to my locker and started crying. Two of my friends came out and tried to comfort me. When we got to the hospital, my brother Chris met us at the elevator and told us the grim news. I tried not to cry in front of Mom because it would upset her, and then she wouldn't be able to breathe. I took a deep breath and went in to see her. It was so hard to see her lying there so helpless. I held her hand, and we tried to talk but it was hard for her. I can't even count how many times I told her that I loved her.

When I left her that night, I had the feeling that it was going to be the last time I saw her alive. When I got home, I called her and we talked some more. I remember the conversation word for word. I told her that she sounded better and that I loved her. That conversation was so special.

The next day, Robert and I were called out of school again. I wanted to cry so badly, but I held back my tears. Chris and my dad were in the car waiting for us. I was so scared to face what was in store for us. When we stepped off the elevator at the hospital, I took a deep breath. I just had a feeling that what I was about to hear wasn't going to be good. My sister came out of my mom's room and she was crying. As I got closer, I could see that everyone else was crying, too. I started to shake. My sister came up to me and said, "She's gone. She died." I tried to laugh because I didn't want it to be true. The pain I felt was like no other. My sister asked if I wanted to go in and see her, and I said yes. When it was time for everyone to leave, we went over and gave Mom a last hug. When she didn't hug me back, I knew it wasn't a dream.

Some days I really need my mom. When she died, a part of me died, too. However, I knew that I would have to become an adult very quickly. Sometimes I ask myself, Why her? She did not deserve any of the pain that she went through. She fought hard for her children. We meant the world to her, and I know she didn't want to leave us.

I always thought my mom would be here for special things like homecoming, prom, graduation and my wedding day. It's hard knowing she's not going to be. She's never going to know her grandchildren or see Robert and I grow up. I would do anything to have her back. I miss and love her so much.

Very few people consider the true dangers of smoking. They think it is cool because everyone else is doing it. But it isn't. It really isn't.

I'm sure that at least one of you reading this thinks that life would be so much better without your parents. I have a little tip for you: Live life to its fullest and love your parents. It's hard to go on without them.

~Diana Carson
Chicken Soup for the Preteen Soul

43

Tell Me Why You Cry

They say that everyone has a story that will break your heart. My little brother Nicholas had cancer. His hair had fallen out, and he was so weak that it was hard for him to walk. I couldn't stand to see the pain in his eyes any longer. His childhood memories were not of Christmases, camping trips and toys; his memories were of hospital visits, IVs and blood transfusions.

I remember when it first started, when he was only three. At first, it was the way he was always getting awful, ugly bruises. We didn't think anything of it until they started showing up in places they didn't belong, like in his armpit or on his scalp. Then there were his nosebleeds, which were a constant occurrence. My mom would always have to remind us, "Don't horse around with Nicholas; his nose will start to bleed."

His form of cancer was acute lymphatic leukemia (ALL), which is very curable. Seventy percent of children with ALL achieve remission within one year, and out of those in remission, 50 percent never relapse. Nicky's odds were very good.

He started chemotherapy immediately, to stop the cancer from getting any worse. It went well but it was hard. He was at the hospital Monday, Tuesday and Wednesday receiving treatment, and then he would come home for the rest of the week, sick and completely powerless. He missed preschool that year, but he was in remission in nine months, and we were all happy.

Life was back to normal for a while, until one day during my freshman year. I came home from school to see my parents sitting on the couch, which was odd, because my parents were never home after school. But when I saw the tears, I knew that my worst fear had come true. The cancer was back.

He was five by then and had been in remission for about two years. We all thought he had beaten it, but then they had found a cancerous tumor inside his chest. The doctors were not sure how big it was, so they set a surgery date. They were going to make a small incision on his chest and evaluate the tumor. If it was possible, they would remove it that same day.

The day of the surgery, we all woke up early to accompany Nicholas to the hospital. We sat in the stark white waiting room of B-3, the "cancer hall." I had been there far more than I could handle. In the last two years, I had seen too much of this hall, of cribs occupied by babies whose mothers visit less and less, of children who know they will not make it. The sickening smell of death lines each room, telling past stories of children whose lives were cut short by a silent killer.

We sat and waited for what seemed like an eternity. Finally, after four hours Dr. McGuiness, Nicky's cancer physician specialist, came out of the door marked SURGERY. He was still wearing his operating garb as he motioned for us to follow him, which meant that we needed to talk. As we sat down, fear consumed us.

"Nicholas is out of surgery now, and the medicine will wear off soon," Dr. McGuiness began.

"I'm sorry, though," he continued. "The tumor has grown too large. It has consumed one entire lung, and it has grown all down one side of his heart. There is nothing we can do now."

As I heard those words, my eyes filled with tears. Those words meant that it was time to stop fighting because we would not win. I looked around and knew I wanted to leave. I wanted to run far, far away, but I knew I couldn't. It wouldn't make my problems any better, and it wouldn't make Nicky live.

The doctor left for ten minutes so we could regain composure. When he returned, he asked where we wanted Nicholas to spend his last days. We said we wanted Nicholas home.

The next few months were torture, having to watch Nicky get sicker and weaker. As the tumor grew, his heart stopped pumping regularly and he became short of breath.

The summer went by much quicker than it should have. Nicholas's health remained steady, although still very fragile. We were even able to take a trip to Disneyland, Nicky's One Last Wish. It was so hard, though, trying to be happy for him and knowing it was our last vacation together as a family.

As the year went by, the bustle and jumble of the holiday season kept us occupied. Halloween was fun and Thanksgiving dinner was delicious. Then, as we started preparing for Christmas, Nicky's health deteriorated.

One day as everyone was decorating the tree, I went in to see Nicholas, who was sitting in a chair. The Christmas lights beautifully illuminated his face and brought out an innocent sparkle we had not seen in a long time.

As I came closer, I realized he was crying. I sat down in the chair with him and held him in my arms the way I had when he was younger.

"Nicky, tell me why you cry," I said.

"Sissy, it's just not fair," he blubbered.

"What's not fair?" I asked.

"Why am I going to die?"

"Well, you know that everyone dies," I replied, obviously avoiding the subject. I didn't want him to know, and deep down inside I didn't want to know either.

"But not like me. Why do I have to die? Why so early?" And then he started to cry. He buried his head in my chest, and I started to cry, too. We sat like that for a long time. A very long, lonesome and scary time. Afterwards there was an understanding between us. He was ready, and so was I. We could handle anything now.

In January, he slipped into a coma and we knew we were losing him. One day we sat in his room, holding his hand, because we knew this was going to be his last time with us. Suddenly, a certain peacefulness filled the room, and I knew that Nicholas had breathed his last breath.

I looked outside. The freshly fallen snow somehow seemed brighter. I hated myself for it, but I suddenly felt better. All the pain and sorrow of the past few years were gone, and I knew that Nicholas was safe. He was no longer scared or hurt, and it was better this way.

~Nicole Rose Patridge
Chicken Soup for the Teenage Soul II

44

My Mother:
Her Depression,
Her Strength

grasped my blanket in one hand and my doll in the other as I reluctantly pushed open my parents' bedroom door. I shivered as I stepped into the dim, frigid room and tiptoed to the side of their bed. A single arm cautiously reached from the bundles of blankets and sheets and sorted through the countless bottles of medication on the nightstand. "Oh, hi baby... do you want to come lie down and take a nap with Mommy?" I crawled into the king size bed, snuggled up next to her warm back and laid with her for the next couple of hours. This was the most contact I'd made with my mother for many years of my life. I thought that all families functioned as mine did. It took me several years of frustration and confusion to understand that my mother suffered horribly from depression.

As I began making close, personal friends in school, they shared the details of the relationships with their mothers with me. I realized I was missing out on something wonderful with my own mother and began suggesting to her that we spend more time together. She would continuously find an excuse or dilemma that would hinder her from going out with me. She would then proceed to her bedroom to take medicine and go to sleep for the remainder of the day. I remember sitting in my room crying so many nights because I could not make sense of her broken promises and refusal to spend time with me. It broke my heart to know that she would rather sleep than spend time with her own daughter.

My mother's behavior soon came to affect my entire family. My father would constantly question and quarrel with my mother, not understanding her illness. He built his entire life around pleasing her: cooking her favorite comfort foods and making sure I never made a single noise while she was sleeping. Why did my father put up with my invalid mother all those years? Adopting my mother's ways, my sister began sleeping all day, only coming out for meals or to log on to the Internet. The way things were going, I felt like I was the next in line to be plagued by this disease. So I kept myself active and hardly ever spent time at home. The only way I could face the fear of becoming depressed was to distance myself from the people who were most likely to cause it.

The culmination of my mother's battle with depression came when I was a senior in high school. It was an early Saturday afternoon, and I had just returned home from band rehearsal. I could sense that something was wrong the moment I unlocked the front door. I heard the shower running in my parents' bathroom, which seemed odd because my father was working in the front yard and my mother should have been asleep. As I cautiously walked toward the bedroom that adjoined the bathroom, the sound of someone weeping rushed to my ears. My stomach dropped. I was afraid to go in because of what I might find. I carefully opened the bathroom door to find my mother huddled in the corner of the running shower, fully clothed and sobbing uncontrollably. I rushed outside to tell my father. For reasons I still do not understand, he became angry and stormed inside, shouting at her that he didn't have time for this and to get out of the shower and dry off. We called her psychiatrist and he immediately admitted her to the mental institution wing of Baylor Hospital under a suicide watch. I was in denial about how critical my mother's condition had gotten and explained to all my friends that she had hurt her back and had to stay in the hospital for a couple of days. Visiting my mother behind the secured doors of the institution was the single most difficult thing I've ever had to do.

Wounded and hurt, my mother watched as I could not meet my eyes with hers. I sat across the cafeteria table from her, barely making conversation and fidgeting my fingers. I did not want her showing me the macaroni art that she had created earlier that day in "craft therapy"; I needed her to give me a long, safe hug and tell me that everything was going to be all right. I trudged out the hospital doors that day wondering what my life would be like if my mother had actually followed through with her intended plan. It terrified me.

After her short visit to the hospital, my mother became dramatically healthier. It was not because of any prescribed medication or therapy session; it was because she realized that she did not want to spend the rest of her life in so much emotional pain. We sat down together after the hospital released her, and she attempted to explain to me what was going on inside of her mind and body. She felt that she had nothing to live for and did not see any point of going on. But as she was crying helplessly on the floor of the shower, she saw me standing there and found a reason to go on. She called me her "angel" because, in a sense, I had saved her life. After all those years, I finally understood my mother's pain.

My mother and I have a bond today that surpasses everything that happened in the past. I love my mother more than anyone in the world, and I am so proud that she has overcome her depression and is the remarkable mother that she is today.

~Laura Pavlasek
Chicken Soup for the Teenage Soul IV

Not Your Typical Prom Night

There's no other love like the love for a brother.
There's no other love like the love from a brother.
~Astrid Alauda

It's supposedly the happiest night of a girl's life (aside from her sixteenth birthday, that is). The night when every girl in the free world does her hair for far too long, spends much more time on her face than she ever will the rest of her life, and waits for Mr. Right to whisk her away to a night filled with excitement, music, friends and fun. Ah, prom night.

Strange how things always look good in the theory stage, but never in the execution. When I look back on my prom night, I see those wonderful things that other girls saw—the pretty dress, the date, the car. However, that night I also saw something that a teenage girl should never have to see—a brother slowly dying of cancer.

This isn't as morbid as it sounds. My brother was never the morbid type. Everything was always "fine," even though as prom night approached, he couldn't see more than five inches in front of his face and had limited use of his arms and legs because the cancer pressed on nearly every nerve in his body. It caused him excruciating pain with every touch—every hug.

This is how I found him the night of my prom. As I entered the room, my father was already there, being a dad and sitting there with my brother, watching whatever sports event was on the television. My brother made a feeble attempt to watch; he could even try to convince himself that he could see what was going on. Looking back on it, he had us all (except for my mother who spent twenty-four hours a day with him) convinced that he would get better. That night I fully believed he saw me walk in the room.

"Hi, my Dacy," he said, in the ever-so-cute baby talk tone he always used with me. I greeted him with a smile, which to this very day I am not sure he saw. I wanted to give him a hug, but the pain for him would have been too great. So instead I leaned over and gave him a slight kiss on the cheek. He heard my dress rustling as I did this, and I could see him strain to see it. He always tried to hide this act from us, but you couldn't help but notice it. He had this funny way of tilting his head downward, because to quote him: "It's like the bottom part of my eye is cut off and I can only see what is above this line." And he would hold his large hand up and divide his eye in half horizontally, to try to demonstrate.

As he tilted his head, desperately trying to see me in all my prom night splendor, I couldn't help but sob quietly. A tear hit my red satin gown and I tried to brush it away, absurdly believing that he could see me.

"This sucks, Mom," he said, frustrated. "I can't even see my own sister's prom dress." I took his hand and let him feel the satin of my dress. Being the protective sibling that he was, he felt around the neckline, and noticing there wasn't a neckline, began to chastise me.

"I don't know about this, Dacy," he said protectively. He then tried to look around, and proceeded to call my date over and lecture him on what a gentleman he was going to be that night. I stood back and watched him, this bigger-than-average boy, who couldn't see or even walk on his own at this point, telling my date EXACTLY how he was going to treat his sister. I began to cry. I cried not only for his feeble attempt at protection (actually, as I found out from my date much later, my brother was still able to strike some fear into his heart) but at the fact that God, fate, or whatever was doing this to a boy who all his life just wanted to be normal—who just wanted to live.

I knew at that moment, as I watched him talking, that he would be gone from me soon. Maybe I didn't admit it to myself right then, but I knew—somehow I knew, and I cried even harder. My brother heard me from across the room, and called me over.

"Don't cry, Stace... don't cry." He had changed tones on me. This was the Serious Brother tone now, the you-better-listen-to-what-I'm-saying tone. "It will be okay. It will get better. I know it will." He started crying at this. My mom tried to reassure me that it was his medication that was making him depressed; I wasn't convinced. Those tears were real. He tried to hug me and let me know that it was okay; to let me know that I should go to my prom and live my life. I gave my brother one last kiss and was gone.

~Stacy Bennett
Chicken Soup for the Teenage Soul II

I Wish You Were Dead!

Even my locked bedroom door couldn't keep out the aroma of my mother's homemade spaghetti sauce. As I flipped through the pages of Teen, checking out the latest fashion trends, the celebrity scoop and my horoscope, my mouth began to water.

Just then, I heard my doorknob turn, and then a soft knock.

"Shannon, honey, can I come in?"

My mom hated it when I locked my door. What she didn't understand was that if I didn't, Brian would barge in and destroy my room. Ever since my brother grew armpit hair, he had turned into the biggest jerk in the world. He was either ignoring me or annoying me.

His latest torture was to walk into my room while I was in the middle of talking on the phone or writing in my journal. He wouldn't leave the first time I asked. Instead, he'd lie on the bed and tease me about whoever I was going out with at the time.

Then he would proceed to toss my stuffed animals around the room and move around my knickknacks until I was screaming for him to leave. Last week, he got me so mad that I yelled after him, "I wish you were dead!"

Mom usually sided with him even though I was the youngest and I was used to getting my way. She was probably at my door right then to tell me that I needed to help him set the table or something lame like that.

Instead, she walked in and told me something that would change my life forever. Her eyes were swollen, and she covered her face. I told her to sit down, and I put my arm around her shoulder — not knowing what else to do.

"Mom, you're freaking me out. What is it?"

"Shannon, you know how your brother has been having joint pain and how we've been going to the doctor a lot lately?"

"Yeah, so?" I was really worried now. All along, I had thought his legs and arms were just worn out from tennis tryouts or that he was having another growth spurt.

"Shannon, your brother is sick. He has leukemia."

"What is that? Is that like a kind of cancer or something?" I scooted away from her and stood up to walk around in my room, which suddenly felt a lot smaller at that moment.

"Yes, honey, it is. Don't worry, though. Brian has the good kind."

"The good kind?" I stared at her in disbelief. "There is no good kind." All I had ever known about cancer was that when you got it, you lost your hair and died.

"Shannon, please sit down. I know you're upset. I'm upset too. The only people I've ever known with leukemia were two boys that I grew up with in Ohio who died from it. But treatments have changed so much. He's going to make it. I promise."

As we held each other, my mom's tears drenched my cheek and collar, and I could hear her muffled sobs. When she stood up, wiped her face and took a deep breath, I couldn't tell whether five or thirty minutes had passed. She flashed me a weak smile, told me that dinner would soon be ready and headed back downstairs.

I collapsed onto my bed, feeling paralyzed. I remembered the awful thing I had said to him, "I wish you were dead!" Was this my fault? Had I actually played a hand in my brother's getting sick? At that moment, I would have given anything to be able to take back those words that I had so passionately screamed at him. Then all kinds of images began to swirl around in my head like the flakes in a shaken snow globe.

There was Brian in his magician's cape finishing a trick with me, his "assistant," at his side. There was Brian interviewing me, in his most serious voice, for our taped news broadcast. There was Brian, laughing and smiling his big, bucktoothed grin as we watched *Saturday Night Live* together. There was Brian holding my hand, as we got off the plane to go visit our father in Texas.

In an instant, I knew exactly what I needed to do. I knew how bad I felt, so I couldn't imagine how bad Brian was feeling. I cleaned up my face so it didn't look as though I'd been crying. I grabbed a piece of poster board and my markers and headed downstairs.

When I entered the living room, he was sitting on the couch watching television. I placed all of my materials on the floor and began working on a science project that was due that week.

"Brian?"

"Yeah?"

"Can you help me with this stupid thing? I can't draw an elephant, and I have to have an elephant on it to get a good grade."

"I'll try."

As we sat on the living room floor, drawing and coloring without saying a word, I knew that something had changed — something big. While he was concentrating on the elephant's outline, I watched him.

All those fights. All those cross words. All those times he made me mad. All the times he got to do something that I didn't get to do. They just didn't matter anymore. All that mattered was being next to him, right then, in that moment.

~Shannon Griffin
Chicken Soup for the Preteen Soul 2

[*Editors' note*: Brian fully recovered and to this day is cancer free.]

Chapter 6

Teens Talk

Tough Times

Pushing Forward

*In three words I can sum up everything I've learned about life:
it goes on.*
~Robert Frost

No Matter What Happens

Say you are well, or all is well with you,
And God shall hear your words and make them true.
~Ella Wheeler Wilcox

I remember a time when each day was long,
When the world was a playground and my life a song,
And I fluttered through years with barely a care,
Ignoring the future and what waited there.
School was intriguing and filled with delights.
I played away daytimes and dreamed away nights.
My parents assured me I had nothing to fear,
And that no matter what happened, they'd always be there.
Little I knew of a world outside home,
Where tragedy, sorrow and murder could roam.
All I saw were blue skies, rainbows and stars.
I looked past destruction of buildings and cars.
As a child, my biggest concern was just me;
I had to be happy, I had to be free.
And if I was content, I would not shed a tear,
And no matter what happened, I still would be here.
But as I grow up, darkness starts to set in;
My bright world has turned into concrete and tin.

I now see the violence I looked past before;
My friends start to die and my heart hits the floor.
Deadly diseases claim people I love,
There are landfills below me, pollution above.
I often think back to when life was a game.
But no matter what happens, it can't be the same.
There are days when I just want to break down and howl,
To give up completely, to throw in the towel,
But I hold my head high and I push my way through.
I have too much to give and so much to do.
And I make a vow that, though it'll be hard,
I'll go on with a smile and play every card.
I'll give all I can, help others and love.
No matter what happens, life will bloom again,
And the strength I don't have will come from above.
So come, take my hand, and through darkness we will sail—
If we all join together, we never can fail.
We'll remember to care, remember to feel,
And no matter what happens, our world we will heal.

~Alison Mary Forbes
Chicken Soup for the Teenage Soul II

48

Anything Is Possible

When I was a little kid, I would always come in last when my friends and I ran races. I was never fast at running. I also had a hard time playing basketball because I couldn't jump well. It's hard to jump when your ankles don't move. So I was always picked last to be on a team. I used to get so frustrated and would be really upset about my "fake legs." But I made up for it all when I got my first pair of Rollerblades.

I was born with a condition that caused me to have to be fitted with prosthetic legs and feet. I got my first ones when I was eight months old. Also, my fingers on my left hand were joined together. I had to have surgery to separate them, and as a result, I now have only eight fingers. But for those of you who think that a person with no feet and only three fingers on one of his hands should be in special ed classes—well, you've got me way wrong.

At first it was pretty hard to learn to skate—I kept falling. But I liked the way I felt; while I was on skates, I felt like I was able to move just as fast as the other kids. So, I kept practicing—and I learned how to get up. Soon, I got better and faster. Then, when my friends were running races, I would put on a pair of Rollerblades and skate the race with them. Win or lose, I was able to keep up.

Since skating had become my favorite thing to do, I signed up for the local roller hockey team and then the ice hockey team. I began playing hockey year round.

When I first joined, I thought I would just skate up to the net and take a shot. But I soon found out it wasn't so easy. I didn't score one single goal that whole season.

So, I trained hard in the off-season and the next year I signed up again. When I got through with the tryout, I was actually put into an older age bracket. The problem was, the kids in the older group were huge, and I quickly became intimidated. They actually stole the puck from me during the first game, and I didn't know what to do. I remember thinking, "Aren't we on the same team?" It made me feel like quitting, and I didn't show up at the next game. But my parents and my younger brother encouraged me to get back in there and keep trying.

On the next game day, late in the game, we were losing four to five and I was playing right wing. Finally, a pass came to me and I took the shot. To me, everything went in slow motion. I saw the puck fly into the net just as the buzzer went off. My goal tied the game. When my team came skating over to me with excitement, I realized that I really could become good at this game. It would be the first of many goals.

Now, at thirteen years old, I have played in three all-star games for ice hockey and roller hockey, all on able-bodied teams, and I don't even know how many goals I've scored in my entire career. I play for the American Amputee Hockey Association as well. We play all over the country and we have even played in Canada and Russia. Recently, I got sponsored by Nexed, an inline-hockey skate company. I get free shirts, hats, skates—anything that has to do with inline hockey. And just think, all this stuff started with one little two-second goal—and an awesome prosthetist named Eric.

Eric makes my prosthetics and knows exactly what I want and need. He's always looking for ways to make them function better. Before this year, my prosthetic legs had no bendable ankles. I had to grow to a certain height—and this year Eric made them for me. Now I know what it's like to have my feet on the ground while my legs move around. These new prosthetics with ankles that bend are good for running, jumping, hiking, and golf, which I recently took up. However, the old style, where the ankles don't bend, is great for hockey—and, as a matter of fact, creates an advantage for me over other kids, whose ankles can get strained or even broken during a game. Now, I can choose which prosthetic I want to wear, according to the sport I'm playing!

I can also decorate my legs any way I want. I bring Eric a t-shirt or patches and he laminates them right onto the legs. I used to have the Rangers and Yankee logos—once I even had the American flag. Now I have them with tie-dye and Green Day and Nirvana patches. Everyone thinks they're pretty cool.

I've had some pretty funny things happen, like the time that I joined an out-of-town roller hockey team. Most of the guys on the team and their parents didn't know that I wore prosthetics. (You can't tell with all my equipment on.) So, you can just imagine everyone's faces when one of my legs came flying off during the game, as I was trying to shoot a goal. My leg kept going toward the net, almost scoring a goal! There was dead silence in the arena. I think everyone was in shock! The two coaches came to get me off the rink. One coach carried me, the other coach carried my leg.

When I got off the rink, everyone just started clapping and whistling—they were flipping out! I don't think anyone who was there will forget seeing that! My mom helped me get my leg back on and all we could do was laugh at what had just happened. When the game was over, people kept coming up to me and shaking my hand like I was the "most valuable player" or something.

I have never thought of myself as handicapped. I'm definitely differently-abled. I began skiing when I was only seven, and now I am a black diamond skier. I go to ski camp every year with my amputee friends and for the whole week we ski and hang out. Maybe some day I will train for the Paralympics, which is like the Olympics, only it's just for people who are physically challenged. Whatever I decide to do, I know I would have to train hard to be one of the best—just like any other pro.

As I get bigger, my prostheses get even better, and it gives me more courage to get out and try new stuff.

One day, after I had run in a six mile race, one of my friends asked me where I'd been all day. When I told him that I had just finished a six mile race, he said, "I couldn't do that!"

Someday, I want to go to a good college and eventually play for a team in the National Hockey League. I also want to be on the All-Star Team. But more than anything, I want to beat Wayne Gretzky's record. My philosophy is, you just have to go for it. You'll never know until you try.

Hey, as they say, "Anything is possible!"

~Danny Stein
Chicken Soup for the Preteen Soul 2

Blessed

A smile can brighten the darkest day.
~Author Unknown

Whitney stepped up to the microphone to sing the National Anthem. Her voice was strong and clear, and the high school gym erupted into cheers as she sang the last notes and the basketball teams dashed onto the court. But the loudest cheers in the stadium came from her greatest fans—her father, Tony, her older brother, Jared, and me, her grateful mother.

I never dreamed we'd be sitting here again, I thought, my heart bursting with pride as my daughter took her place with the other high school cheerleaders. After everything she's been through, it's a miracle Whitney is still alive.

Our long nightmare began when Whitney came down with what seemed like a simple sinus infection. After complaining of a sore throat, her doctor prescribed antibiotics, but they didn't help at all.

Whitney's glands swelled. Her whole body grew stiff and achy. I guessed she might be coming down with the flu and put her to bed. But over the next several days, Whitney's condition took an unexpected turn for the worse. Her hands and feet began to tingle… and soon the tip of her nose was tingling, too.

One night, Whitney noticed her upper lip was going numb. The next morning when she awoke, her eyes were crossed and she was seeing double.

We rushed Whitney to our family doctor, who immediately sent her to a neurologist. At the hospital, doctors put Whitney in quarantine and performed a spinal tap. Whitney frantically asked what was wrong with her as she continued to lose feeling in her limbs and face.

She was finally diagnosed with meningoencephalitis and Guillain-Barré syndrome. The doctor told us it is very rare to have either condition; to have both is almost unheard of.

The delicate membrane that was supposed to cushion Whitney's brain was swollen and causing painful pressure. Her motor nerves had been stripped of their protective lining, and her arms and legs were growing weaker by the minute. She couldn't walk or feed herself, or move the muscles in her face to make any expression at all.

Her doctor theorized she may have contracted the mono virus, causing her immune system to overreact and begin attacking her own body. His next words drove a spike of fear through my heart. "I'm afraid it's going to get a lot worse before it gets better."

Whitney was an honor roll student who had made the cheerleading squad every year since she was twelve. She loved performing with her high school's choir, but as she lay in the hospital bed she wondered if she would ever sing or dance again.

Soon Whitney was transferred to the intensive care unit, where a ventilator stood ready to help her breathe. Her doctor explained that sometimes with Guillain-Barré, the paralysis grows so bad that even drawing a breath becomes too difficult. We needed to be prepared—just in case.

For the next three days, I sat at Whitney's bedside praying for a miracle. Whitney could barely speak, her tongue felt so numb and thick in her mouth, and her eyes were mere slits because she didn't have enough motor control to open her eyelids. Whitney's entire body was a single raw nerve, and she sobbed in agony when the pain grew so excruciating that even morphine didn't help.

Whitney's name was added to numerous prayer chains and, miraculously, she survived her respiratory crisis. We all celebrated when it was decided she wouldn't need the ventilator, and Whitney was moved out of the ICU.

Doctors prescribed physical therapy to help her regain use of her arms and legs. Whitney struggled as she tried to grip a toothbrush. When she practiced with her walker, her legs dangled limply as the physical therapist encouraged her to push against the floor.

Whitney pushed herself as hard as she could because she knew it was the only way she'd ever get well. "Look, Mom—I'm smiling," she said one day. I felt my heart break in two as I forced myself to smile back even though Whitney's face remained a frozen mask of paralyzed muscle.

But I felt a sense of hope for the first time. Despite everything she's been through, I thought, Whitney's still trying to smile. She still has hope, and she's trying to pass that hope along to me. Somehow, I knew Whitney would fight her way back from this terrible illness... and her strength was inspiring the rest of us to be strong.

Doctors told Whitney she'd need a wheelchair to return to school, but Whitney was determined to prove them wrong. "C'mon, Mom, let's go again," she would beg only minutes after her physical-therapy session because she wanted even more exercise with her walker.

"Go for it!" Jared said, giving his sister her handgrips and counting off the reps. "One more," he coaxed again and again. "You can do it. I know you can."

After two weeks, Whitney was transferred to St. Vincent's Children's Hospital, where she continued her therapy and received tutoring from a hospital teacher. Whitney dictated her lessons to me, but one day her hands were finally nimble enough to sign her own name to her homework paper. She beamed with pride, and this time her smile was the real thing.

We threw a big party the day Whitney came home from the hospital. After ten weeks of outpatient therapy, she returned to school—not in a wheelchair or even using a walker, but on her own two feet with only leg braces for support.

Before long, Whitney was singing again with the school choir, and by the following fall when cheerleading tryouts came around, she made the varsity squad. This year she's a member of the All-Star Team.

Whitney uses only a single word to describe how she feels today: "Blessed." Blessed for the doctors who fought to save her life. Blessed for the prayers of friends and schoolmates... and blessed for the family who was always there for her.

~Jerrilyn Thetford as told to Heather Black
Chicken Soup for the Christian Teenage Soul

Academic Excellence Begins with a '51 Studebaker

In September 1956, my best friend David Ford and I were playing kick-the-can on our way to our third grade class. It was a typical September morning in Jal, New Mexico. The smell of crude oil and dust hung heavy in the desert morning air. Until that time, I had been an A student and liked school, but this year things were different. Although we didn't do many difficult things, school was turning out to be a place I would rather not be. These long fall days were spent coloring, adding, subtracting and looking at a dead snake in a pickle jar. I was a towheaded boy with a cowlick that would not quit. My jeans were worn through at the knees before it was popular to wear them that way.

Our classroom was also known as Mrs. Writt's dungeon of torture. Mrs. Writt was a stickler for proper appearance and pointed out daily the sins of untidiness. I seemed to be her favorite target and to my chagrin, she would inevitably find dirt under my fingernails and my Keds improperly laced.

Although I didn't recognize its significance until much later, this one particular day was to be a defining time for me. This would forever be the moment at which I could look back and say, "That's when it happened."

We had all colored the same picture the day before: a curly-haired, dimple-faced girl sitting on a hobby horse. The same image was used, no doubt, for comparison purposes. Now, I never saw the purpose in coloring; it was something I had decided that girls did. David and I had discussed this at length and had decided that, indeed, boys couldn't be good at this activity. Any boy who was adept at coloring a curly-haired, dimple-faced girl most certainly wasn't capable of excelling at "boy things" like shooting rabbits or playing football.

When I took a seat, my classmates were giggling and pointing at the chalkboard. To my surprise, my rendering of color on the curly-haired girl was taped prominently on the left side of the chalkboard, and labeled with broad chalk lettering: "Terry's picture." On the right side of the board was another coloring of the same picture, labeled "Sherry's picture." Sherry's picture had been done by "perfect" Sherry Peirson. Sherry was pretty, clean and always well dressed. Her coloring was always perfect, with the correct hues and of course, always within the lines.

As Mrs. Writt called roll, I got a knot in the pit of my stomach and I felt my face getting hot as I slid further down into my seat. Suddenly, I felt like my feet were grotesquely oversized and I didn't know what to do with my large, dirty hands, so I put them in my pockets. I felt dizzy and my vision narrowed to where all I could see was my coloring taped to the chalkboard. There it was, the girl with curly purple hair and green lips sitting on a red hobby horse, crayon marks irregularly straying over the lines. Oh how I wished that I had done better, or had a chance to do it again. Maybe the principal would call a fire drill or even better, the school would catch fire and burn down. Maybe now the Soviets would drop the bomb on us and we could jump under our desks and watch the searing heat burn all the paper products in town. Before salvation could come in any form, Mrs. Writt called my name. "Terry, Terry Savoie, come and stand under your work. I want the class to see who is responsible for this."

"Sherry, please stand next to your work. Now class, which of these is acceptable, Terry's work or Sherry's work?"

"Sherry's, teacher."

"Class, please notice how the appearance of the person matches the appearance of the work. I want you to be like Sherry; she is a shining example of excellence. Don't do what Terry has done; Terry is an example of failure. This is what failure looks like and this is what excellence looks like. Okay, children, you may take your seats."

So this was my position, the class failure. Oddly, at the moment I sat down I felt comfortable with my new position. My parents had told me, "Do what you do well." I could most certainly do this well. I could, in fact, be the best class failure Jal Elementary ever had. It was a liberating feeling. I would have this position unchallenged and indeed be a clown, or sleep, or work feverishly at failing and forever own the official title of Class Failure. I found that I was particularly good at my newfound talent. I took pride in my position and never again had to feel that knot in my stomach for poor performance.

David, being my best friend, was impressed with my new ability and began to compete with me for my position, but he was never any real competition because he had never gotten the recognition from the authority on this subject like I had. I was the best at failure and had the credentials to prove it.

I found that there was a price to pay for my position. I had to deal with my parents' disappointment every six weeks. I spent many long hours being lectured to and also had to endure regular spankings. The most difficult price for me to pay were my mother's tears. But a man's got to do what a man's got to do. My parents continued to tell me that I wasn't stupid. In fact, they went to great lengths to encourage me and tell me I was as smart as anyone else, even smarter than most. But they were my parents and they were supposed to say that. The "professionals" knew better and had spoken.

Life turned out to be relatively easy once I had calloused myself to my parents' grief. The school moved me on with my friends and annotated on my records "chronological promotion," which meant I was old enough to move to the next grade. They did hold me back when I failed the seventh grade and again in the ninth grade. This is when my problems began to catch up with me. My friends were leaving me, even David moved up, and I was left with the younger kids. After I failed the ninth grade, Mom suggested that I get a tutor in algebra and English. It was then decided that I would spend the summer of 1964 in summer school, and that until my grades came up I would spend every summer in school.

The high school principal, Mr. K. B. Walker, called a meeting with my parents and me. He got so close to me that I could smell the oil in his red hair, and he said some very scary words to me that went something like this: "Savoie, you need to understand that I don't care how long it takes, you will stay in the ninth grade until you meet the same standards everyone else does before you move on." Then he looked at my dad and said, "Herman, you're backing me on this, aren't you?"

"Yes sir."

At this time my interests were in cars and trucks. I was fascinated with all sorts of mechanical things. My dad had helped me buy a 1951 Studebaker and we spent many weekends together working on it. When we pulled it into the garage, it was rusty red and nothing worked, but to me its sleek rocket shape was the most exciting thing I had ever seen. We removed the hood and began our project by first removing all the dirt daubers' nests from around the carburetor. We cleaned and scraped and I worked part time at Alexander's grocery store, putting every dime I made into parts.

Eventually the car came back to life. We rebuilt the old flathead six and put in a new six-volt battery. I remember clearly the Friday evening in July waiting on the porch for my dad to get home so we could connect the battery and start the engine. Dad came straight in and we told Mom to skip supper—we had important things to do. I brushed the cables gently with a wire brush. Then I reverently tightened the seven-sixteenth-inch post clamps. Dad decided to check to see if the six volts were now coursing life through the old rocket. He pulled the headlight switch and the right headlight burned brightly. The light reflected my white T-shirt and Dad spit some Beech-Nut tobacco out the driver's side window and raised his eyebrows. He stuck his head out and said, "Son, pour about two tablespoons of gas in that carburetor and let's see if she cranks."

He pumped the accelerator pedal twice and pulled the choke half closed, turned the key on and pushed the chrome-plated start button. The starter rotated the engine once, then twice, the rotations quickened. A bright orange flame shot from the open exhaust pipe, the engine spun to life with a cloud of black smoke and then the air cleared. The engine settled to a smooth, even idle. I whooped, Dad grinned and Mom came into the garage. She put her arm around my shoulder and said, "It's running, you made it run, you're good at this, aren't you?"

I said, "Yeah, with Dad's help, I guess I am." We went on to paint the car and with the help of wet concrete mortar for rubbing compound, we got all of the tarnish off the chrome bright work. It was truly a work of art.

I tell you about the Studebaker because the work I did on this car became a recurring topic of conversation during my algebra summer school. To understand the metamorphosis that was to take place the summer of 1964, I must introduce you to Montrella Ruffner. My parents never gave up on me and they weren't afraid to try anything. Montrella was a member of our church and was also a teacher. My parents talked her into helping me. She didn't tell me anything my parents hadn't told me but since she was a teacher, she was the expert on success and failure. Montrella was a robust and enthusiastic woman. She was rather large and usually the first thing she did when I arrived for tutoring was to give me a hug. When Montrella hugged you, you didn't come unhugged for a week. We would start each session by talking about my favorite subject, my Studebaker. Montrella was as mechanically inclined as most thirty-five-year-old algebra teachers but she seemed to really enjoy hearing me talk about connecting rods, piston rings and carburetors. She sat enthralled as I spoke eloquently about firing order and ignition timing.

Then she would ask, "Is this what you really love to do? Would you like to be a mechanic when you grow up?" Well, to me, being a mechanic wasn't anything special. Most of my friends were mechanics on their own cars. I allowed, though, that it might be what I would do. After all what else could an academic failure like me do?

This robust authority on success began to paint pictures in my mind. She talked about how it was almost magical how automobiles worked and how people who could fix them were like powerful doctors. She asked me to imagine what a world without mechanics would be like. "Why, surely we would still have to hitch up a wagon and bail our drinking water out of an open well," she said authoritatively. She talked about the mechanical magicians that had fixed her car over at the Kermit Chevy House. How they wore the professional blue coveralls with their names and "Chevy Mechanic" embroidered on them.

She told me, "Son, you are going to be one of those guys. Not only that, I think I see you being a Master Technician one of these days. Can you see yourself in those clothes doing that with a reputation for being the best? Why, look at Jimmy Lewallen. He is one of the smartest, most respected men in Jal." Jimmy was our small town's resident mechanic and a man of excellent reputation.

It was at this point she caught me, she gently nudged me into algebra by saying, "You're gonna be the best, aren't you?"

"Yes ma'am."

"Son, do you know there are steps you have to take to get there?"

"Yes ma'am," I said, nodding enthusiastically.

"Son, you know what you've got to do first to be top of the line?"

"What's that, ma'am?"

"You gotta do this algebra. Anyone that can do the kind of magic you do with a broken down old car can do this algebra and do it well, do you understand that son? Do you?"

"Yes, ma'am."

Then she said, "Let's tear this algebra down and breathe some life into it, okay?"

I went on that fall to get a B in algebra—the first B that I had gotten since the second grade. It turns out that I was a solid B student with occasional abilities for receiving As. I joined the Air Force in 1969. They didn't know that I had been stupid once and I didn't tell them. In basic training, I was overjoyed when I was told I had a high aptitude for mechanics and that they were going to send me to jet school at Chanute AFB Ill. To me, this was like getting drafted to play linebacker for the Dallas Cowboys.

The victories, though, didn't end in mechanics. I had many different and interesting jobs in my twenty-five-year career and in 1987, I was selected as the USAF First Sergeant of the Year, "Top of the Line." I earned two college degrees going to night school and now that I'm out of the Air Force, I'm a teacher of aerospace science at Central High School in San Angelo, Texas. Academic excellence sometimes begins in strange and unorthodox places. To me, academic excellence began with a 1951 Studebaker.

~Terry A. Savoie
A 5th Portion of Chicken Soup for the Soul

My Mother's Strength

A mother is the truest friend we have, when trials heavy and sudden,
fall upon us; when adversity takes the place of prosperity;
when friends who rejoice with us in our sunshine desert us;
when trouble thickens around us, still will she cling to us,
and endeavor to dissipate the clouds of darkness,
and cause peace to return to our hearts.
~Washington Irving

When I was just fourteen, I watched my mother age ten years in a sickly green hospital room. It was cancer, and I knew it was bad because although I had seen my mother bear many crosses in her life, I had never seen her face look so drawn, tired and hopeless.

For my mother, though, this cancer was more than another cross to bear. She believed she was watching me, her youngest daughter, die.

Through the glass walls of my hospital room I could see the doctor and my mother. As the young resident started talking, my mother's head fell back, and tears started streaming down her face. Her arms flailed in despair.

When she walked into my hospital room with the doctor, she looked like she had just been dealt the knockout blow of her life. Her eyes stared pleadingly at the doctor. She wanted me to know—I had that right—but she just couldn't be the one to tell me.

And when the doctor sat on the side of the bed and put his cold, clammy hand on my arm, I knew I was really, really sick. But it was when I looked over at my mother's face—which had gone from a youthful, smiling one with dancing eyes to the haggard, lackluster one before me—that I knew I was dying.

It was Hodgkin's disease. My fourteen-year-old body was riddled with cancerous tumors. The doctor sugar coated nothing. He told me of the incredible pain I would endure. He told me of the weight I would lose and all the hair that would fall out. The doctors would try to shrink the existing tumors with chemotherapy and radiation therapy, but that was no guarantee. There was a very good chance that I would never turn fifteen.

My head fell back on the pillow, and I closed my eyes. I wanted to shut it all out and run away. When the doctor left the room, I wanted to believe that all the ugliness was walking out the door with him. Maybe, I thought, when I opened my eyes, my mother's face would look young again, and we could go home and bake one of my infamous lopsided cakes.

Instead, when I opened my eyes, my mother, sitting beside me, took my hand, pursed her lips and said determinedly, "We'll get through this."

During my stay at the hospital, my mother arrived in my room every morning and stayed there until the last seconds of the last visiting hour at night. For most of the day no words passed between us except for the occasional, "Pat, you should eat something." I spent my days staring out the window while my mother sat and read or watched television. There was absolutely no pressure to talk about the situation. It wasn't profound words of support and love that entwined our souls. It was simply my mother letting me be.

Three weeks later, on the morning I was to be released from the hospital, my mother brought me my favorite bell-bottom jeans, tie-dyed blouse and earth shoes. Seeing them perked me up like no medication in that entire hospital could. I couldn't wait to wear them.

My mother drew the curtains, and I, like any other clothes-crazy teenager, dressed with great glee. When I pulled up the jeans and buttoned them, I could tell right away that they were not mine. They couldn't be, because they fell off the once rounded hips they used to hug so nicely. I was incredulous. In the hospital gown I hadn't noticed the ravages of illness.

I yelled at my mother as though it was her fault. "You brought the wrong jeans! These are too big!" I screamed.

My mother just walked out of the room and went out to the nurse's station, returning immediately with two safety pins. "Look," she said, "it will be all right. All we have to do is pin them up here in the back. Your top will cover them."

"No, I don't want to pin them. I want them to fit right," I sulked, and folding my arms, sat on the bed and cried to the wall.

When I finally looked over at my mother, her eyes boring into mine, I realized that I had to pin my pants. Without saying a word, she was telling me: No matter how much you pout, cry and stomp like a mule, these pants are not going to fit right without these pins. You are sick. Your body is not the same. You have to accept this.

It was then that I learned to compromise with my mother, and with a force larger than myself—a force I could not see, or hear, or touch, but a force that nonetheless had taken control of my life.

Though I left the hospital knowing the doctors believed that I would only return to die, none of it ever felt completely real. My body was disintegrating, I could barely walk and I couldn't keep food down, but death felt as far away from me as grandmotherhood. I don't know why I had this feeling. Maybe it was because my fourteen-year-old mind couldn't grasp the concept of mortality, or perhaps I felt something telling me that this wasn't going to be the end.

I quickly slipped into the normalness of everyday life at home, surrounded by my mother and my sisters. And my mother and I, in the face of my illness, discovered a special way of being together.

We knew what was destroying my body, but we never said the words cancer or death. Still, on a day when I was too weak even to feed myself, I looked up at my mother as she was feeding me some mashed food, and something in me felt that one, if not both, of those words needed to be spoken.

"Mommy," I finally said after about the third swallow, "am I really going to die?"

My mother dropped the bowl of food, spilling it all over me and broke into uncontrollable tears that would not stop, no matter how hard I pleaded with her.

I was frozen with fear. I couldn't take back what I had said. Besides, I really wanted to know. If my mother would just confirm it one way or another, whatever she said would be what was real.

Finally, she looked up at me and said, "My baby is not going to die. Do you hear me? I don't ever want to hear you say that again. Do you hear me?"

I heard her. I never said it again. I simply went about the business of fighting for my life.

Yet as my body withered to eighty-two pounds and my hair fell out, I could see how helpless my mother felt. Her hair grew grayer. She even matched me, pound for pound, with the weight she lost. And yet, it was her strength that jumpstarted my will to make my frail body walk instead of ride in a wheelchair. It was her strength that helped me walk into school wearing a wig amidst stares and whispers from pretty, healthy-bodied girls. And it was her strength that made me see that in the larger picture, those stares and whispers didn't mean a thing.

More than a year went by before I finally went into remission. When the doctor called my mother and me into his office after the last chemotherapy treatment, we didn't know what to expect. Somehow, though, we knew we didn't need to expect the worst. He went through a long-winded dissertation about shrunken tumors and good cell counts before he told us, essentially, that I was in remission.

My mother and I didn't cry tears of joy. We didn't get swept up in a whirl of happiness and giddiness, hugging the stuffing out of each other. We just smiled and squeezed each other's hands. The doctor was really only telling us something that we already knew: that I was not going to die.

~Patricia Jones
Chicken Soup for Every Mom's Soul

Mountain Fever

What is possible? What you will.
~Augustus William Hare and Julius Charles Hare

The coup de grâce of our senior year at Oregon Episcopal School in Portland, Oregon, was an experiential program based in part on the Outward Bound philosophy, a twenty-seven mile hike through the Columbia Gorge, the first event of its kind in the school's history. There was no such thing as a category for disabled teens on this adventure, and I was an amputee with many deformities.

Participation was voluntary, of course, and involved training in both endurance and rappelling. When the idea was presented to our senior class and our principal asked who didn't want to go, only one hand went up in the room, and it wasn't mine. Martha was healthy and capable, but she had no interest: "No way on earth I'm diving off cliffs, hauling a forty-pound backpack through a cold forest in the rain and cleaning bugs out of a sleeping bag in the middle of the night," she wailed. Everyone laughed, but seemed nonplussed and undeterred from what could befall us.

We were given a choice: final exams or the hike. Suddenly the room fell silent and everyone stared straight at me, their laser eyes like pin pricks in a voodoo doll. My classmates were waiting for my hand to go up in the nervous air. They stared so hard I was sure they could see my underwear. I said nothing. I didn't move.

I wanted to go so badly I could almost taste the moisture in the trees, but I feared that I would drain the patience and strength of my friends who had the luxury of taking navigation for granted. I knew it was a crazy idea because it held so much risk of disappointment, but I was determined to go. Later that day, after math class was over, I was walking by the faculty lounge and stopped to pick up a book I dropped. The door was barely cracked and I froze when I heard my name.

"Janet didn't raise her hand," said Sam Dibbins, our tennis coach.

"What the heck are we going to do? There's no way on this green Earth that girl can hike those trails, cross those creeks and carry forty pounds on her back with just one leg," said one of the science teachers. "If she collapses or takes a bad fall, we'll have to carry her out," he said. "It isn't prudent." Suddenly the room grew gravely quiet. "Maybe, if we're lucky, her father won't sign the permission form," he added.

As the conversation continued, they discussed the fact that Outward Bound was all about people pushing the limits, breaking set boundaries and realizing their potential.

"We'll figure it out," said Dibbins. "I say she goes! It may drag down the other kids, but it will also teach them teamwork." I limped off down the hall, hoping they hadn't heard the noisy click of my artificial knee.

One night during spring break, I waited until after dinner and took the permission form into my father's study. "What's this?" he asked.

"Oh, it's for an off-campus event," I said. "Just scribble your name. It's no big deal," I added, fumbling my words as I uttered this little white lie. He signed the form with the flick of his wrist and went back to sorting through his mail.

Since it was the month of May, we were hoping for nice weather; instead, we were met with relentless rain, so heavy it looked like falling apples against a backdrop of emerald silk. Between showers, we were surrounded by gnat clouds as thick as bedroom drapes. The forest was all-consuming to me, lush green ferns like peacock fans rustling in a light wind. The terrain wasn't terribly steep, but the hiking path was narrow and relatively untraveled. My body had never been free to write its own rules, and the uneven ground only exacerbated the problem. Each step was a problem to be solved. My friends kicked boulders and sticks out of my way as we hiked, in a vain attempt to prevent my falls. I was always on the ground and always wet from the moss, but the majesty of our surroundings and the smiles of my friends kept me afloat. They took turns helping me up. We dried my outer clothes at night by taking turns fanning them over what tiny campfires we could manage to keep ablaze.

At one point the trail narrowed to a foot-wide path of loose dirt, which was the only ledge we had against the wall of a very steep cliff. It was a long way down. The belly of the gorge looked like something in a jungle movie on a wide, wide screen, but this was no movie we could turn off or ignore. Dibbons roped our backpacks together and we crossed it in a slow line, stomachs flat against the wall, one at a time, barely breathing as we moved. I tested each twig in the mountain's side for the surety of its hold. Most came out of the earth at the slightest pull. When I slipped, the others tightened the ropes in one quick, impulsive jerk, bringing me back to standing.

That night, when they thought I was fast asleep in our tent, two of the boys snuck in and took more weight out of my backpack. They sensed the fragility of my pride; they would do nothing to make me feel ashamed or burdensome. The second night of the trip, the temperature dropped and it began to snow—first in tiny white grains, then in doughy flakes larger than our fingertips. I was soaked to the proverbial bone from falling in creeks along the way, and that night they stripped me naked and put me in someone's dry sleeping bag. Two of the others had to double up in one. (You don't take extra bags on a hike like this!) In a pretty short time, laughter was echoing through the frosted trees as the two of them squirmed and jostled for a little precious space inside one bag.

Because of the weather, some of us were in grave danger of frostbite, and so we had to hike out in the middle of the night anyway. Because our trip had been cut short, our teachers promised us another one in the summer—a hike in the Wallowa Mountains, where we would get to rappel.

Graduation night, in front of hundreds of parents and relatives, I received more awards than my hands could carry down the aisle, and my father, sitting in the audience at Trinity Church, listened as the principal told the story of our hike and our choir sang "Amazing Grace."

When it came time for the second hike, Dad signed the forms with a flourish of pride, and I crossed out any "I can't" memories from my childhood.

~Janet Buck
Chicken Soup to Inspire the Body and Soul

53

Getting the
Most Out of Life

Dear Authors of *Chicken Soup for the Teenage Soul*,
I love your books! They are so wonderful!

When I started the first *Teenage Soul*, I was going through a really hard, depressing time, and suicide had popped into my head more than once. I read the stories about teenagers who had committed suicide, or attempted suicide, and they really made me think. I realized how incredibly stupid it would be for me to end my life for my own selfish reasons, just so I didn't have to face my problems and reality. I would have hurt so many people who love me. I thank you from the bottom of my heart for making me wake up and face my reality.

I'm fifteen years old, and I have cystic fibrosis. It's not contagious—I was born with it. This disease affects the lungs, the respiratory system and the digestive tract. I have been in the hospital several times, and it can be a lonely feeling. A part of me has felt alone all my life because of this disease. Sometimes my friends say, "Oh, I understand," but they don't really. No matter how hard they try, or how hard they want to, they can't understand what it's like to live with a life-threatening disease. I'm lucky, though: On the outside you can't tell anything is wrong with me. Some people with this disease aren't as lucky because they can look anorexic. Some die young, in their twenties. I am a very healthy cystic fibrosis kid.

Sometimes I even forget I have it, but other times I can't help but be reminded.

During one of my first stays in the hospital, I made friends with a girl my age who had cancer. I remember her shiny bald white head in contrast to her bright blue hospital gown. We played together all the time, racing down the hospital corridors on our IV poles, kind of like scooters. The nurses would just laugh and let us have fun. I can't remember exactly why, but she went away and we didn't see each other anymore.

Later, I was moved to a different room. I shared it with another CF girl, Kate, who was sicker than I was. Even though I was in the hospital, the time we spent together was one of the best times of my life. It was cool just to have someone like me with the same illness. We would take our medicine together and have therapy together. She taught me how to blow smoke rings out of my nebulizer. We spent an endless amount of hours just talking and hanging out with one another. Our friendship was special. My health eventually improved, and I was able to go home. Kate was not so fortunate. She had to remain in the hospital. I lost contact with her after I left the hospital. The following summer I found out she had died. I was so sad not knowing how she died — or if she died alone. The whole time I was in the hospital I never really saw anyone come visit her, maybe a telephone call once in a while but that was it. She was only fourteen when she died. When I think about it sometimes it scares me to know that she died at fourteen and I am now fifteen. I get this lonely feeling that sometimes smothers me. None of my friends have to think about or wonder if they will live to see their sixteenth birthday. I do, almost every day. I think about Kate and the fact that she will never get to drive or freak out over SATs. She will never marry or have kids. I live in two worlds — one of which is very lonely and scary. But no matter how lonely or scary it may seem, I will survive. I've promised myself many times that I will live to see another day.

Today I enjoy playing soccer for my high school team. I long jump and throw the javelin. I act, sing and dance. I love to read and write, and I live my life to the fullest. From reading your books, I have learned that it's possible to do anything you want to, and that everyone is made of "Tough Stuff."

Sincerely,

~Emily R. Monfort
Chicken Soup for the Teenage Soul Letters

Chapter
7

Teens Talk Tough Times

Lessons Learned

Other people may be there to help us, teach us, guide us along our path.
But the lesson to be learned is always ours.
~Melody Beattie

54

Already Perfect

Use what talents you possess;
the woods would be very silent if no birds sang except those that sang best.
~Henry van Dyke

Everyone can identify with the need to fit in. Each one of us struggles with self-esteem and self-worth to some degree. I spent much of my time striving to achieve perfection in every aspect of my life. What I did not realize was that in my desperate need to be perfect, I sacrificed the very body and mind that allowed me to live.

I was a happy kid with lots of friends and a supportive family. But growing up was really hard and even scary sometimes.

During my childhood, I was constantly involved in something that included an audience viewing my achievements or my failures. I was into acting by age seven, and progressed to training for and competing in gymnastics, horseback riding and dance—all of which required major commitment, discipline and strength. My personality thrived on the high energy required to keep up. I wanted everyone's praise and acceptance, but I was my own toughest critic.

After I graduated from high school and moved out on my own, my struggles with self-esteem and happiness increased. I began to put pressure on myself to succeed in the adult world. Meanwhile, I was feeling very inadequate and unsuccessful. I started to believe that my difficulties and what I perceived to be my "failures" in life were caused by my weight. I had always been a thin-to-average sized person. Suddenly, I was convinced that I was overweight. In my mind, I was FAT!

Slowly, my inability to be "thin" began to torture me. I found myself involved in competition again. But this time, I was competing against myself. I began to control my food by trying to diet, but nothing seemed to work. My mind became obsessed with beating my body at this game. I slowly cut back on what I ate each day. With every portion I didn't finish or meal I skipped, I told myself that I was succeeding, and in turn, I felt good about myself.

Thus began a downward spiral of my becoming what is known as anorexic. The dictionary defines it as "suppressing or causing loss of appetite, resulting in a state of anorexia." When taken to an extreme, anorexia can cause malnutrition and deprive the body of the important vitamins and minerals that it needs to be healthy.

In the beginning, I felt great—attractive, strong, successful, almost superhuman. I could do something others couldn't: I could go without food. It made me feel special, and that I was better than everyone else. What I didn't see was that I was slowly killing myself.

People around me began to notice my weight loss. At first they weren't alarmed; maybe some were even envious. But then the comments held a tone of concern. "You're losing too much weight." "Elisa, you're so thin." "You look sick." "You'll die if you keep this up." All their words only reassured me that I was on the right path, getting closer to "perfection."

Sadly, I made my physical appearance the top priority in my life, believing that it was the way to become successful and accepted. As an actress, I am constantly being judged by my appearance. The camera automatically makes people appear heavier than they are. So I was getting mixed messages like, "Elisa, you are so skinny, but you look great on camera."

I cut back on my food more and more, until a typical day consisted of half a teaspoon of nonfat yogurt and coffee in the morning, and a cup of grapes at night. If I ate even a bite more than my allotted "crumbs" for the day, I hated myself and took laxatives to rid my body of whatever I had eaten.

It got to the point where I no longer went out with my friends. I couldn't—if I went to dinner, what would I eat? I avoided their phone calls. If they wanted to go to the movies or just hang out at home, I couldn't be there—what if food was around? I had to be home alone to eat my little cup of grapes. Otherwise, I thought I was failing. Everything revolved around my strict schedule of eating. I was embarrassed to eat in front of anyone, believing that they would think I was gluttonous and ugly.

My poor nutrition began to cause me to lose sleep. I found it hard to concentrate on my work or to focus on anything for any length of time. I was pushing myself harder and harder at the gym, struggling to burn the calories that I hadn't even eaten. My friends tried to help me but I denied that I had a problem. None of my clothes fit, and it was hard to buy any, since I had shrunk to smaller than a size zero!

Then one night, like so many nights before, I couldn't sleep, and my heart felt as though it might beat its way out of my chest. I tried to relax, but I couldn't.

The beating became so rapid and so strong that I could no longer breathe. The combination of starving myself and taking pills to get rid of anything that I did eat caused me to nearly have a heart attack. I stood up, and immediately fell down. I was really scared, and I knew I needed help. My roommate rushed me to the hospital, beginning the long road to my recovery. It took doctors, nurses, nutritionists, therapists, medications, food supplements... and most important, a new sense of what was really true about myself to get back on track with reality.

Recovering from what I did to my body and reprogramming the way I think about myself has been a very slow and extremely painful process. I still struggle with the effects of anorexia every day. Although it has been a couple of years since that hospital visit, it is by no means over for me. I must be honest with myself and stay committed to being healthy.

I had used my anorexia as a means of expression and control. I used it as my gauge for self-esteem and self-worth. It was my identity.

Now I realize that the way to success lies in my heart, mind and soul, rather than in my physical appearance.

I now use my intelligence, my talents and acts of kindness to express myself. This is true beauty, and it has nothing to do with the size of my body. With my experience of trying to be "perfect" on the outside, I had sacrificed who I was on the inside. What I know now is, we are—each and every one of us—already perfect.

~Elisa Donovan
Chicken Soup for the Teenage Soul II

Life Is a Gift

It is the friends you can call up at 4 A.M. that matter.
~Marlene Dietrich

My hands trembled as I let the phone fall carelessly on my unmade bed; this had to be a mistake. There was no way Gray could be dead!

At that moment, everything in my life seemed insignificant. How could anything else matter when my best friend—someone I had known, trusted and loved since eighth grade—was gone forever? I looked down at the clothes I was folding and saw Gray's national soccer team jersey lying on my bed. My whole body froze. How could this be true? I wanted to cry, but I was in complete shock.

It took a month after Gray's death before I was emotionally ready to visit his grave site. It was a cold Sunday afternoon and the rain bounced off the pavement as I stared at my muddy black boots. The fifty feet from the car to the grave seemed like fifty miles. I looked around at all the different tombstones and flowers, and I thought about just how many people must have done exactly what I was here to do. They had all endured the pain of visiting loved ones who had passed away. Tears streamed down my face as I began to walk toward my best friend's grave. My legs felt like they weighed one hundred pounds each, and my stomach twisted into a knot so tight that I thought I was going to be sick. I did not want to look up and see his name written on the temporary headstone. I wanted to savor my last moments of hope that he would come back.

The rain turned into a downpour, and it was cold enough that I could see my breath. I did not feel a thing; my entire body was numb. I shut my eyes, hoping, praying this was all some horrible dream. When I opened them, I was still in the cemetery, blurred by the shield of tears that covered my eyes. Taking a deep breath, I glanced up to the sky and made one last desperate wish that I would wake up from this nightmare. Then I slowly turned my eyes downward and looked at his name written on the headstone, the fresh hay lying over his body, the wilting flowers with water dripping off their petals and splashing into the soil covering his casket.

The moment I saw his grave, I finally stopped fantasizing that he would come back, and the reality sank in that I would never again see my best friend. I knew this was goodbye, but I could not leave. I did not want to walk away; I yearned to stay by his side forever. I stood there and let my mind drift to all of our experiences together, from the time we fell in love to our first real fight. The memories came in crystal clear torrents.

"Do not tell him that I like him! Pinky swear?" I told my best friend Falon in eighth grade. I was in love. He was taller than all the other boys and had shoulder-length blond hair just like Taylor Hanson, from my all time favorite band, Hanson. Sure enough, by the end of the day Falon had told him how I felt. Word was now out that I had a very serious crush on Gray. Every time we passed in the hallways, my cheeks would turn a soft pink. I had no idea what was happening; this was definitely not like me. I never liked guys; I was always "one of the guys." My friends would try to get me to talk to him, but no words would come out. Then our eighth grade dance made all my dreams about him come true. Gray dedicated "All My Life," by KC and Jo Jo, to me and asked me to dance. I was on cloud nine. We dated for about three weeks and then broke up. (In middle school, a week was considered a long-term relationship.)

After we got through the soap opera breakup, Gray and I were inseparable. Even distance did not hurt our friendship. In the tenth grade, Gray was offered the opportunity of his lifetime; he was asked to be the captain of the United States Junior National Soccer Team.

He had to move to Florida to attend a special training center. He frequently traveled to tournaments in Italy, China, France and other locations throughout the world. Despite his distance and hectic schedule, he was there for me during all of my most difficult hours, and he always took the time to call with encouraging words.

I'll never forget the time I spent the night at Falon's house in tenth grade. We were lying in bed talking about our past relationships, teasing each other about our old boyfriends and laughing for hours. It was around 3:30 A.M., and right as we were about to drift off to sleep, Falon said something that will stay with me forever. "LP, you know that Gray loves you more than anybody ever will. You are lucky to have such a good friend." At the time, I didn't think much of this statement, as I took our friendship for granted. I never recognized just how lucky I was to have a friend that I could call at any time of the night, who would talk with me until I fell back asleep. Only now, in his absence, do I realize what an incredible friend and person Gray truly was.

Just two months ago, I approached Gray for advice, as I had frequently in the past. I was caught in a dilemma, debating whether or not I should transfer to Appalachian State University. Gray's words were simple and wise; he told me to follow my heart and that, no matter what, he would always be there to support and guide me. I then asked if he knew that I loved him, and he told me that he never doubted it. If I only knew that this was the last time I would talk to him, I would have driven to Furman and spent the entire night with him! However, I know I can't live regretting the past or wishing I had done more.

I have learned to cherish every moment I have with the people I love. I take time to fully enjoy life, and I try to appreciate each minute I am given on this planet. I did not "lose" Gray. He is still my best friend, only now he is guiding me from above. I can talk to him every night and know he is listening, and I still see him in my dreams. Gray was my angel on earth, and now he is my angel in heaven.

~Lindsay Ann Parker
Chicken Soup for the Teenage Soul IV

56

Blameless

People are not disturbed by things, but by the view they take of them.
~Epictetus

I was a freshman in college when I met the Whites. They were completely different from my own family, yet I felt at home with them instantly. Jane White and I became friends at school, and her family welcomed me, an outsider, like a long lost cousin.

In my family, when anything bad happened, it was always important to place blame.

"Who did this?" my mother would yell about a mess in the kitchen.

"This is all your fault, Katharine," my father would insist when the cat got out or the dishwasher broke.

From the time we were little, my sister and brothers and I told on each other. We set a place for Blame at the dinner table.

But the Whites didn't worry about who had done what. They picked up the pieces and moved on with their lives. The beauty of this was driven home to me the summer that Jane died.

Mr. and Mrs. White had six children: three sons and three daughters. One son had passed away in childhood, which may be why the surviving five siblings remained so close.

In July, the White sisters and I decided to take a car trip from their home in Florida to New York. The two oldest, Sarah and Jane, were college students, and the youngest, Amy, had recently turned sixteen. The proud possessor of a brand-new driver's license, Amy was excited about practicing her driving on the trip. With her endearing giggle, she showed off her license to everyone she met.

The big sisters shared the driving of Sarah's new car during the first part of the trip, but when they reached less populated areas, they let Amy take over. Somewhere in South Carolina, we pulled off the highway to eat. After lunch, Amy got behind the wheel. She came to an intersection with a stop sign for her direction only. Whether she was flustered or distracted or just didn't see the sign no one will ever know, but Amy continued into the intersection without stopping. The driver of a large semi tractor trailer, unable to brake in time, plowed into our vehicle.

Jane was killed instantly.

I survived the accident with only a few bruises. The most difficult thing that I've ever done was to call the Whites to tell them about the accident and that Jane had died. As painful as it was for me to lose a good friend, I knew that it was far worse for them to lose a child.

When Mr. and Mrs. White arrived at the hospital, they found their two surviving daughters sharing a room. Sarah's head was wrapped in bandages; Amy's leg was in a cast. They hugged us all and cried tears of sadness and of joy at seeing their daughters. They wiped away the girls' tears and teased a few giggles out of Amy as she learned to use her crutches.

To both of their daughters, and especially to Amy, over and over they simply said, "We're so glad that you're alive."

I was astonished. No accusations. No blame.

Later, I asked the Whites why they never talked about the fact that Amy was driving and had run a stop sign.

Mrs. White said, "Jane's gone, and we miss her terribly. Nothing we say or do will bring her back. But Amy has her whole life ahead of her. How can she lead a full and happy life if she feels we blame her for her sister's death?"

They were right. Amy graduated from college and got married several years ago. She works as a teacher of learning-disabled students. She's also a mother of two little girls of her own, the older named Jane.

I learned from the Whites that blame really isn't very important. Sometimes, there's no use for it at all.

~Kathy Johnson Gale
Chicken Soup for the College Soul

57

Forgive

Forgive the sun who didn't shine
The sky had asked her in to dine
Forgive the stars that heard your wish
The moon prepared their favorite dish
Forgive the rain for its attack
The clouds have tears they can't hold back
Don't hate the birds 'cause they are free
Don't envy all the things they see
Don't block the wind, but hear its cry
Or else that wind may pass you by
Forgive the storm it means no harm
Could not resist to show its charm
Forgive the earth that never turns
Don't hate the sun, because too much burns
Life intends to not cause pain
The flowers bloom from all the rain
The storm will come and it will pass
The sun that shines, it grows the grass
The wind it cannot help but cry
The stars at night light up the sky
Forgive the world in which we live
We'll all find peace if we forgive

~Danielle Rosenblatt
Chicken Soup for the Teenage Soul III

Hot Potato/Cold Potato

A happy person is not a person in a certain set of circumstances,
but rather a person with a certain set of attitudes.
~Hugh Downs

"I hate you!" I yelled, as I ran up the stairs to my room. Throwing open my dresser drawers, I pulled out a clean t-shirt and jeans, threw them in my backpack and ran back down the steps. Mom and Dad stood there, looking like they were in shock.

"Where are you going?" Mom asked.

"Anywhere but here," I shouted as I ran out the door. They weren't fast enough to grab me, and I slipped away into the night. It was cold, but my hot temper warmed me, and I didn't feel it. Not at first, anyway.

I hit the streets with my thumb out. Hitchhiking wasn't safe, but I didn't care. It was the only way I knew, at fourteen years old, to get away from them. We'd moved three times in the last four years, so I was always the new kid in class, the one who didn't know what chapter we were working on or what project was due next week. I was always playing catch-up and trying to fit in.

Worse than trying to fit in at school was trying to make new friends wherever we moved. There were cliques of popular students who had known each other since grade school. Then there were the geeks and jocks who just didn't seem to interest me. I wasn't athletic and didn't excel at anything, really. Just an average high school kid looking for friends. Deep down inside, I knew my parents loved me, just like God loved me, but it wasn't enough.

I slept curled up on a park bench the first night I took off. It was hard as a rock, and I was surprised to find that I wasn't alone. With my arms wrapped tightly around me for warmth, I huddled on the bench closest to the streetlight. Peeking through half-closed eyes, I could see other homeless people just like me, only they looked like they'd been there a long, long time. Some of them looked kind of scary, with dirty beards and baggy clothes. Some pushed grocery carts filled with their entire life's treasure. I didn't sleep much that night, and when the sun rose, I washed up in the park's restroom and hit the road.

By the end of the second day, I'd made my way to another city sixty-five miles away where I found a halfway house for runaways. I was tired, cold and hungry. By the time I got there, the kitchen was closed. All that was left on the table was a cold potato. I lifted it to my lips and bit into the wrinkled skin. It was crumbly and dry and stuck in my throat when I tried to swallow. That night I slept on a cot in a room with four other runaways. It wasn't a whole lot better than the park. The cot was hard and the blanket was scratchy, and those other kids looked like they'd been there a long, long time. I tossed and turned all night.

The next day, I changed into the only clean clothes I had and was shown how to use the washer and dryer to do my own laundry.

"The soap is over there," Carly told me. She was one of the other four runaways in my room. "Don't use too much, just half a scoop is all you need."

I wanted to ask her how long she'd been there, but she interrupted my thoughts.

"I've been here almost four months now," Carly said. "We have rules for what you can and can't do, so you better get used to it. You can't use the laundry before 8:00 in the morning and you can't watch TV after 10:00 at night. You have to be down at the kitchen table right at 12:00 and 5:00, or you don't eat, and you have to rotate chores every week. This is my week on kitchen duty. I help make lunches and dinners, and I clean up afterward. So, don't go makin' a big mess in there."

"When are you going home?" I asked her.

"I don't know and I don't care. My parents know I'm here but won't come by to even talk to me, and so what! You got something to say about that?"

Carly glared at me as she talked.

"No," I responded, but I felt sad for Carly. Her parents didn't even care! I was scared. Maybe my parents didn't care, either.

Three days later, my dad showed up at the front door of the halfway house. I don't know how he found out I was there, but part of me was glad he did, though I wouldn't admit it out loud. After gathering my few things, we drove home in silence. I could almost see the questions running through his head. Why did she run away from home? What was so awful there that we couldn't talk about it? I could see by the look on his face that he felt responsible for all my anger and sadness. I regretted shouting at my parents the night I ran away. It wasn't their fault that I felt this way.

I had a long time to think as we drove those many miles home, and I wondered why I hadn't seen all the things Dad had done for the family. He was trying to make a better life for us, moving us from one city to the next so he could get a better job. He was doing his best to put clothes on my back and shoes on my feet. It was up to me to make the best of a new school and to open up to new classmates. Hanging my head in the halls and not talking to anyone who even said "hi" wouldn't help me make friends. Maybe I could make more of an effort to reach out to others.

When we finally reached our house, Mom opened the front door as we walked up the stairs. I smelled a roast cooking and knew there'd be hot baked potatoes to go with it. As I stepped inside, she opened her arms wide and I fell into them. Dad was right behind me and put his arms around both of us. Ordinarily, I'd pull away, but this time I didn't.

They both released me a few moments later, and that's when I saw the tears in Mom's eyes. I lowered my head and blinked twice really fast, trying to hide my own tears. I made a promise to myself not to hurt them like that again. They were doing the best they could. It was up to me to meet them halfway.

I knew the changes I had to make wouldn't take place overnight, but as I looked at my parents and felt the warmth in my house, I realized there's no place like home.

~B. J. Taylor
Chicken Soup for the Preteen Soul 2

Crying's Okay

It is such a secret place, the land of tears.
~Antoine de Saint-Exupéry

My parents made me go to school that day even though I felt as if I couldn't stand to be around anyone. Where can you get away from people in a schoolhouse?

Finally, I wandered into the room where I have English because no one was there except Mrs. Markle, and she was busy grading papers. I sat down across the desk from her. She just looked up at me and smiled as if there was nothing strange about a kid coming to the English room when he didn't have to.

"He's dead," I said in a strangled voice.

"John?"

I nodded. "He was my best friend."

"Yes, I know, Kirk." She walked over and closed the door, then came back to her desk.

"I miss him," I said.

"I know," she said again, "and that hurts. When something really hurts, it's all right to cry." She put a box of tissue in front of me and went on grading papers while I broke down and bawled. I was relieved that she didn't look at me.

"Nothing like this ever happened to me before," I said. "I don't know how to handle it."

"You don't have much choice," she told me. "John is gone and he won't be back."

"But what do I do?"

"Just keep on hurting until you begin to heal a little."

"I don't think I'll ever get over his death."

"You will someday, even though right now you can't believe you ever will."

"I guess."

"That's because we know with our minds," Mrs. Markle said, "but we believe with our feelings."

I sat and thought about that for a while.

"You might make things easier for John's family by visiting them," Mrs. Markle gently suggested.

I hadn't thought about John's family until now. If this was rough on me, what must it be for them?

"John's parents don't like me," I explained. "They think I was bad news for John."

"And probably your folks weren't wild about your running around with John."

"That's right." I was surprised at how much Mrs. Markle seemed to know. Just a plain old English teacher.

"That's how it is with parents," she said. "Young people together do things they wouldn't have the nerve to do by themselves. So parents get the idea that their sons and daughters are being led astray by their friends."

"Hey, that's about it."

"Go see John's family, Kirk. They'll change their minds about you now. You'll see. And if they don't, you will have at least given it a try."

"I feel guilty about some of the things John and I did," I said. "Maybe God makes us feel guilty to punish us."

Mrs. Markle shook her head. "I don't think God plans for us to carry big loads of guilt along through life. He does give us a conscience, though, so we can ask forgiveness, and so we can profit from our mistakes. That's how we grow into better human beings."

That seemed to make good sense, but I didn't know how to quit feeling guilty. Mrs. Markle seemed to know what I was thinking. She said, "Guilt can be a crutch, you know."

"A crutch?"

"Yes, indeed. Guilt is a sort of self-punishment. If you feel guilty enough, you don't have to do something about yourself."

"'Something about yourself'?"

"Like improving your behavior, for instance."

The first bell rang. I stood up to go.

"By the way," Mrs. Markle said, "I'm glad you weren't with John in that car when it crashed."

"That's something else I feel guilty about," I admitted. "About John getting killed and not me."

Mrs. Markle said, "That's one thing you should not feel guilty about—being alive when someone else dies."

"Oh," I said. "Well, thanks for helping me. My folks didn't understand how I felt."

"How do you know?"

"They made me come to school."

"Perhaps that's because they did understand. They probably figured you'd be better off at school with classmates to share your grief."

"Oh. I didn't think about that. I wonder..."

The thought of going to see John's family was the hardest thing I can remember having to do. I wanted to talk to my parents about it, but I was afraid they wouldn't understand. Still, Mrs. Markle had said they might be more understanding than I realized.

At dinnertime Mom said, "We know you feel bad about John. Is there anything you'd like to talk about?"

That gave me the opening I needed. "I ought to go see John's family, but they probably don't want to see me."

"Why not?" Dad asked.

"On account of how John and I got into trouble sometimes."

"Sorrow sometimes brings people closer together," my mother said. "If I were John's parent, I'm sure I'd appreciate your coming."

So I forced my legs to take me to John's house. A lady I didn't know opened the door and took me to the living room. John's mother, father and sister sat there like broken dolls, staring into space. I didn't know what to do, but I tried to imagine they were my parents instead of John's. Then it seemed natural to go over and put my arm across Mrs. Roper's shoulder. When I did that, she began to cry. She put her arm around my waist and her head against my shoulder. "Forgive me for breaking down," she said. "I thought I was all cried out."

"It's all right to cry," I told her. And all of a sudden I was crying, too. John's sister, Adele, was only eleven, but she came over then and put her arms around her mother and me. I began to feel sorry for John's dad, sitting there all by himself. After a little while I went over to him and put my hand on his arm.

"I'm glad to hear you say it's all right to cry," he told me. "I keep wanting to do that."

Some other people came into the room about that time, so I said I guessed I'd better go.

Mrs. Roper walked to the door with me. "Kirk, it was so comforting to see you."

"I was afraid you didn't like me too much," I said.

"We love you because John loved you. And Kirk, don't fret about the past. You and John weren't perfect; you were just acting like teenage boys, that's all. It's no one's fault John is dead."

"I'll come again," I promised.

"Oh, Kirk, will you? It would mean so much to us."

I walked home feeling better than I had since that end-of-the-world minute when I heard that my best friend was dead. Tomorrow I would tell Mrs. Markle about the visit to John's family.

~Kirk Hill
A 5th Portion of Chicken Soup for the Soul

Learning from a Teenager

You give but little when you give of your possessions.
It is when you give of yourself that you truly give.
~Kahlil Gibran, The Prophet

Instead of hanging out at the mall with her friends, fifteen-year-old Carly spent most of her spare time taking care of her dad.

Andy had been a strong, healthy, physically fit man who excelled at sports and loved outdoor activities. But one day he noticed his right hand was numb, and he dropped his cup of coffee. Over the next few months, several similar incidents happened to the point he could no longer ignore the strange and alarming symptoms. After months of exhaustive tests, a neurologist confirmed the terrible news that thirty-eight-year-old Andy had ALS, or Lou Gehrig's disease. When he learned this incurable illness would result in progressive neurological deterioration of his body, Andy tried to conceal it from his family as long as possible. He was separated from his wife, and his three teenage children lived with him. Despite his efforts, it soon became impossible to hide his illness, and the effect on his youngest child, Carly, was the most profound.

He soon lost the ability to use a knife and fork. Carly would quietly lean over to cut his meat. She couldn't wait to come home from school to see him. At first, her friends were intrigued by the close relationship she enjoyed with her father. They patiently waited while she attended to him before she went with them to the mall or the movies. Little by little, though, Carly started declining invitations from friends. Doing homework, helping out with the household chores, and helping her dad button his shirts and tie his shoes took most of her spare time.

Andy was acutely aware that Carly needed to live a normal teenager's life and not be his private duty nurse. Her older brother and sister were more typical teenagers, and although they loved their father, they were less involved in his care. An old childhood friend of Andy's worked for the local Visiting Nurses Association as a home health aide. She made the referral to initiate home-care services. I became Andy's visiting nurse. Over the next several months, I arranged for a physical therapist, an occupational therapist, a speech therapist and daily home health-aide services. In spite of our best efforts, including a course of experimental drug therapy, Andy's disease progressed. He became weaker and weaker each passing month.

Home-care services only provided help six to eight hours per day and none at night, so Carly continued to devote all of her spare time to her father's care. As professional caregivers, we were expected to teach the family members all aspects of care, but Carly had already learned how to dress her father, assist him in the bathroom, prepare his easy-to-chew foods and feed him. We frequently deferred to her to show us an easier method of dressing him.

When I advised that it was time to get a hospital bed for ease of transfers in and out, Andy insisted on having a double bed so that his children could sleep next to him after they had helped turn and reposition him every two hours at night. The professional caregivers conferenced and decided it was inappropriate to have his teenage children sleeping in his bed with him. Carly taught us by her admirable behavior that closeness and warmth with her dad were more important than our stuffy rules. My persistent recommendations to hire private caregivers for nighttime duty also fell on Carly's deaf ears. She was only a freshman in high school. Lack of sleep and leisure time was taking its toll on her physically and academically, but her perceptive guidance counselor informed all of her teachers of the extraordinary conditions Carly faced at home.

All of us professionals worked diligently to keep Andy at

maximum safety and function. However, nobody was as percep-tive to Andy's subtle changes and deteriorations as Carly. When his speech became slurred, Carly understood him best. When he started to choke and have difficulty swallowing, a feeding tube was surgically implanted in his stomach. We taught Carly to prepare and instill the feedings into the tube. She taught us how to do it in the way he toler-ated it best. When his lungs became weak and congested, we taught her to use the complicated portable suction machine. She taught us that she could learn anything needed to care for her father.

I had a lump in my throat watching this fragile, 98-pound girl hoist her 155-pound father out of his wheelchair and into bed day after day after day. I wondered where she got her strength. "From my dad," she answered.

Finally, the day came when it was impossible for Andy to remain at home. Carly had spent most of the night suctioning the mucus and giving him his oxygen treatments. He could no longer breathe unassisted, so he was hospitalized and agreed to go on a ventilator for a short time, just until his family could accept the fact that he was dying. Carly had to be forced to go to school, but as soon as her last class ended, she hustled to her father's hospital bedside to sit with him, along with her brother and sister.

Andy went into a coma on the last day of his life, and his devoted daughter told him one last time how much she loved him. But she did not need to say the words; her love and dedication had been proven countless times. As experienced professionals, we had taught her the techniques needed to care for her dad, yet a fifteen-year-old taught all of us a poignant lesson in love, caregiving and devotion.

~Alice Facente
Chicken Soup for the Caregiver's Soul

Behind the
Bathroom Door

stepped onto the cold tile and silently closed the bathroom door. There I was again, staring into that deep hole. I jolted forward, releasing all my sadness and anger that had somehow turned into food. I flushed the toilet, washed my mouth, wiped my eyes and walked back into reality. I forced a smile on my face and sat down with my family. They didn't know what really happened when their perfect daughter closed the bathroom door.

Dreams of being perfect had filled my head since elementary school. By the seventh grade, my dreams of being beautiful had taken me to unhealthy extremes.

It began like any other diet. I felt the need to be skinny because I was a gymnast and cheerleader and all of my best friends were always skinnier than me. I weighed eighty-eight pounds in seventh grade, when counting calories and reducing food intake became the main priority in my life. I stopped eating. Once the first pound was lost, there was no turning back. Every tip of the scale managed to put a smile on my face.

The thought of being "fat" soon became my biggest fear. I grew afraid of eating in public. I always thought the person next to me was thinking, "Gosh what a pig! No wonder she's fat!" I wouldn't eat anything at all for days, craving food the whole time. I would finally give in to my cravings and find myself with a half-eaten bag of chips and an empty tub of ice cream in my hands. Then I would stop eating again. This went on for about five months until I decided that there was only one thing left to do. I taught myself to throw up. I would starve myself until I couldn't stand it anymore and then eat everything I could get my hands on. After every food binge, I would walk up the stairs, step onto the cold tile and close the bathroom door.

Ironically, my eating disorder pulled me further and further away from the perfection and acceptance that I worked so hard toward. Convinced that I was incapable of being loved, I isolated myself from the world. Everyday, I walked through the hallway at school with my head down. I didn't enjoy talking to anyone. Not even my family. When the day would end, I would lock myself in my room and cry. I sometimes even pressed a sharp blade upon my skin in a strange attempt to feel something besides hunger and unhappiness. I never slept. I stayed awake every night praying for a change in my life.

I continued to hold this dreadful secret through my freshman year. I would stop eating for days, then binge and purge. This lasted my entire ninth grade year. Then, in my sophomore year, I quit starving myself and just binged and purged.

Fortunately, after years of starving, throwing up and crying endless tears, I realized that I needed to rid myself of this demon that ate away all my happiness. I had always thought that I was alone and nobody loved me enough to care. Strangely enough, through the years, I managed to overlook my family and friends reaching out to help me for so long.

December 9th of my sophomore year began just like any other day. However, it was the day my life would change. As I sat in the hall during activity period, someone brought me a message from the guidance counselor. I made my way to her office, and as I opened the door, I found my best friend sitting in the middle of two chairs. The counselor sat to the left of her. The chair on the right was for me. As they looked at me, they didn't need to say a thing—I knew what was going to happen. There was no more running away. I sat down, stared at the floor and began to cry. For the first time in four years, I revealed my secret. I finally began the long journey I would have to take to get well.

Recovery drove me down a dark difficult road. It was a journey consisting of lessons and life-altering decisions. At first, I continued to lie to myself, as well as to my family, and denied every medication and doctor I came close to. My family never gave up on me. They continued to give their support and love to make me better. Luckily, I began to see the truth behind this deadly illness that I had. My family's support gave me the courage that I needed to open my eyes to a life without anorexia or bulimia.

Through the tough times, I learned a lot about myself, self-control and self-acceptance. I finally understood that for other people to accept me into their lives, I had to accept myself. I came to know that my striving for perfection would never end. However, taking it out on myself would never offer me comfort. I began accepting compliments, refrained from comparing myself to others and eventually began to smile again. Rather than letting my eating disorder control me, I finally learned to control myself and the terrible thoughts that previously had owned my mind.

As I walked onto my high school's football field at the beginning of my senior year, cheers erupted from the crowd as the former Homecoming Queen carried a brand new tiara in her hands. As I waited in anticipation, I closed my eyes as memories of my five year battle with the horrible demon ran through my mind. I remembered all the self-hatred, lack of control, and then all the lessons that I learned about myself and my disorder on my road to recovery.

When I opened my eyes, I found the beautiful tiara being placed upon my head. My heart began to race as the announcer shouted my name as the Homecoming Queen. Cheers erupted from the crowd as all my friends ran toward me. Tears ran down my cheeks as I realized that I had finally won my battle with the demon because I had found the strength inside of me to overcome it.

~Katy Van Hoy
Chicken Soup for the Girl's Soul

Pulse

Think big thoughts but relish small pleasures.
~H. Jackson Brown, Jr., Life's Little Instruction Book

I am not an unusual teenager. I've never been given an award for anything special or nominated for an important position. I've had my share of problems and, like most teenage girls, spent countless nights crying over lost friendships, unrequited love and just everyday teenage stress.

One night I was watching a show on TV about an angel. The angel was trying to convince one of the characters not to kill himself. The man thought that dying was the easiest way out. I thought about how many times I have considered the same thing. I put my finger up to my pulse. A thought struck me: This is what will keep me alive. No matter how many breakups I go through, no matter how many times my "dream" soccer team rejects me and no matter how many times I can't pull off my I'm-tough-and-I-don't-cry attitude, that pulse will still be there. Blood will still be pumped through my body. I can survive.

This isn't to say that I will never think about quitting or never go through a day where all hope seems to be lost. But there is one thing I know for sure: In the times of greatest sorrow, or melancholy, or hopelessness, or lifelessness, I only need to use one finger to know that I can survive it all. The steady flow of my healthy, thirteen-year-old heart is the most comforting feeling in the world.

~Adrianna Hutchinson
Chicken Soup for the Christian Teenage Soul

Lucky After All

Dear *Chicken Soup for the Teenage Soul,*

I have been reading your books for a couple of years and have found great comfort in the stories of people overcoming adversity. Your books always put me in a good mood. They give me a bit of perspective on my own problems and the energy to live a "normal" teenage life. Over the last thirteen years, I have grown to accept myself for who I am. I am at the stage where I am comfortable with myself, but it was only two years ago when I was extremely concerned about my appearance.

At the young age of four, I was introduced to hearing aids. With nerve damage to my eardrums, my hearing was cut by 30 percent. During my early childhood, my parents noticed that I never played with my sister or brother and I never watched TV with them. They never really thought about it until one particular afternoon. I was about two years old, and our whole family was outside. I ran out onto the street and into oncoming traffic. My grandpa was calling to me, but I wasn't listening to him and I almost got hit by a car. That made my parents think. They insisted our doctor perform test after test until they determined that I was deaf.

The damage is the same in both ears, so my mom believes I was born with it. My dad, however, chooses to voice a different opinion. He thinks my nerves were damaged during my delivery, with the doctor's forceps. Either way, the damage is called sensorineural hearing loss, in which a deterioration of the inner ear is present. It will never get better, but it will never get worse either. I was searching on the Internet a year ago when I found out that this type of misfortune is irreversible. I cried quite a bit at first because a part of me always dreamed about the day when I could have an operation that would make me "normal." But in a way I expected it. I was sure that my audiologist would have mentioned the option had there been one.

Finding out my condition has no cure isn't the worst thing I have been through, however. Throughout my childhood, many kids have teased me. The worst memory I have is when I was in seventh grade, and a few boys were very loudly imitating the quiet "beep, beep" noise that my hearing aids make. I still remember calling my mom crying and begging her to come take me home.

That may have been a few years ago, but even today many people are still openly curious about "those strange things in your ears." A lot of people don't seem to understand that hearing loss is a physical health problem, not a mental health problem. I try very hard to make eye contact with anyone I am talking to, but their eyes always seem to wander off to one of my ears. This makes me feel very self-conscious so I will try to distract the person by turning my head, scratching my ear or shaking my hair over my ears so they have to look at me. Now I have started being more comfortable with exposing my ears out in the open. Last year I hardly ever wore my hair back in a ponytail because I thought people were looking. These days I'll still do the odd ear-scratch or head-turn to get people out of their daze, but not nearly as often.

Obviously there are many disadvantages to hearing aids. I can't swim or sleep with them. It is also extremely hard to hear in public gatherings and the classroom with all the background voices. Even with a group of friends, I find it difficult to follow the conversation at times. I often have to ask people to repeat what they say. But there is one huge advantage that I think I take for granted sometimes: being lucky enough to wear my hearing aids so that I can hear. I hate wearing the aids, but knowing that I am able to, and that my hearing is not going to get any worse makes me so happy. Another advantage that not too many people know about is being able to shut my aids off whenever I want. If I'm trying to concentrate on counting or reading, one quick, swift move and no one knows. My own personal silence. That's always fun.

Sure, I would like to be able to wear a hearing aid that is a little less noticeable than the one I wear today, but the most important thing is being able to hear as well as I can.

All my life my one wish was to just be a "normal" teenage girl. But since I have entered high school, that wish has changed. I have been getting good grades since I was in preschool. I have a great family, great friends and a boyfriend who is more than comfortable with my hearing aids. I play hockey and rugby, and I am able to work at my family's business. When you put it all together, I would have to say that I am pretty normal, after all.

Sincerely,

~Tara Sangster
Chicken Soup for the Teenage Soul Letters

Teens Talk Tough Times

Loss and Grieving

Silence is no certain token that no secret grief is there;
Sorrow which is never spoken is the heaviest load to bear.
~Frances Ridley Havergal

64

Why Didn't You Try?

We all need each other.
~Author Unknown

They say that you were depressed
And that you had been for a while
They say that you weren't happy
That you couldn't take it anymore

But you were only sixteen
And way too young to die
You had your whole life ahead of you
So, why didn't you try?

They say that you felt all alone
And as if no one cared
But don't you know you weren't alone
For I was always there

They say that you put on a smile
To put everyone at ease
But at night when you were all alone
You'd cry yourself to sleep

But you were only sixteen

And way too young to die
You had your whole life ahead of you
So, why didn't you try?

After a while you decided to give up
You didn't think life was worth the pain
So you climbed the stairs two at a time
Went to your room and ended it all

I was at camp enjoying myself
When I got the call from Mom
I completely lost it and fell apart
I hadn't even known something was wrong

So now I sit here all alone
And think of all I've lost
You took your life and left me here alone
Now all I can do is cry

But you were only sixteen
And way too young to die
You could have had an amazing life
If you had only tried.

~Mandy Pike
Chicken Soup for the Teenage Soul: The Real Deal Friends

65

Cancer, the Only Word I Can't Say

When you are sorrowful look again in your heart, and you shall see that in truth you are weeping for that which has been your delight.
~Kahlil Gibran

I remember the day so vividly. It was early fall, and it wasn't too cold yet—the kind of weather when all you need is a spring jacket and you'll be fine. I was in the third grade. When I walked into the kitchen to look for my mom after school, I heard her talking on the phone.

"She's home, I have to go," she said.

She hung up the phone and gave me a tiny smile. "Do you want to go for a drive?" she asked me. "I need to tell you something."

I nodded my head, feeling that whatever she was going to share with me wouldn't be good, but I knew I had to hear it.

We drove around listening to music. When we reached my school, she drove into the parking lot, stopped the car and looked at me.

"Remember what Grandma had?" she asked.

"Cancer, right?" I replied.

"Yes. Well, when I was in the shower the other day, I noticed an unusual bump on my breast. I went to the doctor's, and he has diagnosed me with cancer," she said. Then she started to cry.

I wanted to cry too, but I didn't. I felt like I had to comfort her and reassure her that she'd be okay, so I needed to stay strong. As long as I kept telling her it would be all right, I felt like it was.

And she was okay—for a while. She had radiation and chemotherapy. It made her throw up everyday and she lost her hair. But the cancer disappeared. The whole time I was in the fourth grade she was completely fine.

Then I went into fifth grade. One day when I got home from school, my mom was sitting on her recliner, crying.

I knew it was back. "It's back... the cancer, isn't it?" I asked.

She nodded her head, and I began to cry. I ran over to her and gave her the biggest hug I have ever given anyone. She told me that it was still breast cancer, but the cells had moved to her liver.

Again, she lost her hair because of the chemotherapy and radiation. We also sent her to Chicago once a month to get a special treatment.

Then in March, my mom went into the hospital. She was only there for one and a half weeks, but during her stay she got a lot better. The doctors sent her home. She was doing great... until one day she couldn't move without hurting.

She was at the point where she had to be in bed all the time, and she couldn't even talk without it hurting like 100 stabbing knives. My family got ready to say goodbye because we all knew she wouldn't be around much longer.

One morning, my mom seemed to be in more pain than usual. My brother Josh and I sat by her bed for over three hours, while I held her hand. Then she became quiet. Josh called the hospital and asked if someone could come over to check on her.

A short while later, a nurse arrived and checked her heartbeat. "She's gone. I'm sorry," he said quietly.

I actually started to laugh because I couldn't believe it. I was eleven! Eleven-year-olds only lose their moms in movies—not in real life. Even though I knew that it was going to happen, it still didn't seem true.

Some days, I am great. Other days, I just can't believe she's gone. On those days, I want her back so badly that no words can do it justice. I'm sure that sometimes you probably think your parents are just out to ruin your life. Believe me; it's really hard to go on without them.

Cancer, the only word I can't say without crying or wanting to cry. I just hope my children, or other people I may love in the future, will never have to go through the same pain that I have had to. Many people survive cancer. I guess my mom just wasn't lucky enough.

~Sammi Lupher
Chicken Soup for the Girl's Soul

Emergency 911

Remember that the road to healing winds through pain, anguish,
sickness and many tears.
~Amanda Ford

I never thought the day would come. You stop by me as I get on the tennis bus. "Would you like a ride to practice?" you ask.

"No, Stephanie—but thanks, anyway." My parents would freak if they found out I got into a car with a sixteen-year-old driver.

You drive away after promising to come to our tennis match tomorrow. I wave out the bus window as you head down the hill.

Five minutes later, our bus is slowing down as we pass a crash on our left side. Crashes are really cool, especially if they are really bloody and gory. The car, a red Honda Civic, looks like yours, but there are lots here in Valley Center. The side is all bashed in, and everyone's faces are covered in blood. People are walking around with cell phones, calling 911. The bus moves on to tennis practice.

My mom is working at the hospital tonight. She calls home to say that two girls from my school are dead, and one is in critical condition. The other was released earlier. I blow it off. The next morning, my mom comes home. She says that you are dead, Stephie, and so is Jenn. I don't believe her and go to school. When I get to school, I suddenly believe her. I start crying as my friends look at each other in amazement. I never cry, at least I haven't in about three years. But this is real. They have a room open for people who can't handle classes.

But I'm Danni. Of course I can handle them. But I can't. I can't last five minutes through first period before I start bawling.

I spend the day in the memorial room making cards for your families. Reporters come up to me and ask me how I feel. I say words not befitting a girl. Your family comes in, Stephanie. I am surprised by how much your sisters look like you. I almost mistook your older one for you. But you weren't there. I laid roses in the quad for you. I wrote countless poems and cried countless tears. Did you know you had so many friends?

The memorial service was held today. The song they played was "Lately"—a song about death and learning to live again. It was our favorite. As I step off of the bus back at Ramona High School, the last chords of "Lately" can be heard.

I won all of my matches for you today. I met a guy the other day. You sent him from heaven, didn't you? His name is Tyler. He helped me through this. I wanted to be with you, and almost succeeded. But he helped me realize that life is worth living to the fullest. After all, that's what you did.

Each day I forget a little more, but in my heart will always be the memory of your love and kindness. Oh, and Stephanie: I don't think crashes are cool anymore.

~Danni Villemez
Chicken Soup for the Teenage Soul III

67

A Friendship to Remember

Now I am light, now I fly, now I see myself beneath myself, now a god dances through me.
~Friedrich Nietzsche

Her name was Emma. She was the new girl in school. I remember feeling very sorry for her because every student was staring, pointing and whispering about her. She was extremely small, very thin and, worst of all, she was a twelve-year-old girl who had no hair.

Emma ended up in my homeroom. She was introduced to everyone that first day and was then told to find an empty seat. Emma took a seat two rows away from me, one chair up. She lay her head down on her new desk, crossed her legs and put her hands over her face. She tried to conceal her embarrassment but everyone could sense it.

At lunch, Emma sat at a table alone. I think she was too frightened to approach anyone, while at the same time everyone was too frightened to approach her. About ten minutes into lunch, I decided to leave my table and walk over to her. I pulled out a chair and sat down. I said, "Hi, my name is Veneta. Do you mind if I sit with you?" Emma didn't answer, but nodded, never picking her head up or raising her eyes to see me. Trying to make her feel more comfortable, I began talking just like I had known her forever. I told her stories about our teachers, the principal, and some of my friends. By the end of the twenty minutes that we sat together, she was actually looking at me right in the eyes, but there was still no expression on her face. She simply looked at me with a blank stare.

When the bell rang and it was time to go to our next class, I stood up, told her it was nice to get to talk to her and went on my way. I felt terrible walking away, as I had been unable to get her to talk or even smile. My heart was aching for this girl because her pain was so obvious to me.

It wasn't until about three days later, when I was at my locker getting things ready for class that Emma finally said hi to me. "I just wanted to say thank you for talking to me the other day," she said. "I appreciate you trying to be nice to me." When she began to walk away, I gathered my things and chased her. From that day on, we were inseparable.

This girl just captured my heart. She was loving and caring, compassionate and honest, but most of all, she was lonely. We became best friends, and in doing so, I set my twelve-year-old self up for the most devastating thing I would ever experience. I found out that Emma had cancer and was not given a very good chance of beating her disease.

For five months, Emma and I were the best of friends. We were together at school every day and then together almost every night to study or just hang out—and, of course, every weekend. We talked, we laughed, we joked about boys and we fantasized about our futures. I wanted to be her friend forever but I knew that it was not to be the case. After five months of being best friends, Emma became very, very sick.

I spent all my free time with her. I would go to the hospital when she was there and sleep over at her house whenever she was home. I knew in my heart I had to make sure she understood that she had become my best friend in the whole world—the sister I never had.

I was at home one Sunday, sitting with my dad watching football. The phone rang and my mom answered it. I could hear her mumbling and then she hung up. She walked into the room, her eyes red and tears streaming down her face. I knew instantly what had happened.

"Is Emma all right?" I asked. Mom's inability to reply answered it all.

Emma had been rushed to the hospital. She had gotten a very high fever. The news was not good. Her cancer was not responding to any treatments—it was spreading. Emma was losing her battle to stay alive.

Three days later, Emma passed away at home, in bed. She was just twelve years old. I remember feeling numb, knowing that she had passed on, but not quite understanding the finality of it all. Over the next couple of weeks, I quickly learned the hardest lesson I have ever had to learn in life.

Not only did I have to learn to deal with death, mentally and emotionally, I had to learn to grieve. I hadn't yet been able to do that. Then one day, her mom came over and handed me a box. She said she had found it in Emma's things. There was a note on it, saying to give the box to me when she was no longer here. I took it up to my room, stared at it for an hour or more, and then finally got up the courage to open it.

Inside, I once again found my best friend.

Emma had put several pictures of her and me in the box, some of her favorite jewelry and, most important, a note to me. I began to sob but I managed to read it.

I never thought I would ever know true friendship. I was always treated like an outsider, a circus freak. If anyone talked to me, it was usually to ask what was wrong with me or, even worse, to ask me if I was going to die.

You are my very best friend in the whole world and I will never forget you. If you are reading this, I am in heaven. Please don't cry. I'm happy now, and I'm no longer sick or bald. I'm a beautiful, perfect angel.

I'll watch over you every day of your life. I will be there for you during your first heartbreak and I'll watch with joy on your wedding day. You deserve the best, Veneta. Never change and never forget our friendship. I'm so grateful God allowed me to know you. I will be waiting to see you again.

Love,

~Emma

Reading that letter changed my life. Although she was the one who was sick and losing her life, she had taken the time to make sure I would be okay. She wanted to make sure I could cope with losing her.

Her death was the hardest thing I've ever had to experience. But I believe that God put our lives and our hearts together for a reason. We needed each other. Emma needed a friend, and I needed her strength and courage. Even to this day I thank God for Emma. I also still talk to Emma every day. I know she hears me and I know she looks out for me. Our friendship will never fade or die away. People may come and go, lives may change in an instant, but love and friendship will last forever.

~Veneta Leonard
Chicken Soup for the Preteen Soul 2

68

I Never Knew

She was my best friend, and I loved her. She was the coolest girl in junior high and everyone wanted to be like her... and she chose me to be her best friend. Her name was Cindy. She was beautiful with her black hair and tall, thin body. While the rest of us in eighth and ninth grade were still looking amorphous, trying to take shape, Cindy was already beautifully poised in her adult body.

Her mother had died when she was a little girl. She was an only child, and she lived alone with her father. By the time we would get home from school every day, he would already be at work. He wouldn't come home until two or three in the morning, so we had free reign of the house. No parental supervision was the greatest thing we could ask for as teenagers. Her house was a big two story that was concealed by a large grove of orange trees. You couldn't see the house from the street, and we liked it that way. It added to the mystique and allure that we were always trying to create.

At school she was pretty much the center of attention. One whole corner of the quad was dedicated to Cindy and her "followers." If there was new music, clothes, hairstyles or even new ways to take notes or study, you could be fairly sure that it came out of that corner of the quad. Even the school faculty caught on to the power this girl held and convinced her to run for class president. Cindy and I were voted in as class president and vice president by a landslide.

By day, we were the acting liaison between students and faculty; by night, we hosted social activities at Cindy's house. If we weren't having a party, people would come just to hang out. Kids would be there for all kinds of reasons—to talk about relationships, their parents, to do their homework, or just because they knew someone they liked would be showing up.

After everyone left, I would usually spend the night. My mom didn't like it very much if it was a school night. Sometimes Cindy would come back to my house to spend the night, but my mom didn't like that much either because we would stay up all night laughing and talking. Cindy didn't like to be home alone.

That following summer, after I came home from vacation with my family, things were starting to change. Cindy looked thinner than usual with dark circles under her eyes, and she had started to smoke. The strikingly beautiful girl looked pale and gaunt. She said she missed me a lot. While it was a boost to my ego, I couldn't believe it could be entirely true. After all, there were always people trying to be close to her and get into her circle of friends.

My solution: two weeks at the beach. Our parents pitched in to rent a beach house for two weeks. My mom would be the only supervision. In Cindy's inimitable style, we collected a group of beach friends within a couple of days. We'd all hang out at this local café during the day, when we were not in the water or on the sand, and at night we'd hang out around this fire pit on the beach.

Cindy started to look like her old self, but better. She was tan. She looked great in a bikini, and all the guys on the beach wanted to be around her. But she was still smoking. She told me it calmed her nerves.

One night, Cindy came back to the beach house very late. She was all disoriented and noticeably excited. She told me she and this one guy had been drinking and smoking marijuana, and they had gotten together. She said that I had to try marijuana because it made everything better, clearer, in fact. She said she really liked this guy and wanted to run away with him. I knew she was just high, and she'd feel differently in the morning.

When school started that next year, things weren't the same, and I missed the old routine. Cindy wanted to get into different things than I wanted, and she started hanging around guys more and more. We would still hang out from time to time, but it wasn't as fun as it used to be. Cindy would get really serious and tell me that I just didn't understand how things were. I just thought that she was maturing faster emotionally than the rest of us, like she had physically.

One morning when I arrived at school, there were police cars all around and a lot of nervous activity in the halls. When I proceeded toward my locker, my counselor and another woman stopped me. I was asked to follow them to the office. My heart was pounding so fast and hard that I could hardly catch my breath. My head was racing with the different scenarios that might have caused this odd behavior.

When we all sat down in my counselor's office, the principal came in and took a seat. Was I in some kind of trouble? The principal began by talking about life and maturity and circumstances. Now my head was really spinning. What was he trying to say? And then my world froze in time with the words, "...and Cindy took her own life last night using her father's gun." I couldn't talk; I couldn't move. Tears started streaming from my eyes before my heart could even comprehend the pain. She was only fifteen years old.

As the suicide note explained, her father had repeatedly sexually abused her and she knew no other way out. Months after he was arrested, he finally confessed. The note also said something else. It said that the only family she ever knew and cared about was me. She left me a ring that her mother had left to her.

I cried for weeks. How is it that I never knew? We were closer than anyone and talked about everything; how come she never told me that? I was certain that I could have helped her, and I began to blame myself.

After weeks of grief counseling, I came to understand that the burden of Cindy's sexual abuse was too much for her to bear, especially when she started to become intimate with boys. The counselor explained to me that her shame was too great to talk about, even to her best friend. It dawned on me how alone she must have felt, and it suddenly became clear to me why she never wanted to spend the night alone in her own house.

My own suffering—weeks of pain and confusion—was eased greatly with all the help and support I received. Teachers, counselors, friends and family members all nurtured me. It was clear to everyone that this situation was going to change my life forever, but because I let help in, it subsequently added to my life an aspect of wisdom and compassion. I wish that Cindy could have known the relief that comes from letting others help you with your pain.

Cindy's suicide note also requested that she be cremated. The note said that I should spread her ashes wherever I wanted. I chose the ocean off the beach where we had spent two weeks that summer.

On the day of the memorial, we rented a boat to take us out to sea. The boat was packed with friends and teachers, even though it was a rainy, overcast day. We stood on the bow and took turns sharing our experiences and love for our friend. When it came time for me to free her ashes, I hesitated. I didn't want to turn them loose in a sea that looked dark and menacing. I thought she had had enough of that in her own life.

My hesitancy gained attention, and both my mother and my counselor stepped up on the platform and put their arms around me. With their support I opened the lid and set my friend free. As some of the ashes hit the surface of the water, the sun broke through for a moment and sent beautiful rays of light that sparkled on the surface of the water. The clouds parted some more and soon the whole boat was bathed in warm sunlight. At that moment, I felt calmer than I had in weeks. Somehow I knew that the angels had come for my friend and that she would be all right—and so would I.

~Rosanne Martorella
Chicken Soup for the College Soul

69

Don't Stop the Dance

Believe that life is worth living and your belief will help create the fact.
~William James

Christy Gonzales killed herself in the spring of our senior year.

She was beautiful. She played volleyball. She was homecoming queen.

Everyone was more than shocked. She'd always been so happy, so popular and so active in extracurriculars. She had so much love and light. She always signed her name with a heart above the "i" and included her middle name, which was Valentina.

Why she did it is a human mystery, but the obvious reason given was that she was heartbroken because her boyfriend—some sophomore, no less—dumped her.

I remember the silence in our homeroom class—except for the sounds of people crying: boys and girls, jocks and nerds.

As the hour wore on, Nick Denver, the quarterback, quietly spoke to Fred Gregory through his sniffles.

"Remember," Nick said, "when Christy punched me in the face at the seventh grade dance?"

They both started to laugh, softly. Nick had been making fun of her, and she lost her temper and gave him a sock straight to his nose that started him bleeding.

He was shocked, but recognized he deserved it.

I could imagine Christy doing something like that. Although

she was the sweetest person in the world, she had so much fire — she lived so in the moment of her feelings and emotions.

In freshman year English class, we'd read the other's stories aloud to the class because we were too scared to read our own.

She'd let me cheat off her geometry test my sophomore year. We'd both been caught.

I'd once had a secret romantic view of suicide. I thought that it would be nice to have everyone miss me, to have my name forever bound with the tragedy of a depth no one could fathom. I imagined the kind of silence in the classrooms, the people sobbing in the halls. I imagined how people I didn't know or barely knew would try to remember every detail — what I had said to them, what I had worn the last day.

She had worn red the last day. At lunch the last day, she had said she was tired of always getting the tater tots, tomorrow she was getting fries.

I could not have imagined a better funeral for Christy with the heavens outpouring rain like tears. The entire town was there, mourning.

I just kept thinking about how we all kept on going but Christy's life stopped.

When I want it all to stop, I remember that you can't dance without a body, and you can't cry without eyes, and you can't have the luxury of feeling when you aren't here.

I wish she could have loved herself when she didn't feel it from anyone else.

~Simone Would
Chicken Soup for the Teenage Soul IV

Losing the Best

The deep pain that is felt at the death of every friendly soul arises from the feeling that there is in every individual something which is inexpressible, peculiar to him alone, and is, therefore, absolutely and irretrievably lost.
~Arthur Schopenhauer

My childhood was easy. You might even say I was spoiled, mostly by my mother. She was always in the mood to spoil me. If there was something I wanted, I knew to go to my mother. She was an angelically beautiful woman. She had this heavenly smell, kind of like ripe strawberries. And her hands felt like velvet, like a newborn baby's fat and tender cheeks.

On the other hand, for as long as I've known him, my father has been an overweight, balding man with thick bifocals. According to my mom, he used to be "a real catch," whatever that's supposed to mean. All I know is he has worked hard all his life to make sure my life is full of all the opportunity it can be. He has been saving money for my college education since I was five. I don't think I have ever told him I appreciate him.

My best friend Donny was two and I was three the summer his family moved across the street from ours. One of the first conscious memories I have is of the two of us. It was the Fourth of July. The neighborhood families had a small fireworks show in the street in front of my house. The only part of the evening I remember is when I was lying on my mom's shoulder. I remember looking over and seeing Donny lying on his mother's shoulder, looking at me and smiling.

Later, when we were in school, Donny and I would spend the night at each other's houses on the weekend. This is when we would talk. We had anything goes, no-holds-barred conversations. We talked about what we thought about life and what we wanted to be when we grew up. Donny wanted to be a billionaire, and I wanted to be everything from a teacher to an architect. For me, it changed almost as often as my underwear.

For my sixteenth birthday, my mother wanted to get me a new car. My father said, "Joyce, let him get a job and buy his own car. He will appreciate it more." He has always been an advocate of working hard and earning the things you want. During one of our father-son talks, he told me, "Life has this peculiar way of leveling out. What I mean is, if you work hard in life, like I have, you will get a break. In my case, the break has been our financial stability and our wonderful family. If you take it easy, you will get knocked down later."

I was young, dumb and didn't listen. I rarely did my homework, and I scraped by on the tests. I didn't cheat, lie or steal, not too much anyway. I just took it easy and put forth as little effort as possible to get by.

My mother wouldn't give in on the new car, so my father finally did. Mom bought me this cool, black Toyota 4x4, with an earsplitting CD player and blinding KC lights. I felt invincible. The first thing I did that day was buy a radar detector. It became my "lookout man." I never got pulled over for speeding. With my truck, I found a new freedom. With the radar detector, I acquired a new sense of rebellion.

My seventeenth birthday was the year my father's advice caught up to me. All day I had pleaded with my mom to lift my barely existing curfew for one night. Since I knew exactly what levers to pull and buttons to push, I got my way.

That night, Donny and I went camping with a couple of friends of ours. We took my truck and John's truck over Cook Mountain and down into the Lake Abundance campground. John and Rick made a stop in Cook City, while Donny and I drove on to the campsite. We had been to the site at least one hundred times with our Boy Scout troop, and knew the forty-five-minute drive like the back of our hands.

Donny and I started setting up camp. About a half-hour after we arrived, John and Rick pulled up. They unpacked John's truck and helped us finish setting up. Then we all relaxed around the huge fire Rick built. That is when John revealed the surprise he and Rick picked up in Cook City. They had found a bum standing at the edge of town with a sign that read, "Why Lie? Need Beer." They made him an offer and he accepted. They paid him the change from what was spent out of fifteen dollars for a twelve pack of Bud Light. He made somewhere around six bucks. I'm sure the whole thing was John's idea because he was always doing the kind of crazy stuff he could get into a lot of trouble over.

None of us had ever had more than a sip of our fathers' beers before, and I was kind of hesitant. My dad had lectured me on the responsibilities and dangers of drinking alcohol many times.

"Don't worry, it won't hurt ya," Rick said, after he was halfway through his first.

That has got to be the weakest argument that has ever come out of anybody's mouth, but it was enough to convince me. I thought to myself, Three beers, what is that going to do to me? At the worst, I'll get sick and puke.

After we had guzzled, chugged and ripped apart three cans each, Rick spouted out, "I'm not feeling anything. We need some more." It was time for a beer run.

Donny and I were voted to go, so we jumped into my truck and went tearing off towards Cook City. We were both kind of excited by this little campsite rebellion. It was the first time we had ever done anything we knew our parents wouldn't approve of—unless you count the time we snuck out of my house and got caught, but that shouldn't count, because we didn't do anything.

I was probably driving a little too fast, but I am not sure because things were a little blurry—not to the point where I don't remember anything, just to the point where things like speed and seatbelts don't seem to matter. Donny suggested we take the shortcut. It would cut at least ten minutes off the trip, so we cut across Rattlesnake Field.

It was mostly grass, the waist-high kind, perfect for lying on your back and watching the clouds roll by or a good game of hide-and-seek. The field was a whole lot steeper than the access road we had come in on. My truck would have made it on any given day, but it was night and we couldn't see very well.

The truck came to a quick stop with a loud thud. We had hit something and were hung up. I looked out my window. "I don't see anything; you got anything over on your side?" I asked Donny.

"Yeah, you hit a tree," he said. "There is a rather large tree just behind your right front wheel." It wasn't really a tree; I wasn't that drunk. It was a log that had been hidden by the tall grass.

At this point, I wasn't exactly sure what to do so I did what any young driver would have done: I floored the gas. The tires were ripping and spinning, and I was rooting for my truck. The log slipped out of place and threw my truck off balance. The truck started to roll. As I felt the truck start to fall off balance, I remember that feeling of panic you get when you know something bad is inevitable. I was almost immediately thrown from my door. Donny went through his window. I was thrown up the hill and out of the path of the truck; Donny was thrown downhill, under the truck and crushed as the truck rolled over him and on down. I remember hearing Donny yelp as the truck rolled over him.

I started to run for help, but I heard his voice pleading, "Don't leave me! Please, Drew, don't leave me!" I immediately turned back.

I slid down and crawled over to where he was. It was worse than I thought it would be. There was blood, a lot of blood. I think I even saw some bone. I wanted to run and get help, but I stayed there with him. I braced myself against the hill and set his head in my lap. He had a grass stain on his forehead and some blood-soaked dirt in the corners of his mouth. As I listened to him wheeze for air, I caressed his hair, the same haircut he had had since third grade. His broken ribs shifted with pain to the slow and inconsistent rhythm of every breath. I was crying as I held him. I felt like a first grader who had been punched in the stomach by the school bully. An angry, sad, ashamed pit of emotions raged inside me, like a pot of boiling oil. I wanted to scream, but I was crying too hard. I tried to apologize for doing this to him, but I was crying too hard. Then I noticed Donny's breaths were getting fewer and farther between. With one final sigh and quickening tightness of pain, they stopped.

I set his head down and started running. I didn't stop until I had reached the campsite. I am not sure why I went there first. That is just where my legs took me. Rick and John were asleep by the fire. I splashed them with water, explained what happened and started running towards Cook City. John and Rick just laid there stunned into half-soberness and scared into solemn remorse.

I made it to Cook City in about thirty minutes. I went straight to the twenty-four hour convenience store where Rick and John had bought the beer. I asked the clerk to call 911.

I led the police to the accident. Donny's body was still lying there limp and cold, like an old doll nobody wants, tossed into the closet. The police questioned me all night, and then there were more questions the next day. "How did this happen? What did you do then? Why did you do this instead of this?" I was sick of all the questions.

I hate that night. I wish I could forget it ever happened. I don't think I ever talked to Rick or John again. I saw them in the halls at school, but none of us made eye contact.

When Donny died, so did a part of myself. I was a junior in high school, and I nearly didn't finish that year. I could feel the other kids staring. I could hear them in the halls. I cried myself to sleep every night asking Donny to forgive me. The guilt was overwhelming. I dropped out of school my senior year. I just couldn't concentrate, and I couldn't take all the kids asking me if I was all right all the time.

It has taken me a long time, but I have progressed. I don't cry myself to sleep anymore, although sometimes I wake up in the middle of the night in a cold sweat crying out for Donny. My fiancée, Jennifer, has gotten used to it. At first, it scared her even more than it did me, but now she calms my nerves and sings me back to sleep. Tomorrow is our big day. I am going to marry her and begin a new chapter of my life. I only wish Donny was going to be my best man.

~Garrett Drew
Chicken Soup for the Teenage Soul on Tough Stuff

[*Editors' note*: This story is not entirely factual. Some aspects have been fictionalized.]

Stay with Me

Sadness flies away on the wings of time.
~Jean de La Fontaine

]was the new kid in the neighborhood. My family had just moved from the country to a bigger city, so I had to start over making friends. I wasn't sure how I was going to do that, even though I had moved many times before. It was just never easy introducing myself to total strangers with the hopes that they'd like me enough to become my friend.

So I was really lonely until the day that this boy named Brandon came up to me and asked if I wanted to play with him and his friends. After that, we were like best friends. He was a few years older than I was so he always treated me like a little sister. If he wasn't at school, he was playing with me.

A few months passed and then a whole year went by. We were closer than ever, even though Brandon began making more friends at school and they would come over, too. Still, he let me play with him, even when they were around. Brandon never let anyone push me around or pick on me. He was always there for me.

When my mom would call me in for dinner, I would always beg her to let me play for a few more minutes. He would say, "No, go ahead. I'll wait right here for you." I would sometimes think that he would not be there waiting when I was done, but he was always still there.

A lot of times, Brandon would help me with my homework and tell me more about what a certain subject was about. Afterwards, we would ride bikes or skate around our neighborhood together. The most important thing that he ever taught me, though, was to be my own person. He always used to say, "Who cares what others think about you? You should only care about how you feel about yourself." That saying got me through a lot of hard times.

One weekend, I had to go to my grandmother's. A new kid, named Lance, had moved to our neighborhood a few weeks before, and he seemed cool. The day I left, Brandon said he was going over to Lance's house to play video games. I said, "Okay, I'll see ya Sunday afternoon."

Well, things changed forever after that. Brandon spent the night over at Lance's and they played video games and watched movies. That Saturday, they went into Lance's parents' room to play Nintendo 64. Lance noticed that there was a little gun by his dad's bed, so he picked it up to check it out. Just joking around, he pointed the gun at Brandon and pulled the trigger. He thought it wasn't loaded. Well, he thought wrong.

I didn't get back until late Sunday night. I came in to find everyone in my family crying. I was scared because I didn't know what had happened. My mom took me into her room and said there had been an accident. From that moment on, I knew nothing would ever be the same. She finally told me that Lance had accidentally shot Brandon with a gun and that Brandon didn't make it. My mom wouldn't tell me where he had gotten shot but I had a good idea of it.

I started crying, and I ran to my room and hid my face in my pillow. I didn't want to talk to or see anyone.

A few days later, we went to his funeral. I couldn't help but cry. I went up to see him and I realized he was in a better place, because I knew that Brandon knew God, and that was comforting to me. All this happened about six years ago. I am now thirteen. Still, there isn't a day that goes by that I don't think about him. I cry whenever I pass by the cemetery. My best friend is gone, but the friendship that he showed me — the new kid in the neighborhood — will stay with me forever.

~Jaime Fisher
Chicken Soup for the Preteen Soul 2

72

Soul Sisters

Ku'ulei and I were the best of friends. In school, you would never see one of us without the other. It was like we were Siamese twins, going everywhere with each other, stuck together. Even if we ran out of things to talk about, which was hardly ever, it still seemed like we were talking, just not verbally. It was almost like a silent conversation. She always knew what was going on in my head without being told. To me, that's what I call a "true friend." As an example, one time for some reason when I was feeling down Ku'u came over to my house, and I was acting like nothing was wrong. I thought that I didn't show it, but she already knew.

It was like we were meant to be best friends. "Soul sisters" is what I would call us. Since we knew that we were going to be friends forever, we had a saying—Ku'ulei and Kayla, Best Friends Forever! Nothing can tear us apart! Not years, boys, parents, distance or fights! In our world, friendship is #1! In every letter we would write to each other, this was our "P.S." It was true then, and it still is.

I always thought to myself, What would I do without her? Now I know—I am living in pain, grief and sorrow. My life seems like it has ended. But I have to know that this is better than having her live in pain from the accident. God did the right thing and took her back home to heaven so she could live a happier life.

It was July 8th. I was visiting Hilo, a town on the other side of the Big Island of Hawaii, where I live. I was staying at my grandpa's house, and Ku'ulei was at her house, back home where we live in Kona. I woke up that morning and jumped on my golf cart with my cousins to ride around the ranch. As we were coming up the hill, my mom was in the garage talking on her cell phone with a terrible, worried look on her face. My cousins were on the back of the cart screaming, laughing and being silly. I was driving but suddenly felt numb when I saw my mother. I was worried that something bad had happened to my dad back home in Kona. I parked the golf cart and asked my mom what was wrong.

"Kayla, there has been a really bad accident in Kona," she replied.

"Was it Dad?" I asked.

"No."

Since it wasn't him, I wasn't too worried.

"It was at Ku'ulei's," she responded.

I panicked and hoped with all my heart that it was not something that involved her.

"I'm not sure, but either Ku'ulei or Charley (Ku'ulei's older sister) was run over by their truck and killed. One of the twins, Pua or Anela (Ku'ulei's younger twin sisters) was also killed. I think you should call Ku'u's house."

Even as my eyes filled with tears, my heart filled with hope. I was praying as I dialed their number that nothing had happened to my best friend. A girl answered the phone, and I started to breathe a sigh of relief. I thought it was Ku'ulei.

"Hello? Ku'ulei?"

"No, Kayla... this is Charley."

Hearing Charley's voice, I immediately knew. I knew that it was Ku'ulei who had been killed. I started to cry.

"Charley... is Ku'ulei there?" I asked with hope in my voice.

"No... Kayla... didn't you hear?"

"What?" I asked.

"My sisters are dead."

When I heard those words, I choked and fell to the ground. It was as if the world had stopped and my life had crumbled into bits and pieces. For a moment, I thought I was the one who was dead.

"Kayla! Kayla!?! Are you okay? I'm so sorry..." said Charley.

"Yeah, Charley... I'm okay. No, I'm sorry, too...."

"Well, I'll talk to you later," she said in a sad voice.

We hung up, and I walked outside to my mom. As I got closer to her, she asked me who had had the accident. "Was it Ku'u?"

I was speechless. All I could do was nod my head. She grabbed me and hugged me tight. "I'm so sorry."

As I hugged her back, confusion ran through my head. I didn't know how to act. I couldn't handle it anymore. I took a walk down the road. I thought of our memories and wondered, Why did this happen to me?... to her?... to us?

It was like she was perfect. She did rodeo, sports, volunteered at gardens and took great care of her sisters. She was sweet, optimistic, loving and fun to be around. She was EVERYTHING!

I walked back and told my mom that I wanted to go back home so I could go to Ku'ulei's house to see her family. When we got there, everybody was there; they were digging a hole for her ashes and bringing in a special rock to place on top. I went to her parents and gave them my love. I sat next to her dad, looking at everything.

"No more your buddy," he said to me.

I looked up at him and replied, "Yeah."

Tears rolled down my face, but I knew she was up there doing better than she would be down here, where she might have been suffering. I just wished that it could have been different—that it wouldn't have happened to her.

The funeral came, and hundreds of people showed up to honor my friend, who had been such a special girl, and her little sister. Then it was over, and the days went by. It has been very hard for me. At times, I still can't believe it, and I often think that she's just in another state but that I can't call or write. It's as if she will come home any day.

Two years have gone by now, and I still go to her grave and visit her and her sister. When I sit on the bench and stare at the rock on the grave with the beautiful flowers that are always fresh, I feel that Ku'ulei is with me. It's like our "silent conversations" from the past, but without her body there. I now understand that my soul sister had to go back home.

Now I go through school without my pal, my best friend, my soul sister, my buddy, my everything. Her spirit is always by my side, in my heart and in my mind.

So hang on to the friends that you know are good and true and give them what they deserve. You never know when God will decide to take them back home.

My poem to you, Ku'ulei:

It's been two years since you went away
I still remember that very day.
I remember that moment, that time and place
I remember trying to picture your sweet gentle face.
My whole body sank to the ground
And my world was dead, all around.
I couldn't believe how fast this all came
I couldn't deal with all of the pain.
We were so young, childish and carefree.
We lived our lives with joy and glee
This didn't come into our heads
It wasn't what was being talked about or said.
I wish we could go back to how it was
Writing each other letters, "Just Because."
Now I am here, sad and lonely
You were my trusted friend, my one and only.
Whenever I was down and blue
I would always turn to you.
I wished this hadn't happened, from the start.
Now the only way I can keep you is here in my heart.
I can only wait 'til it is my day to see you again
As for now... take care, my friend.

I LOVE YOU! GOD BLESS! R.I.P.
Ku'ulei Kauhaihao
1990–2002

~Kayla K. Kurashige
Chicken Soup for the Girl's Soul

73

The Little Red Bunny

Even though I haven't lived my entire life yet, I know that I will never have a worse day than that January 4th.

It was a frosty Saturday morning, and we woke up to the sweet smell of pancakes and fried bacon. My friend Justine and I jumped out of bed at the sound of plates clattering and skipped down the stairs of her cabin in McGregor, Minnesota. We had just finished our huge breakfast when we decided it was too nice to stay inside. So we got bundled up and went out.

"I wanna go four wheeling so badly!" moaned Justine, knowing her dad would never let her drive. "Let's go ask Krissy and see if Dad will let her drive us!"

"Sweet! Let's go!" I said, not knowing my life was about to horribly change.

Krissy, Justine's cousin, only fourteen at the time, was allowed to drive the four wheeler, so we decided to go for a quick ride on the trails. I was on the back with Justine in the middle. Being on the back was scary. It was almost like I knew something bad was about to happen. I had butterflies dancing in my stomach.

"We should go on the North Road!" Krissy yelled over the roaring engine.

Without reply, Krissy sped out of the forest trails and stopped on the side of the road. I was looking at Justine. She was so happy, so full of life. She was laughing the whole time.

"Yeah, we should!" Justine replied happily.

Krissy looked both ways for cars and then hit the gas. The road was half gravel and half ice, and it scared me because I knew we were going very fast. But when I heard Justine's laughter over the screaming engine, I started to feel better.

If she isn't scared, then why am I? I asked myself.

When we got to the end of the road, we made a loop around and went again. I was just starting to have fun when we hit an icy patch. Krissy lost control near a ditch, and the whole four wheeler fell over with Krissy, Justine and me on it!

When I woke up, I was lying in the middle of the road. My head was throbbing, but I got up fast and tried not to cry at the excruciating pain to show the girls I wasn't a baby. It felt like I had been stabbed in the head a thousand times. I couldn't even see straight. I had to cry. But before I could, I saw Krissy. She was standing there, looking at the ground in horror. So I looked down. The sight of my best friend lying there helplessly sent chills through my body. I just stood there staring at the body of my friend who had once been so full of life. I was in total shock. I couldn't move. I couldn't breathe. All I could do was stare. It felt like I was having a nightmare until I started to cry, but not because of the pain in my head. Krissy was crying, too.

A car drove up, and I saw that it was Justine's dad. Soon her cousin drove up on another four wheeler. An ambulance drove up, then another. Krissy and I just stood there, sobbing and holding each other. Everyone was huddled over my best friend, but Krissy and I started to walk back to the cabin.

"I'm so sorry," Krissy said between sobs.

As she said that, we could feel the cool breeze from the helicopter overhead. I could tell that Krissy knew something I didn't.

Death hadn't even crossed my mind. I pictured Justine in a hospital, never a coffin.

Krissy and I sat on the couch staring blankly at each other, not saying a word. But we both knew what we were thinking. We were waiting to hear the news from Justine's father when her aunt came back crying and made me put ice on my head. That was the last thing I cared about.

The ambulance came and took us away. The medics asked if I was okay, but I was still in complete shock. I couldn't cry. As much as I tried to tell myself what had happened was real, I couldn't be convinced. I never thought this would happen to me. I just wanted to go home and forget about the whole day.

When we arrived at the hospital, they did a bunch of tests on Krissy and me. I was lying in the bed all alone, and a nurse came over with a stuffed, little red bunny. She said that a church had donated it and I could have it. I waited forever for my parents to arrive. When they came, they were both crying. They hugged and kissed me until I felt smothered. We drove home in silence. I couldn't sleep.

I didn't cry until I went to the funeral and then it hit me... hard.

I saw Justine's whole family there and all of my friends from school. Almost our entire grade skipped school to go to her funeral.

After that, school just didn't feel the same for me. My friends acted like the whole thing hadn't happened. But my whole life changed.

I get headaches and heartaches a lot easier.

I will never forget my best friend. And as much as I wish I could, I'll never forget that horrible day. But I will always treasure the little red bunny that comforted me when I needed it most.

~Anne Braton
Chicken Soup for the Teenage Soul: The Real Deal Friends

74

The Gift of Time

His name was Bryce. I inherited him when I was nine years old. Actually, he became part of our family when my mother married his uncle.

It was a second marriage for my mother, and while it might have been less than desirable for my two older brothers, for me it was a slice of heaven. We moved to a beautiful neighborhood, into a house three times the size of the one in which I had been born and raised. Not only did this marriage come with a big house, a pool and huge yard, it also came with Bryce. He lived in Northern California with his brother and parents, but he visited frequently, sometimes spending entire summers with us.

Bryce became my good friend. He was six years older than I, but we had an instant rapport that belied the gap in our ages. He taught me how to dive and do flips off the diving board, he helped my stepfather build a tree house for me, and he helped me learn how to expertly negotiate my new bicycle built for two that I had won in a contest. By the time I was thirteen, we had become best friends.

Bryce and I spent many summers together, and as the years passed we still remained close. The activities changed—tennis, hiking, beach trips and computers—but our bond didn't. He was handsome, smart and funny, and even though I was only fourteen years old, I fantasized about marrying him someday. I couldn't conceive of my life without him.

Bryce was the elder of two boys, and he was his parents' pride and joy. He lived nearly a picture-perfect life. Achieving in school, becoming an award-winning athlete, and having this incredibly huge, compassionate heart, he was a parent's dream. When his mother's brother decided to marry my widowed mother, Bryce helped create a bridge that served to unite the two families. He was charismatic, funny and a great mitigating influence for two teenage boys who didn't want their mother to marry this man. But his family came with Bryce, and at the very least, Bryce was cool.

One summer, Bryce and I went swimming at a friend's house. They had a pool to envy. Complete with diving boards, a slide, water-falls and a small island in the center, it was by far the coolest pool in the San Fernando Valley. I was fifteen, Bryce was twenty-one. It was one of those perfect days, and we were having so much fun. At one point, I decided to slide down the slide on my belly. Apparently, given the location of the slide, this was not a good idea. I smacked down hard on the bottom of the pool and was knocked out. By the time anyone figured out that I wasn't just playing around (the blood that began to tint the water was probably a good clue) I was starting to drown. Bryce saved my life. He jumped into the pool, pulled me to safety and helped to clear the water out of my lungs so that I could breathe. When I finally regained consciousness, Bryce was kneeling beside me, with tears in his eyes.

He was now my friend and my savior. I grew up with him; he became the first boy that I really loved. He treated me like I was the only person in his life who really mattered, even though I'm sure he had girlfriends.

By the time I turned sixteen, I was already fairly proficient behind the wheel of a car, thanks to Bryce. He made it very clear to me that it was my turn to drive the seven hours it required for us to visit each other. I was more than happy to oblige.

I would drive up to Redding, and we would go to the river and live in the water. We would jet ski, swim, snorkel and sun on the dock until those long summer days finally claimed the sun. Then we'd go back to his parents' house and barbecue, laugh and hang out.

By the end of my senior year in high school, there was only one person I wanted to take me to my prom, so I was thrilled when he finally asked me. I accepted without reservation. Even though there were other boys who had asked, it was Bryce I wanted to share the occasion with. Besides, grad night at Disneyland required someone with the guts to ride all the coasters several times, and I knew he was up for the task.

During that next year, our lives became busy, and we didn't see each other that often. I was starting college, and he was working. We wrote and talked to each other on the phone, but it seemed that our lives were taking us in two different directions. I missed him dearly, so I was overjoyed when I found out he would be coming down for his birthday. My stepfather had a special gift that he wanted to give him.

We had a little party for Bryce, and my stepfather gave him his gift. It was a gold Hamilton tank-style watch that was given to my stepfather by his mother, Bryce's grandmother, when he was younger. Engraved on the back were my stepfather's initials and the date, 11/30/48. It was a special memento that my stepfather held very dear, so the gesture of giving it to his nephew meant a great deal to Bryce. He cherished it. He wore it all the time. And when the band broke, he just put it in his pocket and carried it around that way. He was never without it.

One winter night, Bryce and I were on the phone on one of those two-hour-long telephone conversations. It was around eleven o'clock at night, he was at his parents' house having dinner with them and some guests who were visiting from out of town. Bryce said that he had to go. His mother had asked him to take these friends back to the hotel where they were staying. It was at least an hour out of town and he was already tired. We made some vague plans to meet on the dock in the summer. Sometimes it was the only thing that would get me through a tough school year. Then before he hung up he said something that made me smile. He said, "Just remember, no matter what you do in this life, I will always be there for you if you bump your head." I told him that he would always be my hero, and then we hung up.

Bryce's car was found the next day. He had driven off the road when he fell asleep at the wheel. My sweet Bryce was killed instantly. He was twenty-five years old. The pain and upset that spread through our family was profound. I was left with a huge hole in my heart, a hole I was afraid would never mend.

That summer, as agreed, I went to the dock. I sat on the dock, knowing that Bryce would never come. I sat down and started to weep, my tears falling into the river. I found myself getting angry. How could he have done this to me? Why did he have to die? I was questioning God, Bryce and whomever else was listening.

Then, remembering our conversation the night before he died, I started to hit my head.

"I'm hitting my head... I'm bumping it, where are you? You lied to me! Do I really need to hurt myself?"

In a moment of emotional frenzy, I picked up an oar that was lying on the pier. Suddenly, underneath where the oar had just been, something shiny caught my eye. There was something wedged between the boards. I set the oar down and bent down to retrieve the shiny object. When I finally pried it free, I immediately recognized it. It was the watch my stepfather had given Bryce on his birthday. I sat down and cried. With the object still cradled in my hand, I held it up close to my heart. I soon realized that this little 1948 old fashioned watch that needed to be wound every twenty-four hours was still ticking. Goose bumps covered my skin, and the warmest, most loving feeling came over me. I felt as if I were being hugged from the inside out. There he was, still with me.

I'll never know exactly how that little watch happened upon that pier. But I think that Bryce left it behind for me. I bought a new band for the watch, and to this very day I still wear it. It will always be a symbol of unconditional love, something time could never stop.

~Zan Gaudioso
Chicken Soup for the Teenage Soul III

75

Letting Go

No winter lasts forever; no spring skips its turn.
~Hal Borland

It's been nearly six years. Many people would say I should be over it by now, but I don't think I'll ever be over my sister's death.

I was only twelve when my sister committed suicide. Jeri Lynn was sixteen. She had just started her junior year of high school when she decided to take a bottle of sleeping pills.

Six years later, I was still holding on to some of the feelings I'd kept inside since her death. I had a lot to say to Jeri. I never got the chance to tell her things I would have liked her to know. I had a need for closure, if that was at all possible.

People suggested that I write her a letter, but it never felt right for some reason. However, I finally reached a point where I had to do something to let my feelings out. So one night I sat down and wrote Jeri a letter. I told her everything I had felt since her death. I explained why I felt guilt and sadness, who I was angry with and all of the memories I was grateful for. Then I told her I loved her.

A few days after writing it, I took the letter to the cemetery. I sat down at Jeri's grave and read the letter to her out loud. Actually hearing the words made it more real.

These intentional actions were really helping. I was doing something in an effort to move on with my life. I knew I was doing the right thing. I wanted, though, to take this one step further. I put the letter and my heartache in four helium-filled balloons. I went back to the cemetery and just sat quietly at Jeri's grave with balloons in hand. I told myself I could sit there until I felt ready to let go. I thought of how much I loved Jeri and realized we both needed this.

When it was time, I stood up and released one balloon at a time. As each one made its way up, I could feel my heart becoming lighter. The burden of grief I carried was finally loosening its grip on me.

When I released the last one, I whispered, "I love you, Jeri." And for the first time in six years, I could love her without the pain and guilt that had for so long been attached to that love. I knew Jeri was smiling down on me. I had learned one of the most important lessons about love and life. I had learned the importance of letting go.

~Kelli Czarnick
Chicken Soup for the Christian Teenage Soul

Teens Talk Tough Times

Reaching Out

If you want to lift yourself up, lift up someone else.
~Booker T. Washington

76

It's Tough
to Be a Teenager

It's tough to be a teenager, no one really knows
What the pressure is like in school, this is how it goes.

I wake up every morning, and stare into this face
I wanna be good lookin', but I feel like a disgrace.

My friends they seem to like me, if I follow through with their dare,
But when I try to be myself, they never seem to care.

My mom, well she keeps saying, I gotta make the grade
While both my parents love me, it slowly seems to fade.

It seems like everyone I know is trying to be so cool
And every time I try, I end up just a fool.

I've thought about taking drugs, I really don't want to you know
But I just don't fit in, and it's really startin' to show.

Maybe if I could make the team, I'll stand out in the crowd
If they could see how hard I try, I know they would be proud.

You see I'm still a virgin, my friends they can't find out
'Cause if they really knew the truth, I know they'd laugh and shout.

Sometimes I really get so low, I want to cash it in
My problems really aren't so bad, if I think of how life's been.

Sometimes I'm really lost, and wonder what to do
I wonder where to go, who can I talk to.

It's tough to be a teenager, sometimes life's not fair
I wish I had somewhere to go, and someone to CARE.

~Tony Overman
Chicken Soup for the Teenage Soul II

77

The Rose with No Thorns

A young man carrying a guitar case boarded the afternoon school bus at Maple Street. Obviously ill at ease, he found a seat, placed the guitar on end beside him in the aisle, and held it upright with his arm. He looked around anxiously, then hung his head and began shuffling his feet back and forth on the floor of the bus.

Melanie watched him. She didn't know who he was, but from his looks she decided he must be a real loser.

Melanie's friend Kathy looked up from her book. "Wouldn't you know it? Crazy Carl again."

"Who's Crazy Carl?" Melanie asked, tossing her sunny hair.

"Don't you know your next-door neighbor?"

"Next-door neighbor? The Bells moved into that house. We met them the day we left on spring vacation."

"Well, that's his name, Carl Bell."

The bus rolled on under the big trees along Elm Street. Kathy and Melanie stared at the newcomer and his big guitar case.

When the driver called out "Sycamore," the new boy awkwardly picked up his case and got off. It was Melanie's stop, too, but she didn't budge. When the bus started again, she rang for the next corner. "See you, Kathy."

Melanie ran home, up the steps and through the front door. She called out, "Mom, does that weirdo live next door?"

Her mother came into the hall from the kitchen. "Melanie, you must not refer to anyone as a weirdo. Yes, the Bells have a handi-capped son. This morning I called Mrs. Bell, and she told me about Carl. He has never been able to speak. He has a congenital heart defect and a nervous disorder. They have found a private tutor for him, and he is taking guitar lessons to help improve his coordination."

"Just the pits! Right next door!" Melanie exclaimed.

"He's a shy boy. You must be neighborly. Just say hello when you see him."

"But he rides the school bus, and the kids laugh at him."

"See that you don't," her mother advised.

It was a week before Carl boarded the bus again. Melanie thought he recognized her. Grudgingly, she said hello. Some of the other kids started whispering and making jokes. Pretty soon spit wads were fly-ing. "Settle down!" the driver yelled. Carl shuffled his feet. Each time a spit wad hit him he twitched. When his guitar clattered to the floor, the driver again admonished them to settle down—this time with a warning tone in his voice. The bus grew quiet but the fun didn't stop. The boys seated behind Carl started blowing on the back of his head, making his hair stand up. They thought it was funny.

When Sycamore Street came into view Carl jumped up, rang the bell, put the guitar strap over his shoulder and headed for the door. The guitar case swung wide, hitting Chuck Wilson on the neck. Carl rushed toward the door with his case still crosswise in the aisle. When Chuck caught up and took a swing at him, the shoulder strap tore loose and the case slid down the steps into the gutter. Carl stumbled off the bus and ran down the street, leaving his guitar behind.

Melanie sat glued to her seat. "I'm never getting off there again," she said to Kathy. Once again she waited until the next corner before getting off, then retraced the block back to Sycamore. The open case still lay in the gutter. She walked past it and headed toward home. What a character! she thought. What did I ever do to deserve him for a neighbor?

But by the time Melanie had gone half a block, her conscience bothered her for leaving Carl's guitar where anyone could pick it up. She turned back to get it. Both the handle and the strap on the case were broken, so she had to carry it in her arms with her books. Why am I doing this? she wondered. Then she remembered how terrible it had been when everybody laughed at him.

Mrs. Bell opened the door before Melanie could knock. "Melanie, I am so glad to see you! What happened? Carl was so upset he went straight to his room," she said, laying the case on a chair.

"It was just a little accident." Melanie didn't want to alarm her with the whole story. "Carl left his guitar. I thought I should bring it."

Carl didn't ride the bus after that. His parents drove him to and from guitar lessons. Melanie saw him only when he worked in his rose garden.

Life should have gone more smoothly, but kids still pestered him. They hung around his yard, threw acorns at him and chanted, "Crazy Carl, the banjo king, takes music lessons and can't play a thing."

One hot day as Carl relaxed on the grass with a soft drink, the kids came and started their chant. Melanie glanced out her window just in time to see the soda bottle shatter on the sidewalk at their feet.

The next day at school Kathy said, "Did you hear about Crazy Carl cutting those kids with a broken bottle?"

"No wonder," Melanie said, "the way they keep after him."

"Whose side are you on?" Kathy fired back.

"I'm not choosing sides, but I heard them bugging him."

"Bet you two hold hands over the fence," Kathy said sarcastically.

At noon in the cafeteria line a classmate teased Melanie, "If you're asking Crazy Carl to go with you to the banquet, I'll be glad to take Jim off your hands."

Before the day was over, somebody wrote on the blackboard, "Melanie loves Crazy Carl."

Melanie managed to keep her poise just long enough to get home. She ran in the door and burst into tears. "Mom, I told you it was the pits having a weirdo next door. I hate him." She told her mother what happened at school.

"It hurts when your friends turn on you," Melanie said, "and for nothing!" Then she thought of something she hadn't considered before. "Carl must have cried lots of times."

"I'm sure," her mother agreed.

Why do I feel so mean about Carl? she wondered. Or maybe I don't. Maybe I just think I'm supposed to because everybody else does.

"Sometimes, Mom, I don't bother to do my own thinking." Melanie wiped her eyes. "Jim's coming over. I have to wash my hair." She ran upstairs.

On the last day of school, Melanie came home early. Carl was in his rose garden. When he saw her, he clipped a rose and went to the gate to wait. Melanie greeted him with her usual hello. He held out the rose. As she reached for it, he put up his other hand to delay her, and started breaking off the thorns. He pricked his finger, frowned a moment, wiped the blood on his shirt sleeve, and continued breaking off the thorns.

Tonight was the banquet, and Melanie wanted to get home and be sure her clothes were ready. But she stood and waited.

Carl handed her the rose with no thorns. "Thank you, Carl. Now I won't stick my fingers," she said, in an effort to interpret his thoughts. Touched by his childlike grin, she patted his cheek, thanked him again and walked on home. At the door she looked back. Carl was still standing there, holding his hand against the cheek she had touched.

One week later Carl died of congestive heart failure. After the funeral, the Bells went away for a while.

One day a letter came from Mrs. Bell. There was a special note for Melanie.

Dear Melanie,

I think Carl would have liked you to have this last page from his diary. We encouraged him to write at least one sentence a day. Most days there was little good to write.

Mr. Bell and I want to thank you for being his friend—the only youthful friend he ever had.

Our love,

~Carla Bell

Carl's last words: "Mlanee is rose wit no torns."

~Eva Harding
A 5th Portion of Chicken Soup for the Soul

Their Bullet, My Life

Entering the large assembly room, the motor of my powered wheelchair humming in my ears, I could feel the eyes of every boy, all local gang members, staring at me. I wondered how they would react to my computer-activated voice. Would they listen to what I had to say? Would they understand the violence and pain they were causing? Could I really make a difference?

"Hello, I'm Cruz Carrasco," I began. "As you can see and now hear, I am unable to walk or talk by myself. I wasn't always in this wheelchair, and once I could speak as well as any of you. In fact, up until I was seventeen years old, I lived a life probably very similar to yours. My dream then was to play pro football. I loved it! I started as a sophomore for East L.A.'s Roosevelt High School Rough Riders and was soon their star running back.

"By the time I was in the twelfth grade, UCLA had offered me a full scholarship, and I was ready to take it. I was going to be the first college graduate in my family. I promised my mom I would buy her a big house with a pool when I was a star. And then, without warning, my plans and dreams were literally blown away. I don't remember that day now, so what I am going to tell you is what my family and friends have told me.

"November 4, 1986, was a normal school day. After football practice, I headed home, had dinner with my mom, and then went up to my room to do my homework. I heard one of my football buddies calling to me outside my window. My friends knew Mom couldn't hear them back there. I sneaked out the window to go for a ride with him on his new moped. If I had asked my mom, she wouldn't have let me go. We rode around and stopped to hang out with another football buddy at his house, even though we knew his neighborhood was heavily infested with gangs and drugs. Unfortunately, before we arrived at my friend's house, a bad drug deal had gone down in the neighborhood. Little did I know that this would be the last time I would walk by myself, talk by myself, have normal vision or live the life of my dreams.

"Once the gang realized the cocaine they had bought was really soap, they came back, armed with a .44-caliber Magnum, driving down the street and spraying bullets into the neighborhood. In sheer panic, we started to run for cover. My two friends fell as bullets ripped through their legs. My terror was ended abruptly when a bullet exploded in my head.

"For the next four and a half months, I lay in a coma, machines feeding me and making me breathe. There was not much hope that I would recover. Can you imagine what it was like for me to awaken to the helpless horror of what had become of me?

"The two years after the shooting are a blur to me now. I do know that, throughout the seemingly endless year and a half that followed, I was in rehab; my mother refused to give up on me and vowed to eventually bring me home. Her determination was contagious, and in spite of my suffocating despair, I clung to hope.

"I was nineteen when I finally returned home. I had not become the college football hero I had dreamed I would be. Instead, I was having to start over from infancy, physically. I was filled with grief over the life I had lost. It was agonizing to realize that my friends had all gone to our prom and graduated from high school. Some had gone on to college; some were working; some were living in their own apartments; some were even married with kids. Once home, my mother did what she knew how to do best: She loved me. She enrolled me in a program for disabled adults, and I finished high school. But I still couldn't communicate or move my own wheelchair; I was trapped in my own body. I was filled with anger and frustration.

I realized that Mom's love wasn't enough. It was then that Zoe came to work with me.

"Zoe began as my occupational therapist and became first my friend, and then my partner in life. With Zoe, I finally had someone listening to my dreams rather than focusing on my disabilities. Zoe made sure I received the voice-output computer to speak with and the power wheelchair so I could get around independently. Once I realized I could again interact with people, I wanted to find a way to keep what happened to me from happening to anyone else.

"That is why I am here today, eight years after I was shot, to let you know about the effects of the choices you make. Before you make those choices, I hope you will take the time to think about how they will affect your life and the lives of the people around you. They never caught the guys who shot me, although I did learn a most painful truth: One of the men in the car was my best friend from elementary school! I never dreamed that the boy I loved like a brother would take away my life as I knew it. I'm sure he didn't, either. What a cruel result his choices and mine made on my life. While I had been pursuing football, he had joined a gang. I never thought it was cool belonging to a gang, but I did think it was okay to be friends with gang members. I never realized that simply associating with gang members would change my life forever."

I spoke for about fifteen minutes and showed them a video of myself before and after the shooting. When I was finished, they shared with me that they had never met someone who had been affected by gun violence like I had. They knew they had affected a lot of lives through their violence, but they had never seen the true impact of their actions. When we were finished talking, they all came up to shake my hand. I was filled with hope.

A few weeks later, I received letters from some of the boys thanking me for coming and vowing to get out of the gang. Some even said they wanted to look for a more peaceful way of life. I was ecstatic. What had happened to me finally had some meaning. I would never play football, but I could make a difference in young people's lives.

In May 2000, Zoe and I adopted a child. As I see the wonder

and hope in my son's eyes, I dream of a future when the only gun violence he will know about is the cause of my disability. I'll never be the same as before, but we all have to be the best we can be. When I look out into the audience during a presentation, I hope that this won't happen to any of them. I beg them, "Please stay away from guns, drugs and gangs. Stop the violence! It is the only way we can all live together in peace."

~Cruz Carrasco and Zoe McGrath
Chicken Soup for the Soul Stories for a Better World

Operation
Save the World

I always thought "it could never happen to me." To tell you the truth, I don't think the thought ever crossed my mind. I lived an extremely sheltered life living in a small town, and attended an all girl Catholic high school. It all began the beginning of my sophomore year. It was right around homecoming, when I knew I had met the "man of my dreams," or so I thought. Carl was a living dream with a great personality, who always knew exactly what to say to make me feel like I was queen of the world. He seemed to have it all: star of the football team, captain of the wrestling team and president of his homeroom. He was so perfect and to think that he liked me was incredible! He wanted to spend every waking moment with me. I was a busy girl and a very good student. I was an athlete on the basketball and volleyball teams, student council class secretary, choreographer of my swing choir, and this year I was even elected to homecoming court. My life was picture perfect.

The more time we spent together, the more he wanted me all to himself. I didn't object because I thoroughly enjoyed the time I spent with him. But then it began. It started with swearing and verbal arguments, but quickly escalated from there. I always thought I would never put up with that, but I soon realized there was nothing that I could do. I discovered that Carl had problems.

He confided in me, and I found out all about his divorced

parents and abusive father. I felt it was my duty to take care of him because he wasn't as fortunate as I to have two loving parents who gave me the world. Little did I realize I was sacrificing myself for his punishing behavior. I was also sacrificing the friendships of my three best friends. I was becoming extremely isolated and growing farther and farther apart from my family and younger sister. Carl now took up all of my time, and I considered it my responsibility to rescue him. I'm not the type of person who likes to fail at tasks so I put a lot of time and effort into helping Carl. (I now refer to it as "Operation Save the World," because it was such a huge unattainable task that I took upon myself.) Of course, at the time I didn't realize a person can only help themselves if they truly want to change. I was willing to sacrifice anything and everything because this was "the man I loved," and we were destined to be together forever.

I don't remember exactly when the violence became so intense. He never hit me, so I didn't actually consider it abuse. My bruises were from his excessive pinching, shoving, kicking and hair-pulling. I distinctly remember one incident when I had all four wisdom teeth pulled and the two of us were watching a movie. I said something extremely insignificant and Carl lost his temper, so he began fiercely pinching my swollen cheeks together and slamming my head against the wall.

I was the helpless victim and would never fight back for fear of what else might happen. It soon became a sick cycle, but it always ended in tears and a dramatic apology, promising it would never happen again. Despite my swollen cheeks and the contusions on my head, he had never hit me, but the violence was now occurring more frequently and was getting worse each day. Soon I could barely get out of bed in the morning from my aches and pains, and no one knew how much I was hurting. He always made marks in places people couldn't see, and I always had good explanations if anyone happened to see. I was a tough girl, and I could withstand all this pain for "the man I loved." It wasn't the physical pain that hurt as much as the emotional pain that was tearing me apart on the inside

On the exterior, my life seemed composed and everyone thought our relationship was perfect. Carl had even bought me a diamond engagement ring. He would constantly send me flowers at school and all the girls would always exclaim, "I wish I had a boyfriend like Carl. You're so lucky." Little did they know.

I don't know what made me finally realize that this treatment was inhumane. Maybe it was that my three best friends would no longer speak to me, or that my parents wouldn't listen to me. I was convinced that no one would be there for me if I didn't have Carl. I had become so exclusive and Carl was the center of my life. I do know that God played a role in helping me realize that what Carl was doing was wrong.

One Sunday morning, exactly two years after I began dating Carl, my family and I were sitting down at the breakfast table, and I broke down—it all came out. That was probably the most difficult moment of my life, but also one of the best, even though I didn't think so at the time.

I broke off all ties with "the man of my dreams" and began to piece my life back together. I started going to therapy. At first I thought I would die without Carl, but it only took time, lots of it, to change that. My family and friends were very supportive. They let me back into their lives after I had shut them out completely. I could not have done it without them.

A few months later in my behavioral science class, I had to do an oral exam on a social issue that is prevalent in our society. My speech consisted of my experiences with dating violence. The entire class was in tears even though most of them could not understand my experience. It felt good to come out of my corner of isolation, yet at the same time, it was also very scary. Most people don't understand fully unless they have been in a similar relationship. I was often asked, "Why would you stay in such a relationship and let someone treat you like that?" It's extremely difficult when people judge me in this manner, but it's part of my experience and has shaped who I am today.

I have now moved on to new responsibilities and greater aspirations of college life. I have become more independent and happy, thanks to all of the love and support from my family and friends. It's still difficult to learn to trust people, but I am thankful to all those who are learning and growing with me. I couldn't have asked for more than my supportive family, understanding friends and incredibly patient new boyfriend.

Last week I was checking my e-mail and I received this:

Dear Jenny,

I found your e-mail address in a student directory, and I decided to write you since I never got the chance to thank you for your presentation in our class about dating abuse. This summer I was looking at the handout you gave everyone about the signs of abuse. I began hysterically crying as I realized that my boyfriend matched all too many of the signs. I knew it was a bad relationship, but I could not tell anyone and I thought it was my responsibility to fix it. After hearing your experience, I realized I couldn't. Your story gave me a lot of strength to get out of the relationship before it got worse. Well, at least the story has a happy ending for both of us; we are very fortunate. Thanks again for having the courage to tell your story. You really helped me a lot, even though you didn't know it at the time.

"Operation Save the World" didn't fail after all. I did rescue someone.

~Jennifer Winkelman
Chicken Soup for the Teenage Soul on Love & Friendship

The Walk That Changed Our Lives

It can be hard to break the friendship code of secrecy and make your friend mad at you, but you must do what you feel in your heart is right.
~Amanda Ford

The closer we came to the counselor's office, the more obvious it became that this walk would be one of the most important of our lives. It was one of the last days before school got out for the summer, and eighth grade was coming to an end. My friends and I were all thrilled. Everyone, that is, except our friend, Hannah.

It had started the previous summer, when Hannah had begun to keep to herself a lot. Whenever we would go out, she would insist on staying home by herself just to sit around. In fact, a lot of changes had come over Hannah ever since we had entered junior high. She obsessed about her weight, her complexion and how unpopular she was. She never seemed to focus on the good things she had to offer; it was always about what she didn't have or what she was lacking. We were all concerned that something was very wrong, but at thirteen we didn't exactly understand it or know what we could do to help her. Hannah seemed to be getting worse every day. She hated herself, and it was tearing our friendship apart.

Then one morning not long ago, Hannah came to school and told us she had almost committed suicide. She said she had thought about her friends and could not go through with it. We were in shock and had no idea what to do. Since she told no one else—not her parents or her sisters, just us—we tried to figure out what to do ourselves, feeling that no one else would understand. Though we didn't want to stop being there for her, we couldn't carry the burden by ourselves. We knew that if we made one wrong move, it could cost us our friend's life.

We walked into the counselor's office and waited for what seemed like an eternity until they called our names. We held hands as we walked in, each of us holding back tears. The counselor invited us to sit down, and we began to tell him about Hannah and all that had been going on. When we were finished, he told us that we had done the right thing. We waited as he called Hannah's mother. We were overwhelmed with a million questions. What would Hannah say when she found out that we had told? Would her parents be mad at her for not telling anyone sooner? What was going to happen?

When Hannah's mother arrived at school, she had obviously been crying and her face seemed full of questions. She began to ask about Hannah's behavior and what she had told us. It was awful to tell her how Hannah had been alone at home one day testing knives to see if they were sharp enough to take her life. We all cringed at the thought of not having her in our lives today.

We learned later that after we had gone back to class, Hannah had been called down to talk to her mother and her counselor. It turned out she was relieved and grateful that she didn't have to keep her secret any longer. She began counseling and has gotten better. Since that day we are so grateful to see Hannah's smiling face, or even to simply be able to pass her a note in the hallway between classes.

If we had not taken that long, horrible walk to the counseling office, we may not have been able to share high school memories with Hannah. I know now that when we took that walk, it gave us the ability to give her the greatest gift of all... her life.

~Maggie McCarthy
Chicken Soup for the Teenage Soul on Tough Stuff

Slender Thread

Too often we underestimate the power of a touch, a smile, a kind word,
a listening ear, an honest compliment, or the smallest act of caring,
all of which have the potential to turn a life around.
~Leo Buscaglia

As his mother drove away, eleven-year-old Billy stood by the curb and cried. His mother was an abusive drug addict; still, she was all he had. Now he was to live with his aunt. A wave of desolation mounted in his chest.

Aunt Val had no interest in caring for him, either. Billy was left alone, living off peanut butter, stale bread and cereal. In the evenings he spent his time listening to the voices of the five children who lived next door, the laughter and shouts, and the firm voice of their mama sending them to bed.

On Sunday morning, as they packed into the car for church, Mama noticed Billy watching her kids from the shadow of his doorway. He looked like trouble: His face was defiant and his shabby clothes hung loose on his thin frame. What kind of life did this boy have? He made her uneasy; yet she saw the hurt that showed in his dark eyes.

Billy's face haunted her while she sat through the service. When they got home, he was still there. His eyes followed the children as they piled chattering from the car.

Mama's heart caught as her boy, Cecil, paused and asked, "What's your name?"

"Billy."

"How old are you?" Cecil asked.

"Eleven, almost twelve," said Billy.

"Me, too. Want to come inside? We're going out to play basketball after we change clothes."

Mama bit her lip as Billy followed Cecil inside.

The next afternoon, Billy came home with Cecil after school.

"Billy's aunt ain't never home, so I said he could come over here," Cecil said.

But Billy didn't fit in with the rhythm of their household. When the children did their homework Billy was a distraction, chattering thoughtlessly while they tried to concentrate. He used foul language and bullied the younger children. A sour feeling settled in Mama's stomach. Billy was not going to be a good influence on her kids.

The following day, Mama saw Billy hanging around the front of the apartments when she got back from her job driving the school bus. A cigarette hung in his mouth. He ducked away when he saw her, which only made her dislike him more. After basketball that evening, Billy came inside with Cecil. The boys had found an expensive tennis shoe at the courts and wanted to show it to Mama.

"I'm gonna buy shoes like these some day," Billy bragged. "I'm gonna have all the money I want."

Mama shivered. She could imagine how Billy would get the money to buy what he wanted. She didn't like the man she feared he would become. Cecil was looking at Billy and the flashy shoe with envy. It made Mama angry; she didn't want Billy's kind leading her children astray.

When Billy left, she told Cecil, "I won't have you hanging out with Billy. He's not going where I want you to go."

Cecil's expression clouded. "Don't, Mama. There's something good in Billy. I know it. He needs us."

Mama shook her head. She was adamant. Her family came first, and Billy was bad news.

That night she dreamt of Billy, crying while his mother drove away. He turned to Mama but she only shook her head. In her dream an older Billy faced her, his face hardened, his eyes cold. He wore the expensive tennis shoes. He stared at her in agony with a bullet wound in his chest, then collapsed and lay still on the concrete. Light flashed and an angel stood beside her. He asked: "Did you do your best?"

Mama woke and tried to push the dream from her mind. It could not be erased. Life had failed Billy. Would she fail him, too?

It was early. Light dawned outside. Mama tried to sleep, but when she closed her eyes she saw Billy sprawled on the concrete. She got up and went into the kitchen to start some coffee. The Billy of her dream was fresh in her mind—a lost little boy trying to act tough in a frightening world. Billy's future hung by a slender thread. She could either hold it tightly or release it to the wind. She knew what she would want someone to do for her Cecil, if anything were to happen to her.

Later that morning, when Cecil came into the kitchen she said, "You were right about Billy. But there have to be some rules. You bring him home after school. I want to talk to him."

That afternoon, Mama drew Billy aside. "I think there's a lot of good in you and I want us to be friends. But there are going to be some rules. You come home with Cecil each day and do your homework without any talking. If you have any questions, you ask me. You and Cecil need to help me start supper, and you may stay and eat with us. If you work hard and stay in school, someday you'll get those shoes you want."

Billy looked into Mama's face. She met his searching eyes. Then he nodded.

Mama patted his shoulder. "It won't be easy. If you goof off, I'll send you home. But I really hope you'll choose to stay."

Right off, Billy tested Mama and got sent home. But as the weeks passed, more and more often he stayed for supper. On Sundays he often went with the family to church.

Over the years Billy changed. His hardness fell away, he trusted Mama and her firm guidance, and he came to her whenever he had problems. Mama kept in touch with Billy's teachers and followed his progress at school.

On the day of his high school graduation, Billy grinned as Mama snapped a picture. He raised the edge of the long green robe to reveal a present to himself, bought with money he'd saved from his summer job. Tears came to Mama's eyes when she saw the new tennis shoes. She could almost feel the angel's hand resting on her shoulder. Yes, she'd done her best.

~Karen Cogan
A 5th Portion of Chicken Soup for the Soul

Dad's Gift

When I was fourteen, in a two-week period before Thanksgiving, my dad developed hepatitis and died. It was a shock to all of us. He had always been so healthy. He'd only been sick once before and had bounced back quickly.

As one of eight children, I was usually lost in the crowd. Now, however, adults sought me out to console me. They told me how much I resembled my father and what a good man he had been. There was an outpouring of love, visitors and food to our home. To be honest, the months that followed his death were quite beautiful, in a weird way. I had never felt so immersed in love.

At school, none of my friends knew what to say to me. I did have one friend who came to see me at my house the day after my dad died. She sat quietly beside me. I now realize how much courage that must have taken. Besides her, none of my other friends acknowledged my father's death. They acted awkward around me. It was a strange feeling.

Several months later, one of the cheerleaders in my class lost her father to a massive heart attack. Usually, she was in the midst of a huge crowd. She seemed alone most of the time now.

I approached her tentatively one day during lunch. "I think I know how you're feeling. My dad died a few months ago," I told her.

I didn't know what to expect. I was a little intimidated, to be honest. I didn't mix with "her crowd" too easily. They were all so good-looking and popular.

Abby looked me squarely in the face. Her eyes widened. And then she seemed to relax. We talked until the bell rang.

After that day, we chatted regularly. Sometimes it felt like we were in our own little world. We'd share stories and giggle about our dads. It felt good to have a connection with my dad through our talks. I cherished them.

The next school year a girl named Terry lost her dad. Terry was kind of nerdy. She was tall and skinny. Not even "my crowd" had much to do with her. Once again, I approached someone out of my need to have a bond with my father.

"I heard your dad died. My dad died last year," I told her.

Terry sighed, then gave me a description of her past week. I listened to her every word.

As soon as I could find Abby, I told her about Terry. Abby responded like I did. It was as if we were on a deserted island, and we had caught sight of a shipwrecked victim floating toward us.

We became a threesome. Not in a social way—we didn't really hang out together—but we snatched a few moments at our lockers and in homeroom to share bits of our dads. Just having someone who understood when we were going through a tough week was comforting.

I still have my yearbook in which Abby wrote, "Thanks for being my buddy. I needed you." Occasionally, I hear from Terry. I have continued to reach out to people who are in pain. I've received comfort for myself, too, as a result of connecting with others. Being able to reach out to others has returned blessings to me a hundredfold. I thank my dad for this lasting and life affirming gift.

~Mary Cornelia Van Sant
Chicken Soup for the Christian Teenage Soul

The Dustpan Carrier

What the teacher is, is more important than what he teaches.
~Karl Menninger

"It is always the English teacher who holds the dustpan."

The last time I saw Mrs. Jones was in 1991. I had graduated from college and, proud of my accomplishments, came back to Douglas Anderson School of the Arts to find and thank the woman, the teacher, who changed my life.

I spoke to her classes that afternoon about the importance of self-esteem and setting high goals for oneself. I heard myself speaking, but I was somewhere else in that classroom, five years back, sitting at the corner desk with my fingers twisting and twisting that long black hair I once had.

In December 1986, my father, a rabbi and teacher himself, had brought me to Douglas Anderson School of the Arts in desperation. I sat in the hallway while he went into the principal's office and spoke to her. I only heard a few of those words, in between the clutter of strange faces in the hall and the pit-pat of ballet-slippered feet on the white tile, but I knew why I was there and why they chose to whisper. In a nearby practice room, I heard the rhythmic clicking of a metronome, followed by a hesitant piano scale.

"I don't know where else to put her." My father's voice broke, and then I heard a muffle of a deep, authoritative female voice.

"Rabbi, I understand your position, but we only hold auditions in the summer." For the first time in my life, I heard my father weep.

I pressed my head tight against the green door, felt the cold on my cheek, and closed my eyes, tried counting to ten the way my therapist had taught me only a week before, breathing in on every number, then out, slowly.

My father's voice interrupted at seven. "She was raped by a group of boys at her school a month ago. She can't go back there."

I auditioned for The School of the Arts that day, sitting at the piano in the stuffy little practice room I had heard someone struggling in earlier. I lay my hands heavily on the yellow-stained keys and with my heart, with tears, with pain, I played Rachmaninoff, Beethoven, and finally, my father's favorite Chopin nocturne. The teacher nodded, the principal put her hand up to her mouth and shook her head, and my father's face melted into quiet relief. It wasn't until Friday, however, that I met her, Mrs. Jones, when I was transferred into her creative writing class at 11:00 A.M. In my memories of her, she is always the same. She wore brown sandals, a blue flower-printed skirt, and a wrinkled white blouse with its frilly collar bent. She held a constant confused expression and played with a charm on her necklace, sometimes the wisp of hair that often fell over her eye. As she walked closer to my desk in the corner, I noticed she was pigeon-toed. She didn't bend over me the way the other teachers had, but rather, knelt at my desk, and smiled at me, eye level.

"We'll be working in our journals today," Mrs. Jones said softly. She smelled like soap and mothballs and lilacs. "Do you have a notebook you can use as your journal?"

I could feel the inquisitive eyes in the classroom on "the new girl." A pretty blond girl in the front of the room mumbled loudly to her neighbor about my "special audition."

"Get to work, please," Mrs. Jones told the class. Please, I thought. I believe it was the first time I had ever heard a teacher say "please" to a student!

I pulled a green notebook from my book bag and Mrs. Jones lay her cool, dry hand on mine. "I'm so happy to have you in my class," she whispered.

That journal, I believe now, saved me from insanity. I wrote everything that day and from that day forward; I turned myself inside out and dumped it into my green notebook the way I'd seen my mother plop her matzo balls into her chicken soup. I wrote about "them." I wrote their names down and crossed them out, then wrote them again and again, until it didn't hurt so much to hear them in my head. I wrote the word "rape" in red because it felt hot and burned and it was sore and I knew that even if I ignored it, it would not go away.

Mrs. Jones didn't judge my words the way the district attorney had. She didn't probe and pry and prick me like the psychologists or the nurse examiner at the hospital. She didn't insult and blame and scream like my mother initially had—or weep like my father. Mrs. Jones became much more than my English teacher. She was a partner in my internal battle, guiding me with her red-penned words on the many pages of my always-read, always-understood, journal.

In 1991 I went back. I walked through the bustling hallway (I had arrived just as the bell rang), and was surprised at how young the students looked. Had I been so young just five years ago? No, I believe I was much, much older. By coincidence, Mrs. Jones was just leaving her classroom as I approached. She carried a crumpling cardboard box full of journals. At first, she just smiled, had that confused but friendly look of unfamiliarity. And then it hit her. "Tali, is it really you?"

I've been told that it is the English teacher, always the English teacher, who is directly faced with the at-risk students. The faithful dustpan carrier who picks up the pieces when they fall. Perhaps this is because writing so often mirrors our innermost fears and dark secrets, places where a science or math teacher has no grounds to step.

I chose to teach English because I had no choice.

I will never forget what Mrs. Jones did for me. It's been almost ten years since high school. I have my own group of students now and I, too, carry around a worn cardboard box full of journals. And a dustpan.

~Tali Whiteley
A 6th Bowl of Chicken Soup for the Soul

Homeboy Goes to Harvard

You cannot fully understand your own life without knowing and thinking beyond your life, your own neighborhood, and even your own nation.
~Johnnetta Cole

As I walked into the building, I heard whispering among them. Hidden behind dark glasses with a red bandanna wrapped around my head, I approached the front of the room. I wore a long, black coat, a blue shirt buttoned to the collar, baggy trousers and black patent leather shoes. I strutted across the stage and bellowed out the words, "How dare you! How dare you look at me as if I am a good-for-nothing low-life doomed to be dead!" I looked around again. Their eyes quickly shifted away as my eyes made contact. It was as if I had a disease.

They were educators who had come to hear a speaker talk about gang prevention and intervention, about the increase of violence in schools. They expected to meet Mr. Richard Santana, a Harvard graduate. Their eyes continued to shift.

"They call me Mr. Chocolate... and I'm here to talk to you about life."

I've always known my life was different. My mother died when I was three months old, and my father left before then. I, along with my two older sisters, was moved from foster home to foster home in Fresno, California. My parents were caught in the juvenile justice system and the welfare system. I am a product of the system. I hated it.

I was introduced to gangs, drugs and violence at an early age. My uncle, a tall, strong man covered with tattoos, came into my life after serving a sentence in the state penitentiary. He was part of the largest institutionalized gangs in the state of California. My uncle played an instrumental role in teaching me the rules of the barrio—the school of survival. This, along with drugs and alcohol, gave me strength to deal with the shortcomings of my life.

I grew up fast, and I developed an inner strength that made the homeboys I ran with gravitate toward me, making me the leader of the gang. My homeboys' trust in my leadership gave me courage and a deep sense of comfort. I held them close. I was prepared to die for them.

I was proud of all this, yet I often wondered, Why can't others outside my gang see the strengths that my homeboys see in me? Lack of acceptance by adults around me fed my resentment. So I grew intolerant of anyone who denigrated or disrespected me.

Funny thing is that even while I was rooted in the street life—the drugs, the violence, as well as the love and empowerment of being a gangster leader—part of me was elsewhere. I lucidly saw everything my life was about, as though I were looking at my own life and the lives of those around me from a watchtower high upon a hill. This wasn't a single and sudden moment of lucidity; rather I always had this perspective.

From this watchtower, I saw my homeboys' lives growing shorter each day. Whisper, a talented soccer player who was recruited for the U.S. junior team to compete internationally, gave up his dream when he got his girlfriend pregnant. Menso's ability to take pictures of life with his mind and create beautiful artwork through his hands was lost to his love affair with a syringe. I could name more. Despite how affirmed and familiar I felt with the street life, I knew I wanted another way to live.

One day while looking for a job, I dropped by the Chicano Youth Center (CYC), which offered after-school jobs regardless of my affiliation as a gang member. Through CYC, I went to Washington,

D.C., for a student leadership conference and gave a presentation on issues related to gang violence. This marked a turning point in my life—a point when I realized that I could make a positive contribution to society. As a result of this trip to D.C., I was recruited through the Educational Opportunity Program to attend California State University at Fresno.

In college, I learned about my heritage and the sacrifices made by my race. The protest for access to the university and the struggle for equality had a tremendous impact on my perception of life. I grew to appreciate my culture. Yet I was still heavily involved with the violent realities of the streets. I felt split between being a college student and a street thug.

While in my first year in college, I was approached by the campus police and frisked. When I asked why I was being searched, they informed me that they had received a phone call claiming that someone fitting my description had threatened to shoot a professor for not getting an A in the class. When the officers found nothing, I smarted off, "Well, you better get busy 'cause there's this dude looking just like me about to shoot a professor." Naturally, they didn't appreciate my humor.

If they had checked my student status, they would have found that I was getting straight As. I knew at that moment that I would always be treated differently, dehumanized because of the way I looked. For this reason, I made a commitment to dedicate my work toward breaking down barriers that prevent other homeboys and homegirls just like myself from entering college.

I dress as a gang member, enter a room with an audience and speak to them on a variety of educational issues; I then take off a layer of clothing to reveal a shirt and tie. I make many people uncomfortable; I have caused many eyes to shift, many bodies to squirm. But by presenting my life story, I have been able to teach others ways in which they can put aside those biases and prejudices that push youth down.

~Richard Santana
Chicken Soup for the College Soul

The Shadow

D ear Teenage Chicken Soup,
    I am a nineteen-year-old student from Canada. I battled with anorexia nervosa for nearly seven years and I can now say I am well on my way to recovery. During my slow recovery period, I was able to express my feelings and emotions through writing. Your books have helped me through this process. I have enclosed a poem that really sums up what I was feeling. The title is "Shadowland" and it is the word I coined to describe my life as a student and athlete with anorexia nervosa.

Anorexia is an illness that I have struggled with for many years, one that has jeopardized my life and has even placed me in the hospital. You see, I believe that, in essence, developing an eating disorder is akin to becoming a shadow of one's former self. My experience with anorexia has been a transformation into a silent, thin, gray and flattened body that I call my shadow. In the worst of times, I have felt haunted by this figure lurking behind me, one that, despite my best efforts, I have been unable to free myself from. For years, I have struggled to achieve my many ambitious academic and athletic goals, feeling as though I carry the weight of the world on my shoulders. Anorexia, for me, has been like a journey through a world of shadowy gray.

I have no doubt that many of you are wondering what could possibly drive young and enthusiastic individuals who once belonged to the "real world" down such a dangerous path of self-destruction. I am aware that many images portrayed in the media are the driving force behind a North American dieting industry based on cruel, contradictory and unrealistic ideals. I do not, however, hold them completely responsible for the increasing number of young people who suffer from severe eating disorders today. I believe that the cause of these debilitating illnesses is one that is much deeper than the desire to resemble the models in leading fashion magazines. Contrary to popular belief, people with anorexia are not always vain, frivolous and attention-seeking individuals who feel that their lives would be enhanced if they lost a few pounds. Rather, the skeletal and "shadowlike" physical appearances of people suffering from anorexia are silent manifestations of the difficulty they experience in coping with a wide array of daily pressures. These are stresses that other people may not display the same degree of sensitivity towards, or if they do, handle them in different ways. In my opinion, anorexia is a way of not feeling, of starving until the dull numbness of the "Shadowland" sets in. In this state, victims of anorexia are too starved to feel the frightening consequences of having to deal with issues like relationships, family life, change and responsibility.

Enclosed is a poem I wrote. I hope you will publish it, as it is my deepest desire to know that my words can help others the way your books have helped me.

Yours truly,

~F.J.M.

The Shadowland

She is wire
Easily bent and twisted
And molded and shaped by uncaring hands
She's a coat hanger under the clothes

She's a bird in a gilded cage
Her screams only faintly heard

Unable to fly with one broken wing
She patiently waits for a key

And with eyes like a dried-up wellspring
She is blinded by unshed tears
Too terrified to let even one fall
Lest others should sense imperfection

Her most recent purchase was at the "Gap Kids"
Although she is sixteen years old
Waif-like and innocent, shrunken breasts, hips and thighs
She patiently waits for a key

Undeserving of life's simple pleasures
Seized by terror when she opens her mouth
Jaws bound and clenched, hammered with fear
She recently forgot how to chew

Intent to secure her shrunken self
She learned how to lie in a day
With a cross of her fingers behind her back
She falsely proclaims that she ate

And isn't it strange to talk to
An anatomical representation of skull?
Transparent skin that barely contains
Her delicate package of bones

And only when voices that care sound louder
Than the person who lives in the mirror
Will this hollow-eyed former shadow of self
Summon the courage to grow

The puzzling paradox of the hunger disease
Scales that taunt and reflections that scream

A magical number determines the worth
Of this slave to the gods of perfection.

~F.J.M
Chicken Soup for the Teenage Soul Letters

Chapter 10

Teens Talk Tough Times

Second Chances

You can't turn back the clock. But you can wind it up again.
~Bonnie Prudden

The Long Journey Home

I was like any other twelve-year-old. Girls had cooties. Nintendo and bike riding ruled my life. I had homework that I didn't always do. I won a few ribbons at track and field. I tried to stay up past my bedtime almost every night. I played baseball. I had a continuous craving for pizza. There was one thing that was different, though. I was really tired. I would come home and go to sleep at 4:30, get up and eat, and then go back to sleep until the next morning. My mom started thinking something might be wrong so she took me to our family doctor. He sent us for some blood work. We waited a week or so for the results. When the doctor's office called back, they wanted to do more tests. To this day, I don't know what they actually told my mom, but I just went to the hospital and they did their tests. After some more blood work, they came back and said they needed to do some other tests. One of them was a bone marrow test. They took a big needle and stuck it into my lower back. I was out cold for the entire thing.

I honestly don't remember how people were acting around me during this time. I don't remember my mom or dad being upset or anything. I just thought they were normal tests they did for tired kids. The same night as the bone marrow tests, I was admitted to the hospital. The next morning, the oncologist spoke to my mom and dad and told them that I had acute lymphoblastic leukemia.

I don't remember much of that morning—maybe it's better that way. The doctor and my mom and dad all came into the room, and the doctor explained to me that I had cancer. I just sat there and listened. I listened very closely. I didn't understand much until the doctor explained to me that I was going to lose all my hair. She said she was going to send a team of people to my school to tell all my classmates and my teachers that there was a student who had cancer. They said they would tell everyone that I wouldn't be feeling well and what they could do to help. They would tell them to treat me normally, she said, as if I wasn't sick. I was glad to hear about that because I was really scared about going to school with no hair. I didn't know what people would say or think. Looking back, I'm glad they did that.

I didn't really know what hit me. The next day I was getting lumbar punctures and massive doses of radiation. I had a full-blown transfusion. I received all this medicine and treatment in order to put me into automatic remission so they could begin chemotherapy. The first three weeks were brutal. The days I had treatment I'd come home and be so sick that I couldn't sleep. I'd be throwing up and couldn't eat anything. When I would eventually pass out from exhaustion, I would wake up in the morning and my pillow would be full of hair. That's when it started to hit me. I was really sick. When I would take a bath, I'd see chunks of my hair floating down the drain.

My mom took me to the barber to get my head shaved so it wouldn't look so bad. My older brother Matthew came along for support. After the barber had shaved my head, I looked in the mirror and suddenly got really sad. In an instant, my brother jumped into the barber's chair beside me and instructed the barber to shave his hair the exact same way. He didn't want me to feel all alone. It sounds silly but, by him shaving his head, it showed me that he loved me and he would do anything to make me feel better. That meant a lot to me.

My mom took me to the hospital every other day for the first three weeks. She took care of me because my dad had to work. She was always there for me. When my dad got home from work, he'd sort of take over and help out. Through all the chemo, I made a little friend named Brad Rowe. We went through everything together. We laughed. We cried. We played Nintendo. That made things a little easier for me.

The Sunshine Foundation came to us and offered me and my

family a wish. They said they'd give us whatever I wanted. They said they didn't care what it was, just as long as it made me happy. I wanted nothing more than to meet Patrick Roy of the Montreal Canadiens. They set up this huge dinner and game and two-day trip. I was even going to sit in the team box during the game. Well, I wasn't too lucky there, either. The NHL strike took place and along with the players, my wish walked, too! The people from the Sunshine Foundation felt horrible. We ended up going to Disneyland instead. It was great!

The summer following my first batches of chemo, I went to a baseball camp because I was feeling better. I quickly realized I hadn't grown as much as the other kids. I couldn't run for as long as they could. I couldn't go all day like them. Finally, exhausted, I went to the coach to tell him I was sick and I just started crying. I thought he wouldn't, or couldn't, understand. It was brutal. I was embarrassed and frustrated because I couldn't do as much as the other kids. Through tears I told him I had cancer and that I wasn't able to go crazy all day long like the other kids. He said the most amazing thing to me. It has stuck with me ever since. He bent down beside me and told me, "Phil, God is taking care of you and keeping you here because he has something special planned for your life." Suddenly, I had something I didn't have a whole lot of before: I had hope.

My hope seemed to be built on sand, though. My friend Brad relapsed. He ended up in intensive care for a week, but eventually got out. I remember thinking everything was going to be fine. Then, a few weeks later one morning in class, my teacher pulled me aside and told me that Brad had died. I lost it. He had the exact same cancer that I did, and he didn't make it. I cried all day. I went to the funeral and didn't believe a minute of it. At thirteen, I didn't know what was going on with my life.

I was off treatment in January of my eighth grade year. I actually had a few parties. Strange theme for a party... but, man, did we celebrate "No More Chemo!" One party in particular was huge: my friends, both sides of my family, my brother's and sisters' friends, everyone. I continued to go for my checkups, and I got a pin that said, "I Beat Cancer!"

I'm eighteen now, and my life is just like any other teenager's. I hate exams. I play golf. I'm involved in my school. I do drama and help build stuff for tech. I help out with chaplaincy and all the masses. I have great friends. I will never forget, though, the difference my illness made in my life. I look at things differently now. I value my parents and their love instead of fighting with them. I get scared every now and then when I think that they won't be around forever so I have to be with them now. I do the family trips and dinners, and I am happy to be there. I love my brother and sisters. Yes, they sometimes drive me crazy, but I wouldn't trade them for the world. I am thankful for a school that teaches me lessons and friends who love me.

I think of what that baseball coach told me. Every day I try to figure out God's plan for me and try to live the life that I was graciously given a second chance with. I believe in the goodness of people. Every single one of us has a reason for being here. And anything is possible as long as you keep the faith and never, ever give up hope.

~Phillip Thuss
Chicken Soup for the Teenage Soul on Tough Stuff

A Struggle to Be Me

Courage doesn't always roar. Sometimes courage is the little voice at the end of the day that says I'll try again tomorrow.
~Mary Anne Radmacher

]'m sitting in the dark on my bedroom floor. The musky scent of incense is lingering in the air and Fiona Apple is droning softly in the background. I'm crying without knowing it, and my wrist is bleeding from the razor I've just dragged across it.

I'm a cutter.

That was no particular day. That was four years of my life.

Freshman year was the beginning of my very long struggle with depression. I'd never been good at vocalizing my emotions or expressing pain verbally. Instead, I'd act out by doing things that generally made the situation worse. When I got nervous and anxious, or scared and angry, I'd overreact to the situation because I just didn't know what to do with my feelings.

When I entered high school for my freshman year, I was thrilled because I could make a new start and leave behind my glasses and braces from middle school. I could start anew without my former label of "geek."

But old habits die hard. I was painfully shy and intimidated by the thin blonds who played sports and got drunk on weekends. I wanted to be those girls, but I didn't know how.

Instead, I found a new role as an outcast who rebelled against everything those thin blonds stood for. I spoke out against Catholicism in a Catholic school. I joined the literary magazine while they played field hockey. I dyed my hair purple while they bleached their roots.

And I hung out with other outcasts who rebelled with me.

My mom calls them "that bad crowd" that I used to hang out with. We smoked pot and skipped school functions. My best friend and I often hid in the parking lot smoking cigarettes instead of going to mass with the rest of the school. And it made my embarrassment and shame so much easier when hiding behind rebellion, purple hair, and pot.

But at night, lying alone in my bed, the pain washed over me until it was unbearable. All the insults I'd ever received, every rejection, every stupid thing I'd ever done came flooding back. A voice in the back of my head called me stupid and worthless. But I had no idea how to vocalize the pain I'd been hiding.

And that's when the cutting began.

The first time, it was just an experiment. To see if it made me feel better. And it did.

I can't explain the feeling of relief it was to pour out my misery and punish myself. But it wasn't just about punishment. I needed people to understand that I was silently screaming for help.

I never purposely showed my scars to anyone in order to receive attention, but something like that is bound to get noticed. And it did.

My mom took me to psychiatrists to get me on medication, but for someone who was so used to rebelling, I couldn't stand to be told what to do. Cutting was like an addiction that I was terrified to get rid of and if medication would make me stop, I didn't want it.

I went through many different therapists and antidepressants. I wanted to be happy, but I wasn't willing to give up my pain. Being depressed and shameful was the only way I knew how to be. What I really wanted was just to be like those thin, beautiful blonds, but it seemed like an unattainable goal.

By the end of my sophomore year, things were the worst they'd ever been. And to top it off, my parents told me they were separating. That summer was the turning point of my depression.

I spent the whole summer stoned with my friends. My parents would try to control me, and I'd run away. Then my boyfriend broke up with me because I cut myself after I'd fought with my mom on the Fourth of July. And a month later, my parents caught me smoking weed. I had no choice but to deal with everything.

I spent the next nine months in drug treatment and group therapy. I was finally forced to work through issues without hiding behind my scars or drugs. And anytime I cut myself I had to talk about it in therapy. It made me work on verbalizing my pain and figuring out why I did what I did.

I made a vow that I would be who I wanted to be. I vowed to figure out who I was. And it was really the start of a new life. I can't say I am confident about who I am 100 percent of the time, but I have realized that I can't do everything on my own.

I still get depressed, but I have stopped the cutting. For the first time in a long time, things are better than I could ever have hoped.

~Lizzy Mason
Chicken Soup for the Teenage Soul IV

A Sobering Experience

When most of my classmates were starting their sophomore year of high school, I was just coming out of a
coma. I'd missed the entire summer, and when I woke
up, I was a fifteen-year-old with the mind of an eight-year-old.

A few months earlier, on June 12th, we had just finished our last
day of classes before exam week. To celebrate, I made plans to go to
a party with my friend Dean. I knew my dad wouldn't approve of me
partying with Dean since he was a junior and I was a freshman, so I
said we were going to a hamburger place in town. My dad agreed to
let me go, but said I had to be home by 11:00 P.M.

I don't remember most of what happened that night—a lot of
what I know is pieced together from things I've been told. I do know
that after Dean picked me up, we met up with some guys at a lake
near my house. A few of them, including Dean, were smoking pot. I
knew I shouldn't drive with someone who had been doing drugs, but
when it came time to get in the car with Dean, I guess I figured that if
he thought he was okay to drive, he probably was. So we went to the
party. My brother was there and has since told me that I spent most
of the night sitting in a chair in the garage, watching what was going
on. I was only fifteen, and I was surrounded by all these eighteen-,
nineteen- and twenty-year-olds. I don't remember having anything to
drink, but I do remember seeing Dean drinking beer.

When it was almost 11:00, I told Dean I had to get home, and
he said he'd take me. He invited a couple of friends to come with us,

and we headed for the car. Again, I didn't really think about not driving with this guy, even though he'd been drinking and getting high. You learn about all this stuff in school, but when you're caught up in the moment, for some reason it doesn't really click. I guess I never thought anything bad could happen to me.

But on the ride home, Dean was driving really fast—maybe close to 100 mph. We were on dirt roads and he was making the car fishtail, playing it all cool like it was so fun. That's when I realized I'd made a horrible mistake. I screamed at Dean from the passenger seat to slow down, but he didn't. We got to the top of a steep hill, and Dean was going so fast that the car flew into the air. We landed in the wrong lane and, as Dean swerved to try to get back on the right side, he overcorrected and my side of the car crashed into four trees. My head smacked into those trees one after the other.

The guy sitting behind me in the car broke his leg, but Dean and the guy behind him were fine. For a month after the accident, it was uncertain if I would live. I was in a coma until September, and I don't remember much until October. I had no broken bones, scratches or cuts, just one giant bruise down my chest from the seat belt. I would have gone through the windshield and died without that seat belt.

My parents lived the worst nightmare, constantly by my side, fearing I would die at any moment. When I came out of the coma, I recognized my family, but I was not the same person who got into Dean's car before the accident. My brain had bounced around against my skull, and I suffered a traumatic brain injury. Basically, the side of my brain that sends messages to my body to tell it how to move was severely damaged. I don't know how long it will take me to regain my motor skills entirely, or if I ever will.

Even after going through a lengthy rehabilitation in the hospital, I still walked so badly that people on the street stared and wondered what was wrong with me. It's a miracle that I can walk at all, let alone play sports. When I was a freshman, I dreamed of playing basketball for the WNBA, but that dream died the night of the accident. Now, I'm so glad because I am playing again, and I've worked on getting my stride back. But I'll never get back to the level where I used to be.

My knee jerks back awkwardly when I run, and my coordination will never be the same.

The effects of the brain injury have not been just physical. When I first got back to school, I was put into a special resource room to do communication, speech, occupational and physical therapy. Eventually, I started taking regular classes again—and I will graduate on time—but the accident has messed up my memory and my ability to concentrate, and studying is really hard. I have to write myself notes to remember things, and even after a couple of years of handwriting therapy, my writing is still not very fast or clear. My speech has improved, but it's not great. Most people don't realize it, but all of these little things pretty much make up who you are, and when they're gone, a piece of you is changed forever.

Then again, in some ways I've changed for the better since the accident. I used to think that life was all a big joke. Now I know it's much more precious, and I think Dean knows that, too. He and I weren't allowed to see each other when I returned to school. He never went to jail, but he had to pay a fine. My parents will always be angry with Dean, and I get angry sometimes, too. But I don't necessarily blame him. He once said to me, "I wish I had died in that accident; I wish I hadn't hurt you. But I did and I'm sorry." I know I can't change what happened, but neither can he, so we just have to let go of the things that make us sad or angry and live each day in gratitude.

~Sarah Jackson as told to Jennifer Braunschweiger
Chicken Soup for the Teenage Soul on Tough Stuff

Silence

*Learn to get in touch with the silence within yourself
and know that everything in this life has a purpose.*
~Elisabeth Kubler-Ross

It hits like a tornado hits. And, just like the changes in the atmosphere that signal that there is a tornado on the way, there are signs in a home that a divorce is in the air. There is yelling, crying and arguments, but the worst is the silence. During the silence, even if you try to tell yourself it's not true, you know in your heart that your parents are drifting apart. Then, just like a tornado... after it's over you have to step back and inspect the damage.

The damage that hurt the most was not leaving my friends, school or home. The worst damage was that my parents didn't love each other the way that they did when they were first married, had their four kids, bought a home or sent each kid to their first day of school. Now it was a different love, a love that had been forced way over the line... a tie of love that started thinning out at a slow pace but rapidly became more strained through the years of their tense relationship. The tie finally broke and they got a divorce.

The first few months after the divorce were hard. My relationship with my dad totally changed. Right after the divorce, the calls started... calls from my siblings and me to my dad. After his usual questions like, "How is school?" and "How are your friends?" came the worst question... "How is your mom?" There would be this terrible silence that made me run to my room after each call, to cry my heart out for hours.

My whole life had suddenly changed with one word. Divorce. It was hard to start over. It was hard on us all — my brother, my two sisters and me, but especially for my mom. She still loved Dad, not the same as before, of course, but you have to have some remainder of love for a man you spent almost twenty-three years of your life with.

My dad tried to come to see us every month, but he worked on the railroad, and vacations and time off for him were scarce. I can remember how we would get excited when he said he could come and see us, and be so disappointed when he would have to cancel if someone at his work got sick and he had to cover for them. I never told anyone... but I was a little glad when he had to cancel. I wouldn't have to deal with the awkward conversations... and the silence.

Then my mom met someone. His name is Shawn. At times I hated him when they first started dating. I had been secretly hoping that somehow my parents could get back together again, and things would be like they were before... when we were happy. Shawn became the reason why that would never happen... and I resented him for that.

It has taken a while, but now I see that Shawn is a good man. He was the one who took in a woman with four kids and never complained. At first, my dad hated Shawn and constantly reminded us kids that he still loved our mom. But now, after three years, my dad has released his grip and moved on just like my mom did. It's amazing, but my dad now works for my stepdad, so we get to see him more than we used to. He often eats supper with all of us. I think the silence has slowly turned into a new life for us all and we are finally happy again.

~Elisabeth Copeland
Chicken Soup for the Preteen Soul 2

Cookie Cutter Hands

Turn your face to the sun and the shadows fall behind you.
~Maori Proverb

]t started a few years ago—the cutting. My boyfriend had just broken up with me, and my mother disappeared. She left a note—that was it—and then was gone.

On the outside I was your typical high school freshman. I was in the popular group. Older boys liked me, and I earned straight As. I was told to be grateful, to rejoice that I didn't have to keep a job after school and that I could attend a private college back east after graduation. I was told that everything was going to be okay. I was told to smile, and not to think about Mom or stress out over school. I was told not to care. Except the problem was that I did care. I cared about Mom leaving and my boyfriend dumping me, and not being able to talk to anyone. I cared that my dad was always working and that I was always alone. I cared about everything—and I felt so alone.

On the inside I was tormented by feelings of angst, loneliness and self-loathing. My mother's leaving confused me. I was ashamed and humiliated over my breakup with my boyfriend. In a sense, I felt dead. It was as if I went to school mummified. No one knew that my insides were rotting away, slowly.

I never talked about these feelings with my friends. Why would I? What would they say? How would they react? I was happy and fun to hang out with at school, and nothing was ever wrong. I grew up in a neighborhood where the grass was always cut and sixteen candles on the cake justified a shiny new car.

Somehow, even though I was suffering, I couldn't feel it. I wanted to feel the pain that I could not understand. I wanted to reshape the crooked emotions into a neat little line that stretched across my right arm, a line that curved around my ankle, a line that liberated the caged ghosts screaming inside me. The razor was like a tool, a wrench used to tighten the screws on my innards and keep them in place so that I didn't have to cry in public or talk about my pain or feel alone.

With every red beaded line, I would sigh in calm relief. I didn't cry when I was hurt or upset. Instead, I cut. The complex emotions leaked from my flesh in the form of blood, rather than from my eyes in the form of tears. Anytime I felt empty or stressed or confused, anytime I looked in the mirror—hating myself and my cursed reflection—I would cut. I would cut just to bleed, to know that I was still breathing, to feel my heart race and my nerves stir.

My secret kept me safe. I became addicted to a pain that didn't hurt, but instead felt nice. I sought refuge in the shower with my cookie-cutter-like razor, making imprints on my soft flesh: circles and lines, hearts and stars. I was steady with my razor. The whole world seemed to blur and slow down, and the cuts left me calm as I watched the crimson tears drip onto the white shower tiles.

I hid my scars under designer blouses with long sleeves. Sometimes I let them show.

"Darn cat," I would say if anyone asked. "Darn friggin' cat."

My addiction to self-mutilation lasted all through high school. No one knew that there was a war going on inside of me. I was really good at hiding it. Sometimes I flirted with the idea of pressing the razor harder into my wrist to make the whole world stop. I never did, though, thank God. Instead I got caught.

After four years of hiding my cookie-cutter hands and neatly sliced arms, my father finally noticed my self-inflicted wounds. I couldn't use the same excuse with him. He knew we didn't have a cat.

I felt naked showing my father my scars. I didn't want to share them with him. I was angry with him for being so unaware, for letting my mother leave and for abandoning me with my pain. He scrutinized the red marks under my sleeves and the scabbed lines beneath my socks. And then he cried. My father had never cried before. I cried, too, and at that moment, I snapped. I suddenly realized how unhappy I was. I wasn't happy at school, and I wasn't happy after cutting myself. Cutting had been a release, an ephemeral exhale, a brief hope that I could make it hurt enough to release the pain, so that I could smile again, and that my smile would be for real. I wanted to make myself bleed and then watch myself heal. I wanted to be in control of the wounds inflicted in order to see the pain I felt inside, and yet, I realized at that moment that I wasn't in control of anything.

I started seeing a doctor and learning how to express my emotions and make my pain tangible. I wrote in my diary and played the guitar. I talked to my father and my friends at school. I talked to my new boyfriend. I tried to get out of the house as much as possible, exploring nature and the other side of the window. I took in the air and relaxed. Slowly, it became easier. Slowly, my addiction lessened, and I was okay. It was hard, but I grew stronger each time I faced my pain. I realized that for the past four years, I had been walking through shadows without taking the time to look up at the purple jacaranda trees that cast them.

~Kelly Peters as told to Rebecca Woolf
Chicken Soup for the Teenage Soul on Tough Stuff

91

It Happened to Me

Pretty much all the honest truth telling there is in the world is done by children.
~Oliver Wendell Holmes

Cancer. It's a funny word. It has two meanings. One of those meanings is the life-threatening disease we all know about. The other meaning isn't as accurate. We take it to mean something that happens to someone else, something that happens to your friend's aunt or someone in the newspaper. It's not something that happens to us, and it's definitely not something that happens to our own sister. But it happened to mine.

When I was about eight, every once in a while my eyesight would become blurry. I'd blink a few times and my eyes would go back to normal. I was taken to the eye doctor, and then for a CAT scan and various testing, but no one could find anything wrong. Eventually, it went away.

When my sister, Naomi, was about eight, she claimed to go blind when I hit her in the eye with an old nightshirt. I got in trouble, but when she was taken to the eye doctor, he couldn't find anything either. Eventually, she stopped complaining.

But when my sister, Tali, was about eight, she too began to complain that it was getting harder and harder to see out of one eye. My parents made an appointment with the eye doctor for about a month later, but they weren't too concerned.

But when my sister's complaints began to worsen, my parents

began to get worried and made the eye doctor appointment sooner. When the appointment came, my parents were informed that it was possible that Tali had a form of cancer called melanoma. One of the places that this can form is the eye, though there is no known reason why it forms in a particular person. To ensure that the disease is completely removed from the body, the part of the body infected with the disease must be removed. In this case, it would be her eye. If it was proven, for certain, that she had melanoma, the doctors would have to work fast, or the disease could travel from her eye to her brain.

It was not time to worry yet, though, because all that was the worst-case scenario, and melanoma is very rare among children anyway. Nevertheless, I remember my mom coming home from the eye doctor and crying, along with my grandmother and my aunt and trying not to let my sister see. I remember thinking, "This isn't really happening. She can't really die, this will all blow over." Maybe I was in shock, but it didn't feel like it. It was more like I had never even heard it, never even tried to acknowledge it was happening. Maybe it was crazy to feel like that, but maybe it was better that way, because I, the "unshaken one," was able to be the shoulder to cry on for everyone else. It makes it sound as if I was the brave one, but sometimes if you don't show your feelings on the outside, it means you're the most scared inside.

Well, Tali went in for her tests, and her X-rays, and it was confirmed that she had cancer. Her eye would have to be removed immediately. We knew that if even one cancerous cell was left, the disease could fully return.

The operation took place soon after. My mother waited in the hospital, while I stayed home and answered various phone calls. "No, we haven't heard anything yet," "Yes, she's still in surgery," "Yes, we'll notify you immediately." I still didn't believe it was happening. My sister was in surgery... and I still thought I was dreaming.

We later got a call that she was out of surgery, and just awakening from the anesthesia. All had gone smoothly, and tests had shown that they probably got everything out. She would be fine.

Never during the entire experience did I acknowledge what was happening. People would stop to comfort me, and half the time it would take me a few seconds to realize why. Almost every day, I have people stop me in the halls and ask, "Hey, how's Tali doing?" and I answer, "She's fine, why do you ask?"

Even now, as I write this, she's jumping on the bed across the hall, screaming, "Hey Joanie, you done writing the wonderful story of my life yet?" And though it's a miracle, it seems quite normal that there is nothing wrong at all.

~Joanie Twersky
Chicken Soup for the Teenage Soul II

92

You'll Never Walk Again

Toughness is in the soul and spirit, not in muscles.
~Alex Karras

Dear Teenage Chicken Soup,
My name is Nikie Walker. I am sixteen years old. I'm pretty much like any other sixteen-year-old. I was really involved with my high school, and very much liked by all of my peers. I was elected into many presidential clubs at my school. My mom was always saying that she never saw me. I was either running off to school, work, training or at practice. But, somehow I managed to keep my grades up and stay out of trouble.

One morning, I was off to school early for a student council meeting. I had pulled out of the driveway and proceeded down the road. I was about eight hundred feet from my driveway when a dog ran out of the ditch beside me. My first reaction was that it was a child, so I tapped my brakes. (I was only going about twenty-five miles per hour.) My road happens to be very rough, and I was on loose gravel. Well, my car started to slide and face the other way. I hit a patch of pavement, which flipped my car two and a half times, landing on its roof. I had my seat belt on, but it broke during the first roll, and I suffered a broken back and a crushed spinal cord. I was paralyzed from the waist down.

At the hospital, I underwent a six hour surgery. That night I was told that I would never walk again. I was devastated. I had always been so active, and now I was confined to a wheelchair.

While I was in the hospital, my grandma and my aunt bought me the first two volumes of *Chicken Soup for the Teenage Soul* and the *Chicken Soup for the Teenage Soul Journal*. I read them every night before I went to sleep. After reading all of the encouraging stories, I became determined to prove the doctors wrong. On December 13, I started therapy. I walked five steps that day! I improved as each day passed. Today, I am walking more than one hundred feet. The doctors are putting me in the medical books as a miracle. And I have these books to thank. Without an encouraging story every night about someone who was brave enough to fight against the odds, I probably would not be walking at all today. My next goal is to dance at my prom on May 13th! I will reach that goal, thanks to you. I really appreciate your words of encouragement! They have made a big impact in my life.

Love always,

~Nikie Walker

[*Editors' Note*: We received the following update from Nikie about her prom.]

Dear Chicken Soup for the Teenage Soul,

I am so happy to say that I made it to my junior prom and it was such a blast. My boyfriend, Adam, looked stunning in his little tuxedo. What started out as a frantic evening with all the pictures and making sure family and friends were able to see us, settled down once we were at the prom. The first song of the evening was "Wonderful Tonight," which was our prom's theme, but also happened to be Adam's and my song. He helped me out of my chair and we danced, standing up, for the whole song. It was magical! I tried to dance as much as I could standing up, but I would get tired so I danced the rest of the time sitting in my wheelchair. My friends would gather around me, joining hands with each other and dance with me in a giant circle. Adam did the sweetest thing and sat in one of the chairs from our table and danced with me so that we could be at the same level with each other. All of my friends, especially my boyfriend, really made my junior prom an unforgettable evening.

Thanks again,

~Nikie Walker
Chicken Soup for the Teenage Soul Letters

Teens Talk

Tough Times

You Are Not Alone

Tough times never last, but tough people do.
~Robert H. Schuller

93

Sorrows Underneath

I think of all my problems.
I think of all my pain.
I think of all my sorrows,
Until I go insane.

I think of all the smiles I've worn,
Which hide sorrows underneath.
No one seems to notice,
That I go through so much grief.

My tears seem to keep flowing,
Inside my tired eyes.
Each time I want to tell you,
My words come out as lies.

These days I'm feeling distant,
Far away and weak.
My sadness pulls me further,
From the happiness I seek.

I've just begun to realize,
That my hopes and dreams are gone,
I'm walking down a dead end road
Humming a tuneless song.

I'm standing on a rooftop,
Although I'm scared of heights,
I'm watching the cars beneath me move,
And somehow this doesn't feel right.

Now I think of what I'm doing,
I know I should find a way,
To beat through my depression,
Will I be able to someday?

Someone might be there,
To help me make it through,
Maybe they will listen,
And tell me what to do.

I'm seeing through the darkness,
And I'm starting to trust a few,
I think I'll try to make it,
So I can be there for them, too.

~Zihanna Rahman
Chicken Soup for the Teenage Soul on Love & Friendship

Hitting Bottom

It began when I was eleven. My family and I had just moved to a new town. Making new friends was never difficult for me before, but I was going through an awkward stage, and I was feeling self-conscious about my appearance. I was having a hard time reaching out to meet new people. So when I saw some kids smoking, I figured if I could join them for a cigarette I could meet some potential "friends." We hung out and smoked and continued this ritual pretty much every day. Before long I was introduced to other kids, and eventually I started drinking and getting high right along with them—it seemed the natural, easy thing to do. Soon, drugs and alcohol became my friends, too. A few years later, I was using cocaine and running away from home.

The first time I ran away I was thirteen. I had come home late one evening, and my mom was still up. She saw me sitting in a friend's car in front of our house. She was pretty strict about me being in my friends' cars. I was so stoned I knew at that point I couldn't go into my house, so I left with my friend.

After that night, over the next year and a half, I ran away twenty-three times. I managed to get caught every time, but within twenty-four hours I'd leave again. I was so hooked on drugs that I was afraid if I stayed at home, I wouldn't be able to get the drugs I wanted and needed so much.

I would stay at friends' houses until their parents figured out what was going on. Instead of returning home, I chose to live on the streets with friends or by myself. In colder weather, basements of apartment complexes became my source for shelter.

My mom didn't know why I was running away. I didn't communicate with her. She obviously knew something was wrong, but she just couldn't figure out what it was that was causing me to leave home. She tried putting me in treatment centers. Eventually, I ended up in one. During that first treatment center visit, I told her what was going on.

When I returned home from treatment I was off drugs, but after a few weeks I started using again. I continued this pattern for a while, having relapse after relapse. Finally, my mom quit her job to dedicate all of her time to helping me.

I went through three more short-term treatment programs, each one lasting only eleven to fourteen days. Each time, I was sincere about wanting to quit drugs, but I didn't know how. I felt as if I didn't have enough time in those brief programs to learn how to live my life without drugs. By then, my self-esteem was so low that I was battling an eating disorder as well.

When I turned fourteen, I was receiving intensive counseling, and my mom decided I needed long-term treatment. In my state, at fourteen you're allowed to legally deny medical treatment. So when my mom wanted to put me into a six to nine month treatment program, I refused. I was at the lowest of lows in my life at that point. I had already overdosed on peyote and, not knowing how to turn my life around, I looked at suicide as my only way out. I just didn't see how another treatment center was going to help me.

My mom and I took our battle to court. She told the judge about my past, my drug use and that I was an addict. The next day he placed me in a treatment center. I haven't gotten high since that day, five and a half years ago.

The treatment center was like a big family. We would go to school for half the day and then receive intensive counseling. Prior to my admittance to the center, I had been using cocaine heavily, so I went through withdrawal.

The real turning point in my recovery happened when I met

someone my own age who really wanted to quit. She kept telling me, "Help me, and I'll help you." That moved me so much, and it still moves me when I think about it. Having a peer say, "Hey, you can do it," made me want to do it this time.

I also met a woman in a Narcotics Anonymous meeting who had a major impact on me. She stood up and started talking about what was going on in her life. I remember watching her and thinking that she glowed. It's hard to describe, but for some reason she just glowed. Everything about her life was okay now, even the parts she was not happy with. I remember looking at her and thinking, I just want to be a little bit shiny. I don't need to glow, but just shine a little. That day I decided I was going to do everything in my power to live a healthy life.

Wanting something and following through with it were two completely different things for me then. After I finished treatment, we moved again. I was turning fifteen, and I knew that before long everyone at my school would find out about my past. I was going to be in the same position I was in when I was eleven, with no friends, only this time I couldn't use drugs to help me make them.

I was so determined to stay on track that I sought help from my guidance counselor right away. I told her that I didn't trust myself not to slip back into my old lifestyle. She surprised me by asking me to tell my story to fifth and sixth graders. I told her I had never spoken in front of people before, but she assured me that I would do just fine.

I was really scared about sharing my past with a bunch of strangers, so I asked my mom if she would join me. We sat down that evening and planned the presentation. We had our first heart-to-heart since I was ten years old.

We did two presentations at an elementary school, and it made the front page of all the local newspapers. Suddenly, schools were calling us. I was in awe. I couldn't believe people wanted me to come to their schools and talk, that they considered me to be somebody who could help other kids.

I realized that doing these presentations helped boost my self-esteem and confirmed for me that I never wanted to do drugs again. It hit me that I might be helping to save someone's life or preventing another kid from getting involved with drugs.

My mom and I still speak at schools and treatment centers together. Kids call me at home sometimes after our talks. Some thank me. Some share their own stories. Some even tell me that I shine—and that is the best part of all.

~Jenny Hungerford as told to Susan K. Perry
Chicken Soup for the Teenage Soul on Tough Stuff

95

Staring Back at Me

The willingness to accept responsibility for one's own life is the source from which self-respect springs.
~Joan Didion

When I was fifteen years old, I packed as many of my personal belongings as I could fit into two small backpacks and headed for the easy life. My only goals were to avoid responsibility and have as much fun as possible.

It was the beginning of summer, and I was sitting in my bedroom at my mom's house. We got into an argument over the usual teenage stuff. I didn't want to abide by my mom's rules, and I was feeling frustrated that "nothing ever went my way." When I left my house that day, I left with a feeling of liberation. I had won the battle with my mom. I was now in charge of my life.

I didn't know exactly where I was going, but I figured anywhere was an improvement. I spent the next few months couch-surfing from friend's house to friend's house. I would stay at each place until I had worn out my welcome. In less than a year, no one wanted me at their house, and people were starting to talk. See, I had a little secret, or what I thought was a secret. I had been using drugs quite heavily and supporting myself by stealing and selling my friends' material possessions.

I was a sixteen-year-old with no friends, no home, no self-esteem and no self-respect. I was sleeping in bank machine booths and cardboard dumpsters to stay warm and dry in the winter. I considered suicide. I was overwhelmed by the feelings of hopelessness and despair that I felt on a daily basis. I lost a lot of weight. I hardly ever slept because of the drugs. The longer I was awake, the more desperate I would get. It became a vicious cycle.

I remember vividly the night I ended up at my sister's house. It was the middle of winter, and I had been living in another city in a speed lab—an abandoned house with torn-up plywood floors littered with garbage, dirt and bugs. I hadn't slept for thirteen days. I went back to my hometown intending to do some laundry, then leave. I don't remember how I got there, but I ended up at my sister's house where I was asked to "please stay." I was so confused. I hadn't had anyone want me around for so long that I was suspicious. But it wasn't a difficult decision. Either I went back to the streets, or I had a warm place to stay for a night. She gave me her bed, and I fell asleep.

When I woke up, I looked around until I found my sister. I was kind of in a daze. "What time is it?" I asked her.

"It's 9:30 P.M.," my sister told me.

"Oh, okay, then I've only been asleep for a couple hours," I replied.

"Well, no, Ben. Actually, it's Thursday, and you got here on Sunday," she informed me. "You've been sleeping for four days."

My sister, knowing that something wasn't right, told me I could stay with her for as long as I wanted to. I unpacked all my clothes the next day. I stayed with her and her boyfriend for almost a year and continued to use drugs. Unfortunately, my problem progressed and got worse. I was using every day, and I hated the person I had become. I wrote in my journal that I had a problem and wasn't able to stop. Pain was the only emotion I ever felt. I had been stuffing my feelings down with drugs for so long that I didn't know what feelings were anymore. I wasn't afraid of anything anymore. I prayed that I would die. I was depressed, and I had no motivation, dignity or ambition left whatsoever.

One night I jumped as the phone rang. I picked it up, and my mom was on the other end. I was scared to talk to her. She said she knew I was having a hard time dealing with what my life had become, and she wanted to read me a poem called "Footprints in the Sand."

Instead of using the words "the Lord," she used herself. She told me that she would always be there for me if I needed her and that she would "carry" me through the toughest times of my life if I would let her. I finally understood the madness I had created. I had shut her out for so long because of a stupid decision I had made on an impulse one day over a year ago. But with her love that day, she broke through my walls of insecurity and pain. I just sat there and cried. I finally knew that someone cared.

When I hung up the phone, I felt incredibly guilty for what I had done to myself and the pain I had caused others. I was completely overwhelmed. I didn't know what to do. I was happy one moment because my mom still loved me, yet absolutely terrified the next. Through the tears I saw a knife on the dresser in front of me. Crying hysterically, I picked it up, and a feeling of calm and release came over me.

I woke up in the hospital bandaged and surrounded by people—my mom, my sister, my friend Emily and the nurses. I spent another month in the hospital, only this time I made a conscious effort to get help for my drug addiction. I started going to a twelve-step fellowship and met some people like me who were getting clean but had a while to go before they could rebuild any kind of life. On their recommendation, I decided to move into a recovery house. I lived there for ten months and now live on my own. I am finishing high school and enjoying life.

A lot has changed for me. The biggest change is that I feel good about myself and what I'm doing, and I have lost the desire to use drugs. My self-esteem is growing, and I have a huge group of friends. I have a relationship with my mom again. We talk almost every day. I have a job and people who love me. I spent my nineteenth birthday clean, with my family and friends. Today I can finally look in the mirror and be grateful for the person I see staring back at me.

~Ben Jenkins
Chicken Soup for the Christian Teenage Soul

96

Eternal Light

That's when I learned the most important lesson I will probably learn in my life: One person can make a difference.
~Laura Snell

Three years ago my best friend, Stephanie, was killed on her way to school in a head-on collision. The man who killed her did not have a driver's license and was under the influence. He was driving about sixty miles per hour and didn't even brake before he crossed into oncoming traffic and hit her. She died on impact. She was only sixteen. Painfully alone, somewhere between emotional inertia and complete despair, I struggled to navigate my suddenly unraveled reality.

When I received notice that my mother was at school to see me that foggy March day, my stomach sank. Something was terribly wrong. I immediately turned in my half-finished math test and rushed to the administration building to look for my mother. I found her sitting in the school's parlor. She asked me to sit—I stood. When she told me the tragic news, I could hear my heart pounding. The red walls seemed brighter then, and more fluid, as if they were swirling around me. A peculiar emptiness overtook me that afternoon in my mother's car as I repeated the words she had spoken to me earlier: She died today. She died. She's dead. I tried to make myself believe what I soon realized was the dark and horrific truth: Steph was dead, and she was never coming back.

There was a drastic change in my expectations and hopes for

the future from that day forward. Never had I imagined that some-one with whom I had cried, someone who had been a sister to me through everything from my parents' divorce to my first kiss—my future maid-of-honor—would no longer be in my life. All that was left of my future now were the questions. Who would give me those enormous, suffocating hugs and mischievous grins? What would I do at the times when her laugh was the only thing that could make me smile? Who would catch me when I fell? Who would be there for me when I endured the most crushing experience of my young life—the death of my best friend?

I had never felt so alone, and consequently I chose to look within myself for comfort and understanding. I hoped that some-where, deep inside of me, she was still there and would guide me through the monumental changes occurring in my life. But as I began to peel back layers of my own consciousness, my feelings of isolation and desperation only grew. I had always considered myself a strong person, but I felt completely lost.

I could not focus on my schoolwork or much else in my life except Stephanie's death. Most of my days were spent merely exist-ing with little pleasure or interest in anything. I wrote poetry in math class and scrawled overly dramatic statements like "Have you ever lost yourself?" on my notebook during advanced placement biology. I never bothered or cared about the actual class discussion.

I spent what seemed to be an eternity staring into the eyes of my favorite pictures of Steph. I had every lash and sparkle of those celes-tial blue eyes memorized, but I feared that my memory of the pas-sion and charisma that I searched for so intently within them would fade. Although I didn't cry much, I thought a lot. I tried to figure out why she was gone, how someone could kill another person and have no remorse, what I was going to do with my life. Then, after much thought, I found something. Under all the layers of pain and frustra-tion, something within me briefly twinkled.

A few months after Stephanie's death, her sister gave me a letter that she had found deep in one of her cluttered drawers. This letter was the healing catalyst I so desperately needed. She told me in the letter that she loved me always, that I was her best friend, and lastly, that I was her mentor. Like a piece of stardust, something deep inside of me began to illuminate my soul. Never in my life had I been so flattered, so touched, or felt so loved; it was as though she had left the letter behind to console and encourage me. She had always taken care of me before, and now I knew that her death did not change that. I realized that despite my suffering, I needed to take responsibility, use my talents and participate actively in my life's unfolding.

Now, whenever I'm worried, I ask her for guidance, and I swear that she has helped me profoundly. Whether she gives me the strength to call back after I've hung up on someone or the inspiration to trudge through my advanced placement language test with confidence and clarity, I know she helps me every day. Although it is impossible to verbalize such an abstract, warm confidence, I feel her presence inside of me as I succeed, and more importantly as I cry, longing for her sweet, warm embrace. It is with her strength and support that I am able to forge on in life. I have faith in her presence, and I have faith in myself.

Steph's death caused me to question myself and my own position in life. I now feel that although I have endured an emotional darkness more intense and shattering than most eighteen-year-olds have, it is not the pain that has changed me, but rather Stephanie's love and confidence in me that has inspired my metamorphosis. I can feel her guiding light in my own life as it changes, and thus I have the courage and resilience to embark on a new chapter of my life. I emerge from the darkness as a confident, faith-filled young woman with an especially bright twinkle in her eye.

~Anastasia
Chicken Soup for the Teenage Soul on Love & Friendship

Sleep-Away Camp

The willingness to accept responsibility for one's own life
is the source from which self-respect springs.
~Joan Didion

"I'll have a single scoop of the butter pecan in a cone," I say to the guy behind the counter at the ice cream shop. I look over, and sitting in a booth behind me is a kid in my grade at school. It's Cory, one of the boys who made fun of me all year long after finding out that I had been hospitalized for depression. He used to pass me in the school hallways, look down at the scars on my arms where I cut myself, make karate chop gestures and say things like, "Why don't you go kill yourself?"

The thing was, I never wanted to die. I just cut myself to escape the emotional pain I felt. Some days, I would lie in bed for hours—not sleeping, not reading—just lying there. I would sit in my room, cry, loathe myself and wallow in self-pity while I wrote morbid poetry about how great life would be once I was dead. Then one muggy summer morning, my mom found me lying in bed, blood staining my clothing and sheets. I looked and felt like a zombie. That's how I ended up in the hospital.

It all started when my parents got divorced.

I had always been a daddy's girl, and when my father moved three thousand miles away, I grew numb and angry. To this day, I still don't remember much of what happened during that time, even though I was ten years old. All I remember is that I began to get angry more easily, especially at my mom. After the divorce was final, my mom sold the house and that made me mad. Then we moved to a place where I felt like I didn't fit in. I cried all the time because I was different from everybody else. Being multiracial in a predominantly white town set me apart, but I was also different in how I was. I was a tomboy. I was the kind of girl who spoke up for what I believed in, no matter what the cost. Most of the time, eleven- and twelve-year-olds don't want to hear one of their peers telling them to stop acting out.

Some people write when they feel sad, or they go running to get the pain out. They have constructive ways to cope—but I didn't. My method for dealing with depression was a razor blade and a locked bedroom door. But the deepest scars that I carry are the memories of feeling that nobody else understood me and a sense of feeling abandoned and helpless.

That morning when Mom found me lying in my bloody bed, I was admitted to the hospital where I spent almost an entire month.

At first, I hated the hospital. I thought they were making me worse. Looking back, I think I didn't really want to get better. Being depressed was easy, because not caring meant I was numb; I didn't have to feel the pain inside. I soon began to attend group therapy. We'd talk about our issues, and even though I heard every other kid in the group talk about being sad and lonely and wanting to die or trying to die, I still felt like nobody in the world understood me or cared. My only pain was the blood I released through my arms.

I continued to cut myself with whatever I could find at the hospital, although it wasn't easy since they locked up anything potentially dangerous. I took pen caps and used them to cut my arms. I took plastic knifes out of the cafeteria and cut myself with them. I hated the therapists and didn't open up to them. I blamed everybody and anybody but myself for all of my problems. And I was embarrassed to be in a mental facility. Was I crazy? Maybe. But looking around me, I realized that I was surrounded by completely normal kids.

Nicole, a dancer, was funny and smart; she had stopped eating and wasted away to seventy-two pounds at five foot six. Even Tina, a beautiful soccer player, cut, binged and had attempted suicide. On the surface, the kids at the hospital looked normal, yet there was nothing normal about Tina needing a straitjacket after having an anxiety attack and trying to kill herself. Kids who would normally be playing softball were sitting on couches, looking like zombies because their medication had just been changed.

When one of us was finally released to go home, everybody signed her discharge journal. These were like yearbooks, with inscriptions and signatures in it, promising things like, "Keep in touch" and "Never forget you." Almost like a real summer sleep-away camp, only this one was for the emotionally challenged.

Mental illness doesn't get knocked out like an infection after you take an antibiotic. It's a multistep process, so it's not easy to describe how I got better. Through weeks of intensive therapy, painful sessions in which I let down my guard and let myself cry, and group sessions in which I actually contributed, I began to recover. I was placed on medicines that helped ease my depression. I personally made an effort and slowly it began to show. With the combination of these things and support from family and friends, I learned to laugh again. I stopped hurting myself.

Now I am past my preteen years, and I'm a teenager. I have recovered from my depression. I'm alive. I am enjoying life, and I cannot believe that I was so depressed that I cut myself so viciously. I try to grasp whatever pieces of my childhood I lost in that month in the hospital and the months leading up to it.

Depression is a disease, not an excuse to treat others poorly. People have called me crazy, but I know that I wasn't crazy. I was sick and now I have recovered. I notice other people around me who cut themselves, who write the same dark poetry that I wrote. In science class one day, a girl was being picked on because somebody noticed cuts on her arms. I immediately came to her defense and even caused a disturbance in the class because I felt so strongly that this was not something to harass somebody about.

So today, at the ice cream shop, I get my ice cream and I look back—right at Cory. I realize that I may still have my scars, but I don't have my depression anymore. He can harass me all he wants, but his words can't drive me to drag a blade across my skin like they would have a year ago. I won. I'm a winner, and like Petra Salvaje said, I have the scars to prove it.

Butter pecan ice cream has never tasted sweeter.

~Kellyrose Andrews
Chicken Soup for the Girl's Soul

98

Take Back the Night

For most of my life, I kept all my feelings bottled up inside, and I wouldn't allow myself to acknowledge any anger or pain. I thought that by ignoring the pain, I could somehow avoid experiencing it. What I didn't realize was that I would eventually have to deal with all the emotions I suppressed. Over time, it became increasingly difficult to hide my problems, and I desperately needed someone in whom I could confide. Thankfully, my parents sought counseling for me, and this was the first step in what has become a long, harrowing journey.

For the past four years, I have been striving to conquer my depression and end the mental and physical torture I inflict upon myself. I have begun talking about an issue from my childhood that caused a great deal of anger and self-hatred: sexual abuse by an extended family member. Initially, it was difficult to speak about such a painful time in my life, but the tremendous support I've received from family and friends has made an immense difference. I can't even begin to express the sense of relief I felt once I disclosed this painful secret; it was like an enormous weight was lifted off my shoulders.

As a victim of molestation, I have carried a large burden of shame.

There is something very healing about the words: "It was not your fault; it is a horror that no one deserves." Once I realized how much this insight helped me, I decided I wanted to talk with others who had been through similar traumas. When my mom informed me of a candlelight vigil in New York City to speak out against sexual crimes, I immediately decided to attend. Although I looked forward to participating, nothing could have prepared me for the life-altering experience I would have.

Even though it's been almost two years since I participated in that momentous event, I still think about that night. Recently, while looking through some old journals, I came across the following entry. As I read it, I began to relive the evening I took part in, an amazing event appropriately called "Take Back the Night."

Dear Diary,

I have to write about the unforgettable time I had tonight! At 8:30 P.M., I took a train into Manhattan and then a cab to Greenwich Village.

When I arrived, I was overwhelmed by the amazing scene. The entire area was blocked off, and a huge circle of women sat on the soft earth below. I found a spot among the crowd and took a deep breath. On a small platform set up for this event, women took the stage to share their stories of abuse. I was also surrounded by a multitude of t-shirts, each designed by a victim of sexual crime. Small shirts represented childhood abuse, while larger ones symbolized trauma that took place later in life. These shirts displayed such comments as "It wasn't my fault," "Love and hurt," and "Rape kills."

Repeatedly, my eyes welled up with tears that refused to fall. I was numb from the pain, inundated with shame as I rocked back and forth in fear. I wanted to scream and cry, but I was too embarrassed to do so in the middle of the crowd. When I could no longer hold it all within, I ran inside the bathroom and sank to the floor, sobbing. A few people asked if I needed help, but I could not respond; their voices seemed far away. Eventu-

ally, I picked myself up, grabbed a few tissues and headed back outside.

When I returned to the rally, volunteers distributed white candles for our march through the Village. Women of all ages stood together. We screamed the chants, "Wherever we go, however we dress, no means no and yes means yes!" and "All colors, shapes and sizes, this is the power that rises: take back the night!" As we stormed through the dark city, our unity illuminated the crime-filled streets. Police officers walked beside us, and people came out of clubs and restaurants to see us and listen to our message. I held my candle high in the air and felt a strong sense of purpose. In my mind, I was telling the person who hurt me that he had taken too many years of my life, and I would no longer grant him that power.

I left the Village just after midnight. Even though I am exhausted both emotionally and physically, I feel an immense sense of activism and accomplishment. It was moving to see such a shocking number of people who have endured this pain. Their stories and our common bond have inspired me to continue speaking out! This evening, there were many different emotions amidst the crowd: agony, despair, anger, etc. However, there was one feeling that shone through all of that darkness as a powerful beacon of light: hope. It was a hope so strong and plentiful that everyone could take as much as they needed and store it in their hearts forever.

Life is about giving and taking, and this evening I was able to do both. I let go of the burden and shame I have always felt, and I embraced a new sense of peace and self-worth. I took the power of my future back into my own hands. I recognized that I must no longer live in the shadow of the past, and I refuse to spend one more day of my life as a "victim." The time has come to open *my eyes and acknowledge what I am, always have been, and always will be: a survivor.*

~Lauren Nevins
Chicken Soup for the Teenage Soul IV

99

The Perfect Family

Call it a clan, call it a network, call it a tribe, call it a family. Whatever you call it, whoever you are, you need one.

~Jane Howard

D ivorce. That's a word I dreaded more than any other word in the English dictionary.

All my life, I thought I had the perfect family. Perfect parents, two great sisters and a younger brother. We all got along well. But during the last several years, my parents had started to fight more and more.

My dad came home less and less, working more hours than ever in Vermont. And now here we all were, sitting in the television room as a family, with my parents saying they had an announcement to make. I began to cringe.

There it was: that nightmare word, the one that made me sick to my stomach. They were, they announced, getting a divorce. The big D word. My sisters and brother and I gaped at each other. How many times had I asked my mom and dad: "Are you getting a divorce?" How many times had they assured me that would never happen and given me hugs and kisses?

"This is some sort of April Fool's joke, right?" I said.

My mom's eyes welled with tears and she held me in her arms.

"No, Marc, I'm sorry," she whispered.

I felt betrayed. How could they do this to us? Most of all, I wanted to know what we had done wrong. What had I done wrong?

My mother could see the dread in my eyes, the fear, the hurt and the pain. It all welled within my belly and I felt sick. She promised she would take care of me, of us. All of us.

But how could I believe her now? My family had collapsed before my eyes. We were splintered. Shattered. There would be no more perfect family. And of course, things would get worse rather than better. They'd get a lot worse.

My mom told me that we would have to leave our home. The home I'd lived in all my life.

I felt like I was losing everything. My family. My home. My dad. The good news: My mother would have custody of all of us and my father wouldn't dispute it.

We moved into a tiny home with my mom's parents. At first, I wasn't very happy. The house was small. We were all squished in together. Sometimes I felt there wasn't enough room to breathe. There was one thing, however: We loved each other. My grandparents, Mom, sisters, brother and visiting aunts and uncles tried to do everything to fill the house with warmth and caring. My grandparents paid special attention to all us kids. I'd never felt so close to them in my life.

They asked me about school and were actually interested. They asked me about my friends, my grades. We sat at the kitchen table and talked often. They could never replace my father, but they spread their warmth to all of us.

Still, I carried a lot of guilt. I couldn't understand what bad thing happened to split up my parents. At times, I agonized over it, lying in bed, wondering in a cloud-like state what possibly could have been the reason that my parents quit loving each other. Was it something I had done?

And then more unexpected news: We learned my father was gay.

I was sure as word got around that the other kids would laugh and make fun of me. Some did, but there were a lot of kids who didn't say a word. They still hung around me and could care less what my dad did. They liked me before and they liked me still. I had learned who my real friends were, and the ones I lost were not the kind of people I wanted in my life anyway.

I also learned that I was really loved by my family. They supported me. They cared about me. My grandparents adored me. Eventually, we were able to move out from their home and get a condominium. I started junior high school and started doing well.

I have since learned to redefine that funny concept I had about a perfect family.

Maybe a perfect family really means a lot of love and a lot of support. Maybe it really means giving, sharing and caring. Maybe I still have a perfect family after all.

~Marc St. Pierre
Chicken Soup for the Teenage Soul II

My Loss

Most of us live under the false perception that everyone we know is immune to bad things happening. We see friends and family members as individuals who are so untouched that unfortunate events and catastrophes never dare to prod their everyday living. The media is full of war news, death tolls and freak accidents, but as a nation we merely shake our heads, feel quick sympathy, perhaps donate some money to charity from time to time, then come back to our reality, treating life, ourselves, our loved ones like infinite people we'll never see encased in a coffin.

My earth grounding reality check arrived in the appearance of Victoria, a girl with a charming smile, great hair and a booming, adrenaline-pumped personality. I met her sophomore year when I was still trying to adjust to the high school world. At the time, everyone was going crazy due to the immense workload and cranky teachers pushing us to know the difference between a parabola and a hyperbola.

For some reason, my name was notorious in all of Mr. Farley's English classes. He loved to bring it up because it was unique, and my notes were, in his words, "extraordinarily specific." This is how Victoria heard my name for the first time.

"Ohhhh... so you're Lovely!" she exclaimed with delight when another friend introduced us. "Crazy... Farley mentions you, like, every day in our class."

"Right..." I said uncomfortably, shifting my weight to my other foot, embarrassed that someone knew me through my nerdiness instead of my coolness. "Nice to meet you. Hopefully we can hang out sometime."

And we did. Days later, Victoria knew me not only for my geeky qualities, but also for my love of clothes, my inability to cook and the fact that I write from the heart. We grew closer each day, laughing about things only fifteen-year-olds would understand, braiding hair into cornrows every week to stand apart from the crowd and hugging each other like sisters. Yet all this changed when she decided to switch tracks to pursue her dreams of being a musician. I was definitely distraught, but she reassured me that we would never sever our bond, that we'd see each other in school every two months. So she left with the promise that we were friends deep within our souls, and our relationship could never be tested.

Months passed, and I bloomed into a junior, now sixteen years old and not as lame as before, with a handful of friends and a high GPA to boot. As time slipped away, I forgot Victoria and our friendship—forgetting her existence, forgetting her smile, forgetting her soul. The promise of our endless companionship quickly deteriorated, and I grew indifferent toward her. When I saw her walking in the halls, I'd stride by with an unexplainable bitterness coursing through my veins, believing that she had changed for the worse, that she felt that she was above my level.

The one time I attempted to start a conversation by asking her how she was doing, a mere three words were the only response to my effort before she walked on without even looking back. "Oh, I'm fine," she said simply.

Sometimes I found myself looking at her from a distance when she was alone. I knew that she was looking at me, too, but I blatantly ignored her friendly gestures to inflict the hate back, to be cold and detached, to signify that I'd forgotten her. She was stuffed into the corner of my mind with dust bunnies and worries. I took her for granted, and now I wish I hadn't, that I would've taken the chance to talk to her when she was alive.

In June, Victoria got into a car accident on the California 2 freeway. The car flipped several times and was totaled when it hit the ground. She was on her way to lunch with a bunch of friends she had met a week before, novice drivers who were confident enough to tackle the freeway. She wasn't wearing a seat belt, and she suffered severe head trauma and slipped into a coma. She died a few days later.

When I learned the news, my body went numb, and I just sat there with eyes wide open, spitting the words, "Oh, my God" twenty times over. During the funeral, I held my friend's hand and stared ahead at Victoria's sobbing sister, the mournful priest and the glistening white coffin. I felt ashamed when tears rolled down my cheeks, a sudden disgrace for crying over a person I had purposely forgotten, a friend who passed away not knowing how much her short companionship meant to me. I felt I had no right to cry, no right to visit, for she would never understand why I was there in the first place when I had condemned her as a forgotten friend.

Right after the Mass, I had to go back to the real world, ironically stopping by the DMV office for my sister to take her driving test, seeing teenagers pass by so joyous for their permit, while I, dressed in black, fought with my sadness, clutching in my hand a prayer given for her during the wake.

Nothing lasts forever. We hear this all the time in Hollywood movies and tragic stories in the news, yet so often we turn our backs from this message as if it doesn't apply to our own lives. But look closely and you'll see the world turning in constant turbulence, never stopping for you or your loved ones to glide through life forever. At some point in our lifetimes, we will all experience tragedies, so don't wait until it's too late. We are finite — it's better to love and appreciate now.

~Lovely Umayam
Chicken Soup for the Teenage Soul: The Real Deal Friends

A Smile Can Save a Life

*Treat everyone with politeness, even those who are rude to you —
not because they are nice, but because you are.*
~Author Unknown

The day that changed my life forever started out like any other day for me. I have been a professional speaker for the last four years, since I was eighteen. I travel around the country speaking to middle and high school students about self-esteem, goal setting and helping others. On that day in 1999, I was speaking to a group of students near Fort Worth, Texas. The auditorium was full of applause, hugs and smiles. Such a love-filled morning did not prepare me for the tragedy about to unfold.

After my speech that day, I went back to my hotel room. It was then that I received the emotional phone call that I will never forget.

"There was a tragedy at a youth event, right near where you spoke. Most of the victims were kids. I don't know what their conditions are."

For once, I was speechless. I was also afraid. Were any of the kids I spoke to today involved? I wondered. Even though I didn't really know them, I felt a strong connection with the young people who had been in my audience only hours before.

I immediately hung up the phone and turned on the radio to find out more. A middle-aged man had walked into a youth rally at a local church and started shooting. In only minutes, he had ended the lives of several preteens from the church's youth group.

I bought a map, and drove the few miles to the scene. When I got there, it was a horrible scene. Helicopters were circling overhead, and parents were screaming and calling the names of their children. Everyone was crying. I didn't know how to help, or what to do. Then I noticed a group of young people sitting on the street corner and I walked up to them.

To this day, I don't remember exactly what I said. I do remember that we hugged one another and did our best to comfort each other while the crying and screaming was going on all around us. I will never, for the rest of my life, forget sitting on that street corner with those kids — feeling their pain and confusion — and crying with them.

I knew from that moment on that my life work would be about preventing youth violence.

I began asking questions during my speeches and listening to the students, tens of thousands of them from all over the country. I learned from them what they thought causes violence and especially what they thought could prevent it. Having the students sharing their opinions, and working with them to shape their schools has become a moving experience for me.

I will never forget the eighth grade girl, Jenny, who told me she was more afraid of sitting alone at lunch than being physically hurt, and that no one ever smiled at her. Or looking into the teary eyes of Stephen, who had sat next to another boy for an entire year — a boy who later shattered his school and many lives. He hung his head as he told me, "I never once said hello to him. I never once asked him how his day was. I never once acknowledged him." I started to realize that these kinds of behaviors are the seeds that can later create violence. My belief was confirmed when I got word about the man who had shot the kids at the event in Fort Worth. He had opened fire on those kids just to get attention, and because he had felt that this was a way to get back at people who had ignored him.

The most important thing that I have learned is that young people are amazing. I am always so frustrated that the media often depicts teenagers as lazy, unintelligent and violent. They rarely discuss the millions who work hard to get through school, hold steady jobs, support their families and stay clear of trouble. They overcome all kinds of obstacles, limitations and fears every day, in order to move forward with their lives. Such as Maria, the blind girl, who is a star on her school's track team, or John, the school bully, who turned his life around to become one of my best volunteers. Thousands of students put forth an effort every day to help others, and they never even expect to be acknowledged.

Together we can work to respect all different types of people. We can learn what behaviors can hurt and what behaviors can help. Ignoring others or calling them names can create an atmosphere that fosters violence. And, something as simple as a smile can truly save a life.

Young people do have the potential to make their own schools and communities safer. Most of all, we can sincerely value ourselves and others for who they are. Together, we can connect and end the hurt.

~Jason R. Dorsey
Chicken Soup for the Preteen Soul

Chicken Soup for the Soul

$\mathcal{S}$hare with Us

W e would like to know how these stories affected you and which ones were your favorite. Please write to us and let us know.

We also would like to share your stories with future readers. You may be able to help another teenager, and become a published author at the same time. Please send us your own stories and poems for our future books. Some of our past contributors have launched writing and speaking careers from the publication of their stories in our books!

The best way to submit your stories is through our web site, at

www.chickensoup.com

If you do not have access to the Internet, you may submit your stories by mail or by facsimile.

Chicken Soup for the Soul
P.O. Box 700
Cos Cob, CT 06807-0700
Fax 1-203-861-7194

Teens Talk Growing Up
You have lots of friends in the Chicken Soup family, sharing their stories with you about growing up, meeting challenges, and learning from life. This book contains the best stories from Chicken Soup's library on the ups and downs that you and your friends experience every day.

Teens Talk Relationships
Being a teenager is hard but you are not alone. Read stories written by other teens just like you, who face the same problems and issues. Read how other teens met the challenges of new friends, new love, and changing family relationships.

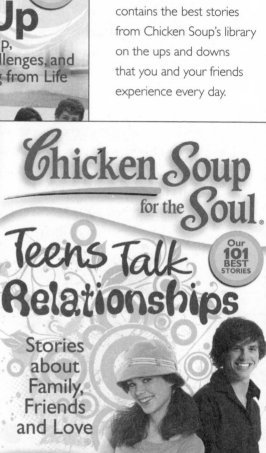

Check out the other books in the

And for Younger Family Members...

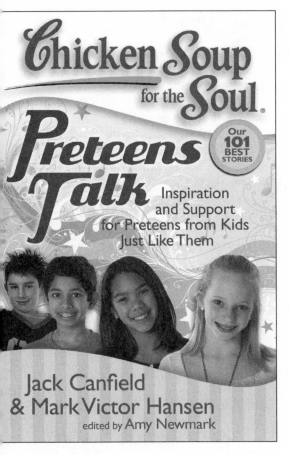

Chicken Soup for the Soul
Preteens Talk

Inspiration and Support for Preteens from Kids Just Like Them

Jack Canfield & Mark Victor Hansen
edited by Amy Newmark

Our 101 BEST STORIES

Preteens Talk

Being a preteen is harder than it looks. School is more challenging, bodies are changing, relationships with parents are different, and new issues arise with friends. This book supports and inspires preteens and reminds them they are not alone, as they read stories written by other preteens just like them, about the problems and issues they face every day. This book contains Chicken Soup's 101 best stories and poems for preteens from its 15-year history. Stories cover friends, family, love, school, sports, challenges, embarrassing moments, and overcoming obstacles.

Our 101 BEST STORIES

Teens Talk Series

More books for *Teens!*

Chicken Soup for the Preteen Soul

Chicken Soup for the Preteen Soul 2

Chicken Soup for the Girl's Soul

Chicken Soup for the Teenage Soul

Chicken Soup for the Teenage Soul II

Chicken Soup for the Teenage Soul III

Chicken Soup for the Teenage Soul IV

Chicken Soup for the Teenage Soul on Tough Stuff

Chicken Soup for the Teenage Soul Teen Letters

Chicken Soup for the Christian Teenage Soul

Chicken Soup for the Teenage Soul Journal

Chicken Soup for the Soul: The Real Deal School

Chicken Soup for the Soul: The Real Deal Friends

Chicken Soup for the Soul: The Real Deal Challenges

Chicken Soup for the Teen Soul: Real-Life Stories by Real Teens

Chicken Soup for the Soul for the Teenage Soul on
Love & Friendship

More of (Our 101 BEST STORIES) for
Teens & Preteens!

Chicken Soup for the Soul: Christian Teen Talk
Christian Teens Share Their Stories of Support, Inspiration and Growing Up
"Our 101 Best Stories" series
978-1-935096-12-2

Upcoming for
Teens & Preteens!

Chicken Soup for the Soul: Teens Talk High School
101 Stories of Life, Love, and Learning for Older Teens
978-1-935096-25-2

Chicken Soup for the Soul: Teens Talk Middle School
101 Stories of Life, Love, and Learning for Younger Teens
978-1-935096-26-9

Chicken Soup for the Soul: Teens Talk Getting In...to College
101 Stories of Support from Kids Who Have Lived Through It
978-1-935096-27-6

Who Is
Jack Canfield?

Jack Canfield is the co-creator and editor of the Chicken Soup for the Soul series, which *Time* magazine has called "the publishing phenomenon of the decade." Jack is also the co-author of eight other bestselling books including *The Success Principles™: How to Get from Where You Are to Where You Want to Be, Dare to Win, The Aladdin Factor, You've Got to Read This Book*, and *The Power of Focus: How to Hit Your Business and Personal and Financial Targets with Absolute Certainty*.

Jack has recently developed a telephone coaching program and an online coaching program based on his most recent book The Success Principles. He also offers a seven-day Breakthrough to Success seminar every summer, which attracts 400 people from fifteen countries around the world.

Jack is the CEO of the Canfield Training Group in Santa Barbara, California, and founder of the Foundation for Self-Esteem in Culver City, California. He has conducted intensive personal and professional development seminars on the principles of success for over a million people in twenty-three countries. Jack is a dynamic keynote speaker and he has spoken to hundreds of thousands of others at more than 1,000 corporations, universities, professional conferences and conventions, and has been seen by millions more on national television shows such as *The Today Show, Fox and Friends, Inside Edition, Hard Copy, CNN's Talk Back Live, 20/20, Eye to Eye*, and the *NBC Nightly News* and the *CBS Evening News*.

Jack is the recipient of many awards and honors, including three honorary doctorates and a Guinness World Records Certificate for having seven books from the Chicken Soup for the Soul series appearing on the New York Times bestseller list on May 24, 1998.

To write to Jack or for inquiries about Jack as a speaker, his coaching programs, trainings or seminars, use the following contact information:

Jack Canfield
The Canfield Companies
P.O. Box 30880 • Santa Barbara, CA 93130
phone: 805-563-2935 • fax: 805-563-2945
E-mail: info@jackcanfield.com
www.jackcanfield.com

Who Is
Mark Victor Hansen?

Mark Victor Hansen is the co-founder of *Chicken Soup for the Soul*, along with Jack Canfield. He is also a sought-after keynote speaker, bestselling author, and marketing maven. For more than thirty years, Mark has focused solely on helping people from all walks of life reshape their personal vision of what's possible. His powerful messages of possibility, opportunity, and action have created powerful change in thousands of organizations and millions of individuals worldwide.

Mark's credentials include a lifetime of entrepreneurial success. He is a prolific writer with many bestselling books, such as *The One Minute Millionaire*, *Cracking the Millionaire Code*, *How to Make the Rest of Your Life the Best of Your Life*, *The Power of Focus*, *The Aladdin Factor*, and *Dare to Win*, in addition to the Chicken Soup for the Soul series. Mark has had a profound influence in the field of human potential through his library of audios, videos, and articles in the areas of big thinking, sales achievement, wealth building, publishing success, and personal and professional development.

Mark is the founder of the MEGA Seminar Series. MEGA Book Marketing University and Building Your MEGA Speaking Empire are annual conferences where Mark coaches and teaches new and aspiring authors, speakers, and experts on building lucrative publishing and speaking careers. Other MEGA events include MEGA Info-Marketing and My MEGA Life.

He has appeared on Oprah, CNN, and The Today Show. He

has been quoted in *Time*, *U.S. News & World Report*, *USA Today*, *New York Times*, and *Entrepreneur* and has had countless radio interviews, assuring our planet's people that "You can easily create the life you deserve."

As a philanthropist and humanitarian, Mark works tirelessly for organizations such as Habitat for Humanity, American Red Cross, March of Dimes, Childhelp USA, and many others. He is the recipient of numerous awards that honor his entrepreneurial spirit, philanthropic heart, and business acumen. He is a lifetime member of the Horatio Alger Association of Distinguished Americans, an organization that honored Mark with the prestigious Horatio Alger Award for his extraordinary life achievements.

Mark Victor Hansen is an enthusiastic crusader of what's possible and is driven to make the world a better place.

Mark Victor Hansen & Associates, Inc.
P.O. Box 7665 • Newport Beach, CA 92658
phone: 949-764-2640 • fax: 949-722-6912
www.markvictorhansen.com

Who Is
Amy Newmark?

A my Newmark was recently named publisher of Chicken Soup for the Soul, after a thirty-year career as a writer, speaker, financial analyst, and business executive in the worlds of finance and telecommunications.

Amy is a graduate of Harvard College, where she majored in Portuguese, minored in French, and traveled extensively. She is also the mother of two children in college and has two grown stepchildren.

After a long career writing books on telecommunications, voluminous financial reports, business plans, and corporate press releases, Chicken Soup for the Soul is a breath of fresh air for Amy. She has fallen in love with Chicken Soup for the Soul and its life-changing books, and found it a true pleasure to conceptualize, compile, and edit the "101 Best Stories" books for our readers.

The best way to contact Chicken Soup for the Soul is through our web site, at www.chickensoup.com. This will always get the fastest attention.

If you do not have access to the Internet, please contact us by mail or by facsimile.

Chicken Soup for the Soul
P.O. Box 700
Cos Cob, CT 06807-0700
Fax 1-203-861-7194

Chicken Soup for the Soul

Thank You!

W e would like to thank the entire staff of Chicken Soup for the Soul for their help on this project and the 101 Best series in general. Among our California staff, we would especially like to single out D'ette Corona, who is the heart and soul of the Chicken Soup publishing operation, and who put together the first draft of this manuscript, Barbara LoMonaco for invaluable assistance in obtaining the fabulous quotations that add depth and meaning to this book, Patty Hansen for her extra special help with the permissions for these fabulous stories and for her amazing knowledge of the Chicken Soup library, and Patti Clement for her help with permissions and other organizational matters. In our Connecticut office, we would like to thank our able editorial assistants, Valerie Howlett and Madeline Clapps, for their assistance in setting up our new offices, editing, and helping us put together the best possible books for teenagers. We would also like to thank our master of design, Brian Taylor at Pneuma Books, for his brilliant vision for our covers and interiors. Finally, none of this would be possible without the business and creative leadership of our CEO, Bill Rouhana, and our president, Bob Jacobs.